DISSENT:

ITS ROLE THROUGH THE AGES

"The term *dissent* may be used with equal validity in describing the ideas and/or activities of such diverse individuals as the twelfth-century cleric Arnold of Brescia, the fomentors of the Peasants' Revolt in Chaucer's England, the critics of American presence in Vietnam, and the Objectivist philosopher and novelist Ayn Rand. Two basic assumptions underlie our volume: that an understanding of the past is especially relevant to any civilization's search for identity, and that, in acquiring this understanding, defeated causes and minority viewpoints are as important as those programs that resulted in policies."

FREDERICK C. GIFFIN
RONALD D. SMITH

MENTOR Titles of Related Interest

☐ **THE CHICANO: FROM CARICATURE TO SELF-PORTRAIT edited and with an introduction by Edward Simmen.** An anthology of short stories offering for the first time a collection of writings devoted exclusively to the Mexican American. These stories often comic, sometimes tragic—present the Mexican-American as an individual caught in a social order that demands he meet that society on its own terms—or suffer.

(#MW1069—$1.50)

☐ **PREJUDICE: TWENTY TALES OF OPPRESSION AND LIBERATION edited by Charles R. Larson.** The twenty stories in this powerful anthology have one common theme as their concern—racial prejudice. The writers represent ten different countries. Included are **Albert Camus, Flannery O'Connor** and **Anatole France.** A biographical sketch of each author is included.

(#MW1070—$1.50)

☐ **BLACK VIEWPOINTS edited by Arthur C. Littleton and Mary W. Burger.** The more than fifty essays in this thought-provoking anthology deal almost exclusively with the Black man of the twentieth century—his aspirations, frustrations and his image of himself. The writers include **Malcolm X, Dick Gregory, Eldridge Cleaver** and **Stokely Carmichael.** (#MW1079—$1.50)

Against the Grain:

An Anthology of Dissent, Past and Present

Edited by
FREDERICK C. GIFFIN
and
RONALD D. SMITH

A MENTOR BOOK from
NEW AMERICAN LIBRARY
TIMES MIRROR
New York and Toronto
The New English Library Limited, London

ACKNOWLEDGMENTS

Gracchus Babeuf, "The Manifesto of Equals," from *The Last Episode of the French Revolution* by Ernest Belfort Bax. Reprinted by permission of The Richards Press.

James Baldwin, selection from *The Fire Next Time.* Copyright © 1963, 1962 by James Baldwin. Reprinted from *The Fire Next Time* by James Baldwin by permission of the publishers, The Dial Press and Michael Joseph Ltd.

A. A. Bestuzhev, "Letter to Emperor Nicholas I," from *Readings in Russian History and Culture,* ed. Ivar and Marion Spector. Reprinted by permission of Ivar and Marion Spector.

Malcolm Boyd, six meditations. From *Free to Live, Free to Die* by Malcolm Boyd. Copyright © 1967 by Malcolm Boyd. Reprinted by permission of Holt, Rinehart and Winston, Inc.

Daniel and Gabriel Cohn-Bendit, selections from *Obsolete Communism: The Left Wing Alternative.* Reprinted by permission of the publishers, Andre Deutsch Ltd. and McGraw-Hill Book Company.

"The Executive Committee to Emperor Alexander III," from *The Russian Revolutionary Movement* by Konni Zilliacus. Reprinted by permission.

Milton Friedman, selections from *Capitalism and Freedom.* Copyright © 1962 by the University of Chicago. All rights reserved. Reprinted by permission of The University of Chicago Press.

Froissart, selection from *The Chronicles of Froissart,* ed. G. C. Macaulay, trans. J. Bourchier and Lord Berniers. Reprinted by permission of Macmillan and Company Limited.

Martin Luther King, Jr. "Letter From Birmingham Jail"—April 16, 1963—in *Why We Can't Wait* by Martin Luther King, Jr. Copyright © 1963 by Martin Luther King, Jr. Reprinted by permission of Harper & Row, Publishers, Inc., and Joan Daves.

Peter Kropotkin, selection from *Kropotkin's Revolutionary Pamphlets,* ed. Roger Baldwin, from the Benjamin Blom Inc., 1968 edition. Reprinted by permission of the publisher.

(The following page constitutes an extension of this copyright page.)

MENTOR TRADEMARK REG. U.S. PAT. OFF. AND FOREIGN COUNTRIES
REGISTERED TRADEMARK—MARCA REGISTRADA,
HECHO EN CHICAGO, U.S.A.

SIGNET, SIGNET CLASSICS, MENTOR, AND PLUME BOOKS
are published *in the United States* by
The New American Library, Inc.,
1301 Avenue of the Americas, New York, New York 10019,
in Canada by The New American Library of Canada Limited,
295 King Street East, Toronto 2, Ontario,
in the United Kingdom by The New English Library Limited,
Barnard's Inn, Holborn, London, E.C. 1, England.

FIRST PRINTING, MAY, 1971

PRINTED IN THE UNITED STATES OF AMERICA

Preface

Simply defined, dissent means "opposition to the status quo." Hence it is a phenomenon which is neither strictly modern nor confined to a particular ideology. The term "dissent" may be used with equal validity in describing the ideas and/or activities of such diverse individuals as the twelfth-century cleric Arnold of Brescia, the fomenters of the Peasants' Revolt in Chaucer's England, the critics of the American presence in Vietnam, and the Objectivist philosopher and novelist Ayn Rand. A "dissenter" sees what he believes to be flaws in the existing order of things and seeks to remedy them—even if only by attempting to bring them to the attention of the upholders of tradition.

This book represents an effort to provide the common reader as well as the student with useful insights into the nature of dissent as it has existed through the ages. Two basic assumptions underlie the volume: (1) that an understanding of the past is especially relevant to any civilization's search for identity, and (2) that, in acquiring this understanding, defeated causes and minority viewpoints are as important as those programs that resulted in policies. The materials included are arranged, roughly, in chronological order and were selected with an eye toward breadth and variety. We have purposely avoided emphasizing a common or unifying theme in favor of a more open-ended (and, we believe, more useful) approach. Though alike in that they may be regarded as dissenters, the men and women whose ideas and exploits are recorded here include a number of widely differing human types. They illustrate what Pascal called "the glory and the baseness in man."

Although the selections present clear and forceful statements of a variety of positions—most of them intensely partisan—the collection as a whole is not meant to represent or support any particular viewpoint. Readers should not assume that any author in these pages is the spokesman of the editors. Nor should they assume that the selections are intended to serve as a comprehensive survey of dissent in all its forms from ancient times to the present. Rather, our aim is to provoke thought on a limited number of dissenting views and activities which we consider significant. Aware that what may be dissent to one man is orthodoxy to another, we do not anticipate that all of our readers will agree with what we regard as appropriate and important examples of dissent.

Grateful acknowledgement is made to the publishers and authors who have allowed us to reprint their materials. While space will not permit us to thank all those who have contributed directly to this anthology, our deepest thanks go to Mrs. Grace Skinaway for typing the manuscript and to our wives for their patience and understanding. We also wish to express our special indebtedness to Mr. Ward Mohrfeld of New American Library for his encouragement and support.

FREDERICK C. GIFFIN
RONALD D. SMITH

Tempe, Arizona

CONTENTS

1.

Attack on Oligarchic Dominance:
Gaius Gracchus Defies
the Status Quo
of Republican Rome*

With the establishment of the Roman Republic toward the close of the sixth century B.C., there began a struggle on the part of the plebeians, or common people, to compel the favored patrician class to grant them a share in the government. The first step in the progress of the plebeians was the election of tribunes of the people. The persons of these officers, ten of whom were elected annually, were declared inviolate, and they were given the power of vetoing legislation—a power intended to protect citizens against detrimental laws.

By the middle of the third century B.C. the plebeians had won the right to hold the highest offices of the state and had attained equality with the patricians before the law. The republic was in large measure what the words res publica implied, an "affair of the people." Yet the Popular Assembly, though it possessed the power to legislate, never had the right of discussion. It could only vote affirmatively or negatively upon measures proposed by the magistrates; debate was reserved to the Senate, a body dominated by the patricians and hence largely devoted to the perpetuation of their interests. Of even greater significance in limiting the powers of the Popular Assembly, by custom all laws had to be screened by the Senate.

While the struggle for democracy within the republic

*From the book *Plutarch's Lives*. Translated by John Dryden. Rev. by Arthur H. Clough. Everyman's Library Edition, pp. 147–48, 150–53, 155–57. Reprinted with the permission of E. P. Dutton & Co., Inc., publishers, and J. M. Dent and Sons, Limited.

was going on, the Roman armies pursued a policy of territorial expansion which not only extended Rome's political dominance, but resulted in a vast influx of wealth, the effects of which were disastrous. The gulf between the rich, to whom the power of wealth and conquest went, and the citizen farmers became wider. Cheap wheat from newly won territories flooded the market of Italy, and small farmers were forced to sell their land to great land-holders who could work it with slaves. These landless individuals flocked to Rome and, together with the slaves who had been brought in great numbers to Italy as a consequence of the long wars, made up the Roman mob which was to be for centuries a constant menace to the peace of the city. Hence, while the wealthier classes of Italy were busy appropriating the riches of the Mediterranean world, a difficult social problem arose in the state.

The first serious attempt to meet this situation was made by the tribune Tiberius Gracchus in 133 B.C. He proposed that the government restore the class of small independent farmers by restricting the amount of land a citizen might occupy and by instituting a greater subdivision of lands. Though he secured the passing of a law devoted to these ends, the violent and unconstitutional means to which he resorted, added to the hostility aroused by his plan among rich patrician landholders, brought about his assassination and the repeal of the measure.

Ten years later, Tiberius' younger brother, Gaius Gracchus, perhaps one of the greatest pre-Ciceronian orators of Roman history, was elected a tribune of the people and not only renewed the agrarian law sponsored by Tiberius, but pursued even more far-reaching reforms. After securing a law permitting the sale of grain from the public storehouses to citizens at half the market price—a measure which won him the political support of the needy—he projected a system of roads and began a policy of establishing colonies of poor citizens in the provinces. While these policies (which one twentieth-century historian has characterized as the "New Deal in old Rome") may be regarded as the beginnings of a wise program, it was pursued by Gaius with little regard for accepted constitutional practices, and proved his undoing. He even wanted to bestow citizenship on the people of the Latin colonies. But the Roman populace saw in this a possible curtailment of their privileges. They refused to reelect him to the tribunate, and he was killed in an ensuing riot.

Had Gaius succeeded in implementing his reform pro-

*gram, the political balance of Rome would have been
altered to a revolutionary degree. The logical fulfillment
of the measures he proposed would have been the establishment of a democratic government in place of the existing
oligarchy.*

Having moved the people's passion with such addresses
(and his voice was of the loudest and strongest), he proposed two laws. The first was, that whoever was turned out
of any public office by the people, should be thereby rendered incapable of bearing any office afterwards; the second, that if any magistrate condemn a Roman to be
banished without a legal trial, the people be authorised to
take cognisance thereof. . . .

. . . Of the laws which he now proposed, with the object
of gratifying the people and abridging the power of the
senate, the first was concerning the public lands, which
were to be divided amongst the poor citizens; another was
concerning the common soldiers, that they should be
clothed at the public charge, without any diminution of
their pay, and that none should be obliged to serve in the
army who was not full seventeen years old; another gave
the same right to all the Italians in general, of voting at
elections, as was enjoyed by the citizens of Rome; a fourth
related to the price of corn, which was to be sold at a
lower rate than formerly to the poor; and a fifth regulated
the courts of justice, greatly reducing the power of the
senators. For hitherto, in all causes, senators only sat as
judges, and were therefore much dreaded by the Roman
knights and the people. But Gaius joined three hundred
ordinary citizens of equestrian rank with the senators, who
were three hundred likewise in number, and ordained that
the judicial authority should be equally invested in the six
hundred. While he was arguing for the ratification of this
law, his behaviour was observed to show in many respects
unusual earnestness, and whereas other popular leaders
had always hitherto, when speaking, turned their faces

towards the senate house, and the place called the com-
itium, he, on the contrary, was the first man that in his
harangue to the people turned himself the other way,
towards them, and continued after that time to do so. An
insignificant movement and change of posture, yet it
marked no small revolution in state affairs, the conversion,
in a manner, of the whole government from an aristocracy
to a democracy, his action intimating that public speakers
should address themselves to the people, not the senate.

When the commonalty ratified this law, and gave him
power to select those of the knights whom he approved
of, to be judges, he was invested with a sort of a kingly
power, and the senate itself submitted to receive his advice
in matters of difficulty; nor did he advise anything that
might derogate from the honour of that body. As, for
example, his resolution about the corn which Fabius the
proprietor sent from Spain, was very just and honourable;
for he persuaded the senate to sell the corn, and return
the money to the same provinces which had furnished
them with it; and also that Fabius should be censured for
rendering the Roman government odious and insupportable. This got him extraordinary respect and favour among
the provinces. Besides all this, he proposed measures for
the colonisation of several cities, for making roads, and
for building public granaries; of all which works he himself
undertook the management and superintendence, and was
never wanting to give necessary orders for the despatch
of all these different and great undertakings; and that with
such wonderful expedition and diligence, as if he had been
but engaged upon one of them; insomuch that all persons,
even those who hated or feared him, stood amazed to
see what a capacity he had for effecting and completing
all he undertook. As for the people themselves, they were
transported at the very sight, when they saw him surrounded with a crowd of contractors, artificers, public
deputies, military officers, soldiers, and scholars. All these
he treated with an easy familiarity, yet without abandoning
his dignity in his gentleness. . . .

. . .When Gaius divided the public land amongst the
poor citizens, and charged them with a small rent, annually
to be paid into the exchequer, they were angry at him,
as one who sought to gratify the people only for his own
interest. . . .

. . .After his return to Rome, he quitted his house on the
Palatine Mount, and went to live near the market-place,
endeavouring to make himself more popular in those parts,

where most of the humble and poorer citizens lived. He
then brought forward the remainder of his proposed laws,
as intending to have them ratified by the popular vote; to
support which a vast number of people collected from all
quarters. But the senate persuaded Fannius, the consul,
to command all persons who were not born Romans to
depart the city. A new and unusual proclamation was there-
upon made, prohibiting any of the allies or Confederates
to appear at Rome during that time. Gaius, on the contrary,
published an edict, accusing the consul for what he had
done, and setting forth to the Confederates, that if they
would continue upon the place, they might be assured of
his assistance and protection. . . .

. . .About that time there happened likewise a difference
between him and his fellow-officers upon this occasion.
A show of gladiators was to be exhibited before the people
in the market-place, and most of the magistrates erected
scaffolds round about, with an intention of letting them for
advantage. Gaius commanded them to take down their
scaffolds, that the poor people might see the sport without
paying anything. But nobody obeying these orders of his,
he gathered together a body of labourers, who worked for
him, and overthrew all the scaffolds the very night before
the contest was to take place. So that by the next morning
the market-place was cleared, and the common people had
an opportunity of seeing the pastime. In this, the populace
thought he had acted the part of a man; but he much
disobliged the tribunes his colleagues, who regarded it as
a piece of violent and presumptuous interference.

This was thought to be the chief reason that he failed
of being the third time elected tribune; not but that he had
the most votes, but because his colleagues out of revenge
caused false returns to be made. But as to this matter
there was a controversy. Certain it is, he very much re-
sented this repulse, and behaved with unusual arrogance
towards some of his adversaries who were joyful at his
defeat, telling them that all this was but a false, sardonic
mirth, as they little knew how much his actions threw them
into obscurity.

As soon as Opimius also was chosen consul, they presently cancelled several of Gaius's laws, and especially called
in question his proceedings at Carthage, omitting nothing
that was likely to irritate him, that from some effect of
his passion they might find out a tolerable pretence to put
him to death. Caius at first bore these things very patiently;
but afterwards, at the instigation of his friends . . . he

resolved to put himself at the head of a body of supporters....

. . .Gaius could not be persuaded to arm himself, but
put on his gown, as if he had been going to the assembly
of the people, only with this difference, that under it he
had then a short dagger by his side. As he was going out,
his wife came running to him at the gate, holding him with
one hand, and with the other a young child of his. She
bespoke him: "Alas, Gaius, I do not now part with you to
let you address the people either as a tribune or a lawgiver,
nor as if you were going to some honourable war, when,
though you might perhaps have encountered that fate
which all must some time or other submit to, yet you had
left me this mitigation of my sorrow, that my mourning
was respected and honoured. You go now to expose your
person to the murderers of Tiberius, unarmed indeed, and
rightly so, choosing rather to suffer the worst of injuries
than do the least yourself. But even your very death at
this time will not be serviceable to the public good. Faction
prevails; power and arms are now the only measures of
justice. Had your brother fallen before Numantia, the
enemy would have given back what then had remained of
Tiberius; but such is my hard fate, that I probably must
be an humble suppliant to the floods or the waves, that
they would somewhere restore to me your relics; for since
Tiberius was not spared, what trust can we place either
on the laws, or in the gods?" Licinia, thus bewailing,
Gaius, by degrees getting loose from her embraces, silently
withdrew himself, being accompanied by his friends; she,
endeavouring to catch him by the gown, fell prostrate upon
the earth, lying there for some time speechless. Her servants
took her up for dead, and conveyed her to her brother
Crassus.

. . .Gaius, as it is reported, was very forward to go and
clear himself before the senate; but none of his friends
consenting to it, Fulvius sent his son a second time to inter-
cede for them, as before. But Opimius, who was resolved
that a battle should ensue, caused the youth to be appre-
hended and committed into custody; and then with a
company of his foot-soldiers and some Cretan archers
set upon the party under Fulvius. These archers did such
execution, and inflicted so many wounds, that a rout and
flight quickly ensued. Fulvius fled into an obscure bathing-
house; but shortly after being discovered, he and his eldest
son were slain together. Gaius was not observed to use
any violence against any one; but, extremely disliking all

these outrages, retired to Diana's temple. There he attempted to kill himself, but was hindered by his faithful friends, Pomponius and Licinius; they took his sword away from him, and were very urgent that he would endeavour to make his escape. It is reported that, falling upon his knee and lifting up his hands, he prayed the goddess that the Roman people, as a punishment for their ingratitude and treachery, might always remain in slavery. For as soon as a proclamation was made of a pardon, the greater part openly deserted him.

Gaius, therefore, endeavoured now to make his escape, but was pursued so close by his enemies, as far as the wooden bridge, that from thence he narrowly escaped. There his two trusty friends begged of him to preserve his own person by flight, whilst they in the meantime would keep their post, and maintain the passage; neither could their enemies, until they were both slain, pass the bridge. Gaius had no other companion in his flight but one Philocrates, a servant of his. As he ran along, everybody encouraged him, and wished him success, as standers-by may do to those who are engaged in a race, but nobody either lent him any assistance, or would furnish him with a horse, though he asked for one; for his enemies had gained ground, and got very near him. However, he had still time enough to hide himself in a little grove, consecrated to the Furies. In that place, his servant Philocrates having first slain him, presently afterwards killed himself also, and fell dead upon his master. Though some affirm it for a truth, that they were both taken alive by their enemies, and that Philocrates embraced his master so close, that they could not wound Gaius until his servant was slain.

2.

The Jews of York:
Mass Suicide*

In the latter half of the eleventh century William I (the Conqueror), seeking to give his country the benefit of a middle commercial class, encouraged the Jews of Normandy, especially of Rouen, to emigrate to England. Although the Jews who responded to his invitation were awarded protection both under the Conqueror himself and under his successor William Rufus (d. 1100), at the beginning of the twelfth century the favored position of this non-Christian "capitalist element" began to excite the opposition of the barons and the clergy. Peter the Hermit aroused the populace against them while touring England to rally support for the Second Crusade (1144), charges were leveled against them for alleged ritual murders of Christian children, and Jewish leaders were exiled abroad as hostages in order to extort money from those permitted to remain. On the day of Richard I's coronation in 1189 a London mob, inflamed with the spirit of the Third Crusade, staged an anti-Jewish riot. As one of the focal points of the day's persecutions, Benedict of York, a wealthy money-lender who had come to witness the coronation, was seized and tortured into undergoing a Christian baptism. Outrages continued, reaching their zenith in 1190 with the organized massacre of the entire Jewish community at York.

Dissent can take as many forms as its consequences. The Jews of York chose death over forced incorporation into the predominant religious-cultural mold of Angevin England. The description of the incident which follows is

*Roger of Hoveden, *Annals*. Translated by Henry T. Riley (London: H. G. Bohn, 1853), Vol. II, pp. 137–38.

*from a medieval chronicle. It is preceded by a short ex-
cerpt from* The New York Times *(September 5, 1967)
concerning a public demonstration in Milwaukee led by
the Reverend James Groppi with the aim of removing
racial discrimination in housing and employment. The
county judge referred to had already established a reputation for meting out stiff penalties to demonstrators whose
activities violated the law. Seen together, the contents
of the two documents offer points of comparison and contrast. According to Judge Christ Seraphim, obedience to
the law—even in the face of persecution and death—is
preferable to "marching."*

County Judge Christ Seraphim sat with his golden
retriever, Holly, on the porch of his Spanish-style house
on a pleasant East Side street [in Milwaukee] this afternoon and made some acerbic comments on 1,000 civil
rights demonstrators who jived and strutted past his front
lawn. . . .

"I think they are disturbing the peace, don't you?" he
asked, looking at the marchers today. "They are loud and
boisterous, are they not? I can't enjoy the peace and
tranquillity of my home, a home I paid a lot for."

As for the Rev. James E. Groppi, the white Roman
Catholic priest who commands the marchers, Judge Seraphim snapped: "He is a criminal, a convicted criminal,
convicted twice by a jury for disorderly conduct."

The demonstrators finally moved out of earshot, and
Judge Seraphim resumed, with a grateful sigh, his reading
of "A History of the Jews" by Abram Leon Sacher, president of Brandeis University, but soon the marchers
returned.

"These people," said Judge Seraphim, this time refer-
ring to his book, "were baked in ovens. But they maintained their dignity to the end. They didn't do much
marching. They are the most law-abiding people in the
world."

In the same month of March, on the seventeenth day before the calends of April, being the sixth day before Palm Sunday, the Jews of the city of York, in number five hundred men, besides women and children, shut themselves up in the tower of York, with the consent and sanction of the keeper of the tower, and of the sheriff, in consequence of their dread of the Christians; but when the said sheriff and the constable sought to regain possession of it, the Jews refused to deliver it up. In consequence of this, the people of the city, and the strangers who had come within the jurisdiction thereof, at the exhortation of the sheriff and the constable, with one consent made an attack upon the Jews.

After they had made assaults upon the tower, day and night, the Jews offered the people a large sum of money to allow them to depart with their lives; but this the others refused to receive. Upon this, one skilled in their laws arose and said: "Men of Israel, listen to my advice. It is better that we should kill one another, than fall into the hands of the enemies of our law." Accordingly, all the Jews, both men as well as women, gave their assent to his advice, and each master of a family, beginning with the chief persons of his household, with a sharp knife first cut the throats of his wife and sons and daughters, and then of all his servants, and lastly his own. Some of them also threw their slain over the walls among the people; while others shut up their slain in the king's house and burned them, as well as the king's houses. Those who had slain the others were afterwards killed by the people. In the meantime, some of the Christians set fire to the Jews' houses, and plundered them; and thus all the Jews in the city of York were destroyed, and all acknowledgments of debts due to them were burnt.

3.

Roger Bacon:

Opposition to Crusades

in an Age of Faith*

At the beginning of the eleventh century the driving force of the Mohammedan states, which had for many years controlled the Mediterranean, began to decline. In contrast, Christian Europe was emerging from the Dark Ages, and its people were gaining a new strength and energy which found an outlet in aggression. During the course of the century the long warfare against the Moslems in Spain was begun, Italian merchants broke the Moslem domination of the Mediterranean and opened up regular trade with the Middle East, and the Moslems were driven out of Sicily. Then, in 1095, Pope Urban II called upon the people of Christendom to carry the war into the enemy's territory in the East, and to regain Jerusalem and the Holy Land from the infidel. The resultant expedition was the first of an extraordinary series of crusades which would occupy much of the attention of the western peoples until the end of the thirteenth century.

The marauding noblemen and peasants who rode eastward against the infidel were prompted by a variety of motives, not all of them commendable. Although the period in question was an age of faith and the prime motive was clearly religious, the adventurous spirit and love of fighting so characteristic of the medieval knight also played an important role. Moreover, the rich East offered landless knights tempting opportunities for plunder, and land to be had for the taking. Nor could the Italian

*Roger Bacon, *Opus Majus*. Edited by John Henry Bridges (Oxford: Williams & Norgate, 1900), Vol. III, Part 3, Chapter 13, pp. 121–22. Translated by the editors.

merchants who aided the crusaders overlook the benefits to be gained from the establishment of safe trading posts in the Middle East. Hence the crusades represented a fusion of three characteristic impulses of medieval man— sanctity, pugnacity, and greed.

Despite the overwhelming popularity of the "holy wars" against Islam, there were some medieval Christians who regarded these grandiose expeditions as a form of barbarism improper to "true Christian faith." One such critic was the Franciscan scholar Roger Bacon (1214[?]–1294), who wrote in his Opus Majus *very pointedly of the abuses of the crusading order of Teutonic Knights. He insisted that the latter's successful conquests were actually harmful to Christianity because they prevented real conversion, which could best be effected by peacefully preaching the Christian faith.*

Bacon was a celebrated teacher at Oxford University, best known for the central role which he played in the revival of scientific investigation during the latter thirteenth century. In 1278, as a consequence of the daring novelty of his teaching and the antagonism aroused by the publication of his Compendium Studii Philosophiae (1271)—*a vigorous assault on the vice and corruption of his day, including the pedantry and false knowledge rife in the schools—he was brought to trial, condemned, and thrown into prison, where he remained for fourteen years. He was released in 1292, but died shortly afterward and was buried in the Franciscan Church at Oxford.*

. . .Furthermore the Greeks and Ruthenians and many other schismatics also grow hardened in error because the truth is not preached to them in their own language, and the Saracens also, not to mention the Pagans, Tartars, and other unbelievers throughout the world. Nor does war avail against them, since the Church is sometimes defeated in its crusades, as often happens beyond the sea, and especially in the last expedition of the King of France, as the whole world knows. And where Christians are victorious, no one remains to defend the conquests. Nor are unbelievers converted in this way, but killed and sent to hell. The survivors of the wars together with their children are embittered more and more against the Christian faith because of those wars and are indefinitely alienated from the faith of Christ and stirred up to do Christians all the harm possible. Hence the Saracens and the pagans in many parts of the world are becoming quite impossible to convert, especially beyond the sea and in Prussia and in the lands bordering on Germany, because the brethren of the German House [Teutonic Knights] hinder greatly all hopes of converting them owing to the wars which they are always stirring up and because they wish to have complete domination. There is no doubt that all the nations of unbelievers beyond Germany would long since have been converted but for the brutality of the German House, because the race of pagans has frequently been ready to receive the faith in peace after preaching. But they of the German House are unwilling to keep peace because they want to subdue those peoples and reduce them to slavery, and with subtle persuasions they have for many years deceived the Roman Church. The former fact is known, otherwise I would not make the charge. Besides, the faith did not enter into this world by force of arms but by simple preaching. . . .

4.

Protesting Entailed Servitude:
The Wat Tyler Insurrection
of 1381*

The people of medieval Europe were busy, almost wholly, with tilling the soil, the overwhelming majority of them constituting a class of serfs in an age that believed in separate jurisdictions and obligations for the different groups which made up the fabric of society. Under the manorial-agrarian structure of European life, serfs were bound by birth to the soil and tied to obligations such as those set forth in 1351 in the English Statute of Laborers:

Every able-bodied man under sixty years of age without means will serve whosoever requests his service or go to jail until willing to do so; any workman leaving a job before his contracted time of service has expired will be imprisoned; the old wages [those of 1346], and no more, shall suffice; any lord of town or manor who violates this statute shall forfeit triple the monetary value of the violation; . . . no person shall give to a beggar able to work; any person who accepts more than customary wages must surrender them to the town where he resides toward payment of the King's tenth and fifteenth.[1]

During the fourteenth century the prevailing system of manorial land usage was challenged by serious uprisings in France and England that, together with urban revolts,

*The Chronicles of Froissart. Edited by G. C. Macaulay. Translated by John Bourchier and Lord Berners (London: Macmillan & Co., 1908), pp. 250–61. Text modernized by the editors. Reprinted by permission of Macmillan & Co., Ltd.
[1] G. G. Coulton, Social Life in Britain from the Conquest to the Reformation (Cambridge: The University Press, 1956), p. 351. Text modernized by the editors.

threatened to produce general social revolution. In England, in June, 1381, a rather obscure individual named Wat Tyler led a protest march on London. On June 14 Tyler and his followers met with King Richard II at Smithfield and demanded of the fourteen-year-old monarch the abolition of serfdom, the removal of restrictions on freedom of labor and trade, and amnesty for rebels.

A detailed and vivid picture of the Wat Tyler "insurrection" is offered in the following selection by the French chronicler Jean Froissart (1339–1410). The reader should pay special attention to the violent anti-noble and anti-clerical nature of the protesters' grievances and the brutal manner in which their revolt was terminated.

While these conferences were going forward there happened great commotions among the lower orders of England, by which that country was nearly ruined. In order that this disastrous rebellion may serve as an example to mankind, I will speak of all that was done from the information I had at the time. It is customary in England, as well as in several other countries, for the nobility to have great privileges over the commonality; that is to say, the lower orders are bound by law to plough the lands of the gentry, to harvest their grain, to carry it home to the barn, to thrash and winnow it; they are also bound to harvest and carry home the hay. All these services the prelates and gentlemen exact of their inferiors; and in the counties of Kent, Essex, Sussex, and Bedford, these services are more oppressive than in other parts of the kingdom. In consequence of this the evil disposed in these districts began to murmur, saying, that in the beginning of the world there were no slaves, and that no one ought to be treated as such, unless he had committed treason against his lord, as Lucifer had done against God; but they had done no such thing, for they were neither angels nor spirits, but men formed after the same likeness as these lords who treated them as beasts.

This they would bear no longer; they were determined to be free, and if they laboured or did any work, they would be paid for it. A crazy priest in the county of Kent, called John Ball, who for his absurd preaching had thrice been confined in prison by the Archbishop of Canterbury, was greatly instrumental in exciting these rebellious ideas. Every Sunday after mass, as the people were coming out of church, this John Ball was accustomed to assemble a crowd around him in the marketplace and preach to them. On such occasions he would say, "My good friends, matters cannot go on well in England until all things shall be in common; when there shall be neither vassals nor lords; when the lords shall be no more masters than ourselves. How ill they behave to us! for what reason do they thus hold us in bondage? Are we not all descended from the same parents, Adam and Eve? And what can they show, or what reason can they give, why they should be more masters than ourselves? They are clothed in velvet and rich stuffs, ornamented with ermine and other furs, while we are forced to wear poor clothing. They have wines, spices, and fine bread, while we have only rye and the refuse of straw; and when we drink, it must be water. They have handsome seats and manors, while we must brave the wind and rain in our labours in the field; and it is by our labour they have wherewith to support their pomp. We are called slaves, and if we do not perform our service we are beaten, and we have no sovereign to whom we can complain or who would be willing to hear us. Let us go to the king and remonstrate with him; he is young, and from him we may obtain a favourable answer, and if not we must ourselves seek to amend our condition." . . . Many in the city of London envious of the rich and noble, having heard of John Ball's preaching, said among themselves that the country was badly governed, and that the nobility had seized upon all the gold and silver. These wicked Londoners, therefore, began to assemble in parties, and to show signs of rebellion. . . .

By this means the men of Kent, Essex, Sussex, Bedford, and the adjoining counties, in number about sixty thousand, were brought to London, under command of Wat Tyler, Jack Straw, and John Ball. This Wat Tyler, who was chief of the three, had been a tiler of houses—a bad man and a great enemy to the nobility. When these wicked people first began their disturbances, all London, with the exception of those who favoured them, was much alarmed. The mayor and rich citizens assembled in council and debated whether they should shut the gate and refuse to admit them; however, upon mature reflection they determined not to do so, as they might run the risk of having the suburbs burnt. The gates of the city were therefore thrown open, and the rabble entered and lodged as they pleased. True it is that full two-thirds of these people knew neither what they wanted, nor for what purpose they had come together; they followed one another like sheep. . . . King Richard well knew that this rebellion was in agitation long before it broke out, and it was a matter of astonishment to every one that he attempted to apply no remedy. . . .

On the Monday preceding the feast of the Holy Sacrament in the year 1381, these people sallied forth from their homes to come to London, intending, as they said, to remonstrate with the king, and to demand their freedom. . . . On entering [Canterbury] they were well feasted by the inhabitants, who were all of the same way of thinking as themselves; and having held a council there, resolved to proceed on their march to London. . . . At Canterbury the rebels entered the church of St. Thomas, where they did much damage; they also pillaged the apartments of the archbishop. . . . After this they plundered the abbey of St. Vincent, and then leaving Canterbury took the road towards Rochester. As they passed they collected people from the villages right and left, and on they went like a tempest, destroying all the houses belonging to attorneys, king's proctors, and the archbishop, which came in their way. . . .

When the principal citizens of London found that the rebels were quartered so near them, they caused the gates of London-bridge to be closed, and placed guards there, . . . notwithstanding there were in the city more than thirty thousand who favoured the insurgents. Information that the gates of London-bridge had been closed against them soon reached Blackheath, whereupon the rebels sent a knight to speak with the king and to tell him what they were doing was for his service; for the kingdom had now for many years been wretchedly governed, to the great dishonour of the realm and to the oppression of the lower orders of the people, by his uncles, by the clergy, and more especially by the Archbishop of Canterbury, his chancellor, from whom they were determined to have an account of his ministry. . . . The knight on receiving this answer [from the king] was well satisfied, and taking leave of the king and his barons, returned to Blackheath, where upwards of sixty thousand men were assembled. He told them from the king, that if they would send their leaders the next morning to the Thames, the king would come and hear what they had to say. . . .

As soon as the mob perceived the royal barge approaching, they began shouting and crying as if all the spirits of the nether world had been in the company. . . .

When the king and his lords saw this crowd of people, and the wildness of their manner, the boldest of the party felt alarm, and the king was advised not to land, but to have his barge rowed up and down the river. "What do you wish for?" he demanded of the multitude; "I am come hither to hear what you have to say." Those near him cried out, "We wish you to land, and then we will tell you what our wants are." Upon this the Earl of Salisbury cried out, "Gentlemen, you are not properly dressed, nor are you in a fit condition for a king to talk with." Nothing more was said on either side, for the king was prevailed upon at once to return to the tower. The people seeing this were in a great passion, and returned to Blackheath to inform their companions how the king had served them; upon hearing which, they all cried out, "Let us instantly march to London." Accordingly they set out at once, and on the road thither destroyed all the houses of lawyers and courtiers, and all the monasteries they met with. . . . Their leaders, John Ball, Jack Straw, and Wat Tyler, then marched through London, attended by more than twenty thousand men, to the palace of the Savoy, which is a handsome building belonging to the Duke of Lancaster. . . . Here they immediately killed the porters, rushed into the house, and set it on fire. . . .

After this they paraded the streets, and killed every Fleming they could find, whether in house, church, or hospital: they broke open several houses of the Lombards. . . . They murdered a rich citizen, by name Richard Lyon, to whom Wat Tyler had formerly been servant in France, but having once beaten him, the varlet had never forgotten it. . . . Towards evening they fixed their quarters in a square, called St. Catherine's, before the Tower, declaring that they would not depart until they had obtained from the king everything they wanted—until the Chancellor of England had accounted to them, and shown how the great sums which were raised had been expended. . . . In the evening, he [the king] and his barons . . . and some of the principal citizens, held a council in the Tower. . . . However, nothing was done, they were really too much afraid of the commonality; and the king's advisers, the Earl of

Salisbury and others, said to him, "Sir, if you can appease them by fair words, it will be so much the better; for should we begin what we cannot go through, it will be over with us and our heirs, and England will be a desert." . . . On Friday morning the rebels, who lodged in the square of St. Catherine's, before the Tower, began to make themselves ready. They shouted much and said, that if the king would not come out to them, they would attack the Tower, storm it, and slay all who were within. The king, alarmed at these menaces, resolved to speak with the rabble; he therefore sent orders for them to retire to a handsome meadow at Mile-end. . . . When the gates of the Tower were thrown open, and the king attended by his two brothers and other nobles had passed through, Wat Tyler, Jack Straw, and John Ball, with upwards of four hundred others, rushed in by force, and running from chamber to chamber, found the Archbishop of Canterbury, by name Simon, a valiant and wise man, whom the rascals seized and beheaded. . . .

While the king was on his way to Mile-end, his two brothers, the Earl of Kent and Sir John Holland, stole away from his company, not daring to show themselves to the populace. The king himself, however, showed great courage, and on his arrival at the appointed spot instantly advanced into the midst of the assembled multitude, saying in a most pleasing manner, "My good people, I am your king and your lord, what is it you want? What do you wish to say to me?" Those who heard him made answer, "We wish you to make us free for ever. We wish to be no longer called slaves, nor held in bondage." The king replied, "I grant your wish; now therefore return to your homes, and let two or three from each village be left behind, to whom I will order letters to be given with my seal, fully granting every demand you have made: and in order that you may be the more satisfied, I will direct that my banners be sent to every stewardship, castlewick, and corporation." . . .

Thus did this great assembly break up. The king instantly employed upwards of thirty secretaries, who drew up the letters as fast as they could, and when they were sealed and delivered to them the people departed to their own counties. The principal mischief, however, remained behind: I mean Wat Tyler, Jack Straw, and John Ball, who declared, that though the people were satisfied, they were by no means so, and with them were about thirty thousand also of the same mind. These all continued in the city without any wish to receive the letters or the king's seal, but did all they could to throw the town into such confusion, that the lords, and rich citizens, might be murdered and their houses pillaged and destroyed. . . .

This day [Saturday] all the rabble again assembled under Wat Tyler, Jack Straw, and John Ball, at a place called Smithfield, where every Friday the horse market is kept. There were present about twenty thousand, and many more were in the city, breakfasting, and drinking. . . . Those who collected in Smithfield had with them the king's banner, which had been given to them the preceding evening; and the wretches, notwithstanding this, wanted to pillage the city, their leaders saying, that hitherto they had done nothing. . . . To this opinion all had agreed, when the king, attended by sixty horses, appeared in sight; he was at the time not thinking of the rabble, but had intended to continue his ride. . . . Wat Tyler, seeing the king and his party, said to his men, "Here is the king, I will go and speak with him; do you not stir until I give you a signal." . . .

His first words were these: "King, dost thou see all these men here?" "Yes," replied the king; "why dost thou ask?" "Because they are all under my command, and have sworn by their faith and loyalty to do whatsoever I shall order." "Very well," said the king: "I have no objection to it." Tyler, who was only desirous of a riot, made answer: "And thou thinkest, king, that these people, and as many more in the city, also under my command, ought to depart without having thy letters? No, indeed, we will carry them with us." "Why," replied the king, "it has been so ordered, and the letters will be delivered out one after another; but, friend, return to thy companions, and tell them to depart from London; be peaceable and careful of yourselves; for it is our determination that you shall all have the letters by towns and villages according to our agreement." As the king finished speaking, Wat Tyler, casting his eyes round, spied a squire attached to the king's person bearing a sword. This squire Tyler mortally hated, and on seeing him, cried out, "What hast thou there? give me thy dagger." "I will not," said the squire: "why should I give it to thee?" The king upon this said, "Give it to him; give it to him;" which the squire did, though much against his will. When Tyler took the dagger, he began to play with it in his hand, and again addressing the squire, said, "Give me that sword." "I will not," replied the squire, "for it is the king's sword, and thou being but a mechanic art not worthy to bear it; and if only thou and I were together, thou wouldst not have dared to say what thou hast, for a heap of gold as large as this church." By my troth," answered Tyler, "I will not eat this day before I have thy head." At these words the Mayor of London, with about twelve men, rode forward, armed under their robes, and seeing Tyler's manner of behaving, said, "Scoundrel, how dare you to behave thus in the king's presence?" The king, also enraged at the fellow's impudence, said to the mayor, "Lay hands on him." Whilst King Richard was giving this order, Tyler still kept up the conversation, saying to the mayor: "What have you to do with it; does what I have said concern you?" "It does," replied the mayor, who found himself supported by the king, and then added: "I will not live a day unless you pay for your insolence." Upon saying which, he drew a kind of scimitar, and struck Tyler such a blow on the head as felled him to his horse's feet. As soon as the rebel was down, he was surrounded on all sides, in order that his own men might not see him; and one of the king's squires, by name John Standwich, immediately leaped from his horse, and drawing his sword, thrust it into his belly, so that he died.

When the rebels found that their leader was dead, they drew up in a sort of battle array, each man having his bow bent before him. The king at this time certainly hazarded much, though it turned out most fortunately for him; for as soon as Tyler was on the ground, he left his attendants, giving orders that no one should follow him, and riding up to the rebels, who were advancing to revenge their leader's death, said, "Gentlemen, what are you about: you shall have me for your captain: I am your king, remain peaceful." The greater part, on hearing these words, were quite ashamed, and those among them who were inclined for peace began to slip away; the riotous ones, however, kept their ground. . . .

While things were in this state, several persons ran to London, crying out, "They are killing the king and our mayor"; upon which alarm, all those of the king's party sallied out towards Smithfield, in number about seven or eight thousand. . . .

When the rabble had dispersed, the king and his lords, to their great joy, returned in good array to London. . . .

John Ball and Jack Straw were found hidden in an old ruin, where they had secreted themselves, thinking to steal away when things were quiet; but this they were prevented doing, for their own men betrayed them. With this capture the king and his barons were much pleased, and had their heads cut off, as was that of Tyler's, and fixed on London-bridge, in the room of those whom these wretches themselves had placed there.

5.

Against Clerical Wealth and Corruption through Sacraments: Waldensian and Albigensian Heresies* and the Radicalism of John Wyclif

Expanding wealth in land and other forms of property had become by the high Middle Ages not only a general characteristic of the Church, but one which played upon the nerves of both laity and government. There were many who found intolerable the striking contrast between the worldliness and materialism of their clerical mentors and the life style of Christ and his apostles. Certainly there was little in the lavishness of the Avignon Papacy (1305–1377) or the conflicting leadership which resulted from the Great Schism (1378–1417) to recommend the Church as a spiritual guide.

At base, the anticlericalism which resulted from such abuses was not irreligious. But, when harassed, critics of the worldly and often ostentatious habits of the clergy frequently moved from dissent against clerical materialism to heretical opposition to Church dogma. Bernard of Clairvaux (d. 1153), a Cistercian abbot canonized in 1171, confined himself to verbal attacks on "backbiting" monks who ate until they vomited and fancy-garmented bishops who displayed themselves like princes of provinces rather than as shepherds of the Lord's flocks. But Arnold of Brescia, a contemporary of Bernard and a former student of the famous Peter Abelard, was so aghast at the materialism of the Roman Papacy that he led a revolt ousting

*James Harvey Robinson, ed., *Readings in European History* (Boston: Ginn and Company, 1904), Vol. I, pp. 380–83.

Eugenius III and supplanting his rule for nearly a decade with a primitive Christian regime.

Since the hierarchy, jurisdiction, dogma, and property of the Church were all closely interrelated, it was difficult for dissenters to challenge any aspect of clerical practice without facing harsh treatment, if not ecclesiastical condemnation. The followers of Peter Waldo (Waldensians) and the Albigensians, a religious sect of southern France, are cases in point. Their criticisms of ecclesiastical wealth and clerical immorality, as much as their religious beliefs, earned them papal enmity and much persecution during the late twelfth and early thirteenth centuries.

John Wyclif (1320–1384) and his followers, nicknamed the Lollards, were also considered a grave threat to the clerical hierarchy. Wyclif, a renowned English scholar described by one of his contemporaries as "peerless in logic," not only attacked the abuses of wealthy religious orders, but questioned the Pope's claims to temporal rule and drew attention to the contrast between the Holy Scriptures and Church dogma. Gregory XI censured a number of Wyclif's propositions during the 1370's, but the popular reformer was saved from the full effects of the condemnation through the support of John of Gaunt and other men of rank who found some of his positions congenial. Gaunt and his fellow magnates were particularly pleased by the logical ground Wyclif had provided for refusing dues claimed by the Pope, then residing in France. However, two developments occurred in the next years which altered the whole situation: Wyclif challenged the doctrine of transubstantiation and the Peasants' War broke out. The fear and uncertainty occasioned by the latter made it impossible for Wyclif to avoid punishment for his widely publicized view of the nature of the consecrated elements (he maintained that the bread did not become the body of Christ, from which it followed that the Mass and the priesthood had a diminished importance). In 1382 Wyclif was condemned by a synod in London and restricted to his residence in Lutterworth, where he died two years later.

And during the same year, that is the 1173d since the Lord's Incarnation, there was at Lyons in France a certain citizen, Waldo by name, who had made himself much money by wicked usury. One Sunday, when he had joined a crowd which he saw gathered around a troubadour, he was smitten by his words and, taking him to his house, he took care to hear him at length. The passage he was reciting was how the holy Alexis died a blessed death in his father's house. When morning had come the prudent citizen hurried to the schools of theology to seek counsel for his soul, and when he was taught many ways of going to God, he asked the master what way was more certain and more perfect than all others. The master answered him with this text: "If thou wilt be perfect, go and sell all that thou hast," etc.

Then Waldo went to his wife and gave her the choice of keeping his personal property or his real estate, namely, what he had in ponds, groves and fields, houses, rents, vineyards, mills, and fishing rights. She was much displeased at having to make this choice, but she kept the real estate. From his personal property he made restitution to those whom he had treated unjustly; a great part of it he gave to his two little daughters, who, without their mother's knowledge, he placed in the convent of Font Evrard; but the greatest part of his money he spent for the poor. A very great famine was then oppressing France and Germany. The prudent citizen, Waldo, gave bread, with vegetables and meat, to every one who came to him for three days in every week from Pentecost to the feast of St. Peter's bonds.

At the Assumption of the blessed Virgin, casting some money among the village poor, he cried, "No man can serve two masters, God and mammon." Then his fellow-citizens ran up, thinking he had lost his mind. But going on to a higher place, he said: "My fellow-citizens and friends, I am not insane, as you think, but I am avenging myself on my enemies, who made me a slave, so that I was always more careful of money than of God, and served the creature rather than the Creator. I know that many will blame me that I act thus openly. But I do it both on my own account and on yours; on my own, so that those who see me henceforth possessing any money may say that I am mad, and on yours, that you may learn to place hope in God and not in riches."

On the next day, coming from the church, he asked a certain citizen, once his comrade, to give him something to eat, for God's sake. His friend, leading him to his house,

said, "I will give you whatever you need as long as I live."
When this came to the ears of his wife, she was not a little
troubled, and as though she had lost her mind, she ran to
the archbishop of the city and implored him not to let her
husband beg bread from any one but her. This moved all
present to tears.

[Waldo was accordingly conducted into the presence of
the bishop.] And the woman, seizing her husband by the
coat, said, "Is it not better, husband, that I should redeem
my sins by giving you alms than that strangers should do
so?" And from that time he was not allowed to take food
from any one in that city except from his wife.

An experienced inquisitor thus describes the Albigenses:

It would take too long to describe in detail the manner
in which these same Manichæan heretics preach and teach
their followers, but it must be briefly considered here.

In the first place, they usually say of themselves that they
are good Christians, who do not swear, or lie, or speak evil
of others; that they do not kill any man or animal, nor anything having the breath of life, and that they hold the faith
of the Lord Jesus Christ and his gospel as Christ and his
apostles taught. They assert that they occupy the place of
the apostles, and that, on account of the above-mentioned
things, they of the Roman Church, namely the prelates,
clerks, and monks, and especially the inquisitors of heresy,
persecute them and call them heretics, although they are
good men and good Christians, and that they are persecuted
just as Christ and his apostles were by the Pharisees.

Moreover they talk to the laity of the evil lives of the
clerks and prelates of the Roman Church, pointing out and
setting forth their pride, cupidity, avarice, and uncleanness
of life, and such other evils as they know. They invoke,
with their own interpretation and according to their abili-
ties, the authority of the Gospels and the Epistles against
the condition of the prelates, churchmen, and monks,
whom they call Pharisees and false prophets, who say,
but do not.

Then they attack and vituperate, in turn, all the sacraments of the Church, especially the sacrament of the eucha-
rist, saying that it cannot contain the body of Christ, for
had this been as great as the largest mountain Christians
would have entirely consumed it before this. They assert
that the host comes from straw, that it passes through
the tails of horses, to wit, when the flour is cleaned by a
sieve (of horse hair); that, moreover, it passes through the

body and comes to a vile end, which, they say, could not happen if God were in it.

Of baptism, they assert that water is material and corruptible, and is therefore the creation of the evil power and cannot sanctify the soul, but that the churchmen sell this water out of avarice, just as they sell earth for the burial of the dead, and oil to the sick when they anoint them, and as they sell the confession of sins as made to the priests.

Hence they claim that confession made to the priests of the Roman Church is useless, and that, since the priests may be sinners, they cannot loose nor bind, and being unclean themselves, cannot make others clean. They assert, moreover, that the cross of Christ should not be adored or venerated, because, as they urge, no one would venerate or adore the gallows upon which a father, relative, or friend had been hung. They urge, further, that they who adore the cross ought, for similar reasons, to worship all thorns and lances, because as Christ's body was on the cross during the passion, so was the crown of thorns on his head and the soldier's lance in his side. They proclaim many other scandalous things in regard to the sacraments.

Moreover they read from the Gospels and the Epistles in the vulgar tongue, applying and expounding them in their favor and against the condition of the Roman Church in a manner which it would take too long to describe in detail; but all that relates to this subject may be read more fully in the books they have written and infected, and may be learned from the confessions of such of their followers as have been converted.

Wycliffite Conclusions, Ten Condemned as Heretical and Fourteen as Erroneous *

I. That the material substance of bread and of wine remains, after the consecration, in the sacrament of the altar.

II. That the accidents do not remain without the subject, after the consecration, in the same sacrament.

*Edward P. Cheyney, ed., *Translations and Reprints from the Original Sources of European History* (Philadelphia: University of Pennsylvania, 1899), Vol. II, No. 5, pp. 9–11.

III. That Christ is not in the sacrament of the altar identically, truly and really in his proper corporal presence.

IV. That if a bishop or priest lives in mortal sin he does not ordain, or consecrate, or baptize.

V. That if a man has been truly repentant, all external confession is superfluous to him, or useless.

VI. Continually to assert that it is not founded in the gospel that Christ instituted the mass.

VII. That God ought to be obedient to the devil.

VIII. That if the pope is foreordained to destruction and a wicked man, and therefore a member of the devil, no power has been given to him over the faithful of Christ by any one, unless perhaps by the Emperor.

IX. That since Urban the Sixth, no one is to be acknowledged as pope; but all are to live, in the way of the Greeks, under their own laws.

X. To assert that it is against sacred scripture that men of the church should have temporal possessions.

XI. That no prelate ought to excommunicate any one unless he first knows that the man is excommunicated by God.

XII. That a person thus excommunicating is thereby a heretic or excommunicate.

XIII. That a prelate excommunicating a clerk who has appealed to the king, or to a council of the kingdom, on that very account is a traitor to God, the king and the kingdom.

XIV. That those who neglect to preach, or to hear the word of God, or the gospel that is preached, because of the excommunication of men, are excommunicate, and in the day of judgment will be considered as traitors to God.

XV. To assert that it is allowed to any one, whether a deacon or a priest, to preach the word of God, without the authority of the apostolic see, or of a catholic bishop, or some other which is sufficiently acknowledged.

XVI. To assert that no one is a civil lord, no one is a bishop, no one is a prelate, so long as he is in mortal sin.

XVII. That temporal lords may, at their own judgment, take away temporal goods from churchmen who are habitually delinquent; or that the people may, at their own judgment, correct delinquent lords.

XVIII. That tithes are purely charity, and that parishioners may, on account of the sins of their curates, detain these and confer them on others at their will.

XIX. That special prayers applied to one person by prelates or religious persons, are of no more value to the same person than general prayers for others in a like position are to him.

XX. That the very fact that any one enters upon any private religion whatever, renders him more unfitted and more incapable of observing the commandments of God.

XXI. That saints who have instituted any private religions whatever, as well of those having possessions as of mendicants, have sinned in thus instituting them.

XXII. That religious persons living in private religions are not of the Christian religion.

XXIII. That friars should be required to gain their living by the labor of their hands and not by mendicancy.

XXIV. That a person giving alms to friars, or to a preaching friar, is excommunicate; also the one receiving.

6.

Peasants Revolt in Germany, 1524–1525*

In 1524–1525 several provinces of Reformation Germany were ravaged by a serious peasant revolt arising from long-standing grievances. Like the rebels who had descended on London in 1381, the German peasants not only demanded an end to the extortionate taxation of the territorial princes, but called as well for the elimination of social distinctions based on birth and wealth. In a spree of vengeance for centuries of repression, they engaged in wholesale pillage and burning of property and either murdered outright, or seized and placed on public "trial," rapacious landlords.

The egalitarian slogans of the revolt were reinforced by notions of the equality of all Christians to which Martin Luther (1483–1546) had given such emphasis. Though Luther saw himself as a restorer of true doctrine and the practices of the early Church, rather than as a revolutionary, his emphasis on Christian liberty was interpreted by the discontented peasants as the freedom to judge what was right in social, political, and economic matters.

As they rose, the peasants drafted their demands for reforms in twelve articles, reprinted below. From the vantage point of the twentieth century, the demands appear neither excessive nor inflammatory. Yet the rulers and landlords to whom they were addressed viewed them as patently seditious, for, taken together, the demands were an attack on the very foundations of existing society.

*James Harvey Robinson and Merrick Whitcomb, eds., *Translations and Reprints from the Original Sources of European History* (Philadelphia: University of Pennsylvania, n.d.), Vol. II, No. 6, pp. 25–30.

Luther, who was far from unmindful of peasant grievances and had at first criticized the lordly greed which had prompted the uprising, soon turned against the rebels and advised the princes to "kill, destroy, exterminate, drown in blood without mercy" the "rampaging hordes of the peasantry." The princes needed little more urging and crushed the revolt with great ferocity.

Peace to the Christian Reader and the Grace of God through Christ.

There are many evil writings put forth of late which take occasion, on account of the assembling of the peasants, to cast scorn upon the Gospel, saying: Is this the fruit of the new teaching, that no one should obey but all should everywhere rise in revolt, and rush together to reform, or perhaps destroy entirely, the authorities, both ecclesiastical and lay? The articles below shall answer these godless and criminal fault-finders, and serve in the first place to remove the reproach from the word of God and, in the second place, to give a Christian excuse for the disobedience or even the revolt of the entire Peasantry. In the first place the Gospel is not the cause of revolt and disorder, since it is the message of Christ, the promised Messiah, the Word of Life, teaching only love, peace, patience and concord. Thus, all who believe in Christ should learn to be loving, peaceful, long-suffering and harmonious. This is the foundation of all the articles of the peasants (as will be seen) who accept the Gospel and live according to it. How then can the evil reports declare the Gospel to be a cause of revolt and disobedience? That the authors of the evil reports and the enemies of the Gospel oppose themselves to these demands is due not to the Gospel but to the Devil, the worst enemy of the Gospel, who causes this opposition by raising doubts in the minds of his followers; and thus the word of God, which teaches love, peace and concord, is overcome. In the second place, it is clear that the peasants demand that this Gospel be taught them as a guide in life, and they ought not to be called disobedient or disorderly. Whether God grant the peasants (earnestly wishing to live according to his word) their requests or no, who shall find fault with the will of the Most High? Who shall meddle in his judgments or oppose his majesty? Did he not hear the children of Israel when they called upon him and save them out of the hands of Pharaoh? Can he not save his own to-day? Yea, he will save them and that speedily. Therefore, Christian reader, read the following articles with care and then judge. Here follow the articles:

The First Article. First, it is our humble petition and desire, as also our will and resolution, that in the future we should have power and authority so that each community should choose and appoint a pastor, and that we should have the right to depose him should he conduct himself improperly. The pastor thus chosen should teach us the Gospel pure and simple, without any addition, doctrine or ordinance of man. For to teach us continually the true faith will lead us to pray God that through his grace this faith may increase within us and become a part of us. For if his grace work not within us we remain flesh and blood, which availeth nothing; since the Scripture clearly teaches that only through true faith can we come to God. Only through his mercy can we become holy. Hence such a guide and pastor is necessary, and in this fashion grounded upon the Scriptures.

The Second Article. According as the just tithe is established by the Old Testament and fulfilled in the New, we are ready and willing to pay the fair tithe of grain. The word of God plainly provides that in giving according to right to God and distributing to his people the services of a pastor are required. We will that for the future our church provost, whomsoever the community may appoint, shall gather and receive this tithe. From this he shall give to the pastor, elected by the whole community, a decent and sufficient maintenance for him and his (*im und den seynen*), as shall seem right to the whole community [*or*, with the knowledge of the community]. What remains over shall be given to the poor of the place, as the circumstances and the general opinion demand. Should anything farther remain, let it be kept, lest anyone should have to leave the country from poverty. Provision should also be made from this surplus to avoid laying any land tax on the poor. In case one or more villages have themselves sold their tithes on account of want, and the village has taken action as a whole, the buyer should not suffer loss, but we will that some proper agreement be reached with him for the repayment of the sum by the village with due interest. But those who have tithes which they have not purchased from a village, but which were appropriated by their ancestors, should not, and ought not, to be paid anything farther by the village, which shall apply its tithes to the support of the pastors elected as above indicated, or to solace the poor, as is taught by the Scriptures. The small tithes, whether ecclesiastical or lay, we will not pay at all, for the Lord God created cattle for the free use of man. We will not, therefore, pay farther an unseemly tithe which is of man's invention.

The Third Article. It has been the custom hitherto for men to hold us as their own property, which is pitiable enough, considering that Christ has delivered and redeemed us all, without exception, by the shedding of his precious blood, the lowly as well as the great. Accordingly, it is consistent with Scripture that we should be free and wish to be so. Not that we would wish to be absolutely free and under no authority. God does not teach us that we should lead a disorderly life in the lusts of the flesh, but that we should love the Lord our God and our neighbor. We would gladly observe all this as God has commanded us in the celebration of the communion. He has not commanded us not to obey the authorities, but rather that we should be humble, not only towards those in authority, but towards everyone. We are thus ready to yield obedience according to God's law to our elected and regular authorities in all proper things becoming to a Christian. We, therefore, take it for granted that you will release us from serfdom, as true Christians, unless it should be shown us from the Gospel that we are serfs.

The Fourth Article. In the fourth place it has been the custom heretofore, that no poor man should be allowed to touch venison or wild fowl, or fish in flowing water, which seems to us quite unseemly and unbrotherly, as well as selfish and not agreeable to the word of God. In some places the authorities preserve the game to our great annoyance and loss, recklessly permitting the unreasoning animals to destroy to no purpose our crops, which God suffers to grow for the use of man, and yet we must remain quiet. This is neither godly nor neighborly. For when God created man he gave him dominion over all the animals, over the birds of the air and over the fish in the water. Accordingly it is our desire if a man holds possession of waters that he should prove from satisfactory documents that his right has been unwittingly acquired by purchase. We do not wish to take it from him by force, but his rights should be exercised in a Christian and brotherly fashion. But whosoever cannot produce such evidence should surrender his claim with good grace.

The Fifth Article. In the fifth place we are aggrieved in the matter of wood-cutting, for the noble folk have appropriated all the woods to themselves alone. If a poor man requires wood he must pay double for it [*or perhaps, two pieces of money*]. It is our opinion in regard to a wood which has fallen into the hands of a lord, whether spiritual or temporal, that unless it was duly purchased it should revert again to the community. It should, moreover, be free to every member of the community to help himself to such firewood as he needs in his own home. Also, if a man requires wood for carpenter's purposes he should have it free, but with the knowledge of a person appointed by the community for that purpose. Should, however, no such forest be at the disposal of the community, let that which has been duly bought be administered in a brotherly and Christian manner. If the forest, although unfairly appropriated in the first instance, was later duly sold, let the matter be adjusted in a friendly spirit and according to the Scriptures.

The Sixth Article. Our sixth complaint is in regard to the excessive services demanded of us, which are increased from day to day. We ask that this matter be properly looked into so that we shall not continue to be oppressed in this way, and that some gracious consideration be given us, since our forefathers were required only to serve according to the word of God.

The Seventh Article. Seventh, we will not hereafter allow ourselves to be farther oppressed by our lords, but will let them demand only what is just and proper according to the word of the agreement between the lord and the peasant. The lord should no longer try to force more services or other dues from the peasant without payment, but permit the peasant to enjoy his holding in peace and quiet. The peasant should, however, help the lord when it is necessary, and at proper times, when it will not be disadvantageous to the peasant, and for a suitable payment.

The Eighth Article. In the eighth place, we are greatly burdened by holdings which cannot support the rent exacted from them. The peasants suffer loss in this way and are ruined; and we ask that the lords may appoint persons of honor to inspect these holdings, and fix a rent in accordance with justice, so that the peasant shall not work for nothing, since the laborer is worthy of his hire.

The Ninth Article. In the ninth place, we are burdened with a great evil in the constant making of new laws. We are not judged according to the offence, but sometimes with great ill will, and sometimes much too leniently. In our opinion we should be judged according to the old written law, so that the case shall be decided according to its merits, and not with partiality.

The Tenth Article. In the tenth place, we are aggrieved by the appropriation by individuals of meadows and fields which at one time belonged to a community. These we will take again into our own hands. It may, however, happen that the land was rightfully purchased, but when the land has unfortunately been purchased in this way, some brotherly arrangement should be made according to circumstances.

The Eleventh Article. In the eleventh place we will entirely abolish the due called *Todfall* [*i.e.*, heriot], and will no longer endure it, nor allow widows and orphans to be thus shamefully robbed against God's will, and in violation of justice and right, as has been done in many places, and by those who should shield and protect them. These have disgraced and despoiled us, and although they had little authority they assumed it. God will suffer this no more, but it shall be wholly done away with, and for the future no man shall be bound to give little or much.

Conclusion. In the twelfth place it is our conclusion and final resolution, that if any one or more of the articles here set forth should not be in agreement with the word of God, as we think they are, such article we will willingly recede from, when it is proved really to be against the word of God by a clear explanation of the Scripture. Or if articles should now be conceded to us that are hereafter discovered to be unjust, from that hour they shall be dead and null and without force. Likewise, if more complaints should be discovered which are based upon truth and the Scriptures, and relate to offences against God and our neighbor, we have determined to reserve the right to present these also, and to exercise ourselves in all Christian teaching. For this we shall pray God, since he can grant this, and he alone. The peace of Christ abide with us all.

7.

Erasmus Satirizes
the Warmongers*

During the first half of the sixteenth century the European world of letters was dominated by Desiderius Erasmus (ca. 1466–1536), a Dutch scholar with a vital interest in the Greek classics who popularized the application of Humanist learning to specifically Christian problems.

Reminiscent of the typical Italian Humanist of the fifteenth century, Erasmus was repelled by much that seemed wrong to him in the life of his day. Yet he disdained the Italian Humanist's escapism. Whereas the typical Italian Humanist had tended to follow the course set by Petrarch ("In order to forget my own time I have constantly striven to place myself in the spirit of other ages"), Erasmus faced up to reality and became—through words if not through deeds—a reformer of his society's ills. And among the ills which most disturbed him were those associated with the Church. But unlike his contemporary Martin Luther, who also deplored the abuses of the Church, he believed that revolt against religious authority could lead only to religious anarchy. Hence he advocated gradual reform from within and appealed to men's reason and sense of humor. In his popular work In Praise of Folly *and in a long list of other books he satirized the weaknesses and contradictions in the lives of the men of his time.*

The colloquy Charon, *which follows, is a clear example of Erasmian satire of war and warmongers. It was written at a time when many of the nations of Europe were tearing at one another's throats. The principal protagonists*

The Colloquies of Erasmus. Translated by Nathan Bailey (London: Reeves & Turner, 1878), Vol. II, pp. 139–45.

*included Francis I, King of France (r. 1515–1547), who,
assisted by Henry VIII of England (r. 1509–1547), was
pitted against the Hapsburg Emperor Charles V (r. 1519–
1556) in a struggle for the control of Italy. As a tireless
proponent of the brotherhood of man and the splendor of
peace, Erasmus found this conflict abhorrent.*

*Charon was the ferryman in Greek mythology who took
the souls of the dead over the River Styx. Alastor was an
avenging demon.*

CHARON, *Genius* ALASTOR

Ch. Whither are you going so brisk, and in such Haste,
Alastor?

Al. O *Charon,* you come in the Nick of Time, I was
coming to you.

Ch. Well, what News do you bring?

Al. I bring a Message to you and *Proserpine,*[1] that you
will be glad to hear.

Ch. Out with what you have brought, and lighten your
Burden.

Al. The Furies have been no less diligent than they have
been successful, in gaining their Point: there is not a Foot
of Ground upon Earth, that they have not infected with
their hellish Calamities, Seditions, Wars, Robberies, and
Plagues; so that they are grown quite bald, having shed
their Snakes, and having quite spit all their Venom, they
ramble about in search after whatever they can find of
Vipers and Asps; being become as smooth as an Egg, not
having so much as a single Hair upon their Heads,[2] and
not one Drop of Venom more in their Breasts. Do you
get your Boat and your Oars ready; you will have such a
vast Multitude of Ghosts come to you anon, that I'm afraid
you won't be able to carry them all over yourself.

---

[1] Queen of the underworld.
[2] The Furies had poisonous snakes for hair. These they sent to
torment the consciences of the wicked.

Ch. I could have told you that.

Al. How came you to know it?

Ch. Ossa[3] brought me that News above two Days ago.

Al. Nothing is more swift than that Goddess. But what makes you loitering here, having left your Boat?

Ch. My Business brought me hither; I came hither to provide myself with a good strong Three-Oar'd Boat: for my Boat is so rotten and leaky with Age, that it will not carry such a Burden, if *Ossa* told me true. But, indeed, what Need was there of *Ossa?* for the Thing shews itself, for I have suffered Shipwreck already.

Al. Indeed you are dropping dry, I fancied you were just come out of a Bath.

Ch. No, I swam out of the *Stygian* Lake.

Al. Where did you leave the Ghosts?

Ch. They are swimming among the Frogs.

Al. But what was it that *Ossa* told you?

Ch. That the three Monarchs of the the World were bent upon one another's Destruction with a mortal Hatred, and that there was no Part of *Christendom* free from the Rage of War; for these three have drawn all the rest in to be engag'd in the War with them. They are all so haughty, that not one of them will in the least submit to the other: Nor are the *Danes,* the *Poles,* the *Scots,* nor the *Turks* at Quiet, but are preparing to make dreadful Havock. The Plague rages every where, in *Spain, Britain, Italy,* and *France*; and more than all, there is a new Fire[4] sprung out of the Variety of Opinions, which has so corrupted the Minds of all Men, that there is no such Thing as sincere Friendship any where; But Brother is at Enmity with Brother, and Husband and Wife cannot agree. And it is to be hop'd, that this Distraction will be a glorious Destruction of Mankind, if these Controversies, that are now managed by the Tongue and the Pen, come once to be decided by Arms.

Al. All that Fame has told you is very true; for I myself, having been a constant Companion of the *Furies,* have with these Eyes seen more than all this, and that they never at any Time have approv'd themseves more worthy of their Name, than now.

Ch. But there is Danger, lest some Good Spirit should start up, and of a sudden exhort them to Peace: And Men's Minds are variable, for I have heard, that among the Living there is one *Polygraphus,*[5] who is continually,

---

[3]In Homer, the goddess Rumor.
[4]Lutheranism.
[5]Erasmus.

by his Writing, inveighing against Wars, and exhorting to Peace.

Al. Ay, ay, but he has a long Time been talking to the Deaf. He once wrote a Sort of *Hue* and *Cry* after Peace, that was banish'd or driven away; and after that, an *Epitaph* upon *Peace defunct*. But then, on the other Hand, there are others that advance our Cause no less than the Furies do themselves.

Ch. Who are they?

Al. They are a certain Sort of Animals in black and white Vestments, Ash-colour'd Coats, and various other Dresses,[6] that are always hovering about the Courts of Princes, and are continually instilling into their Ears the Love of War, and exhorting the Nobility and common People to it, haranguing them in their Sermons, that it is a just, holy and religious War. And that which would make you stand in admiration at the Confidence of these Men, is the Cry of both Parties. In *France* they preach it up, that God is on the *French* Side, and they can never be overcome, that have God for their Protector. In *England* and *Spain* the Cry is, the War is not the King's, but God's; therefore, if they do but fight like Men, they depend upon getting the Victory; and if any one should chance to fall in the Battle, he will not die, but fly directly up into Heaven, Arms and all.

Ch. And is Credit given to all this?

Al. What can't a well-dissembled Religion do? when to this there is added Youth, Unexperiencedness, Ambition, a natural Animosity, and a Mind propense to any Thing that offers itself. It is an easy Matter to impose upon such; it is an easy Matter to overthrow a Waggon, that was inclining to fall before.

Ch. I would do these Animals a good Turn with all my Heart.

Al. Prepare a good Treat; you can do nothing that will be more acceptable to them.

Ch. What, of Mallows, and Lupines, and Leeks? for you know we have no other Provision in our Territories.

Al. No, but of Partridges, and Capons, and Pheasants, if you would have them look upon you as a good Caterer.

Ch. But what is it that moves these People to be so hot for War? What will they get by it?

Al. Because they get more by those that die, than those

[6]The friars.

that live. There are last Wills and Testaments, Funeral
Obsequies, Bulls, and a great many other Articles of no
despicable Profit. And in the last Place, they had rather
live in a Camp, than in their Cells. War breeds a great
many Bishops, who were not thought good for any Thing
in a Time of Peace.

Ch. Well, they understand their Business.

Al. But what Occasion have you for a new Boat?

Ch. None at all, if I had a Mind to be wreck'd again in
the *Stygian* Lake.

Al. How came that about? because you had too large a
Company?

Ch. Yes.

Al. But you carry Shadows, not Bodies.

Ch. Let them be Water-Spiders, yet there may be enough
of them to over-load a Boat; and then you know my Boat
is but a shadowy Boat neither.

Al. But I remember once upon a Time, when you had a
great Company, so many that your Boat would not hold
them, I have seen three thousand hanging upon your Stem,
and you were not sensible of any Weight at all.

Ch. I confess there are such Sorts of Ghosts; those are
such as pass slowly out of the Body, being reduced to little
or nothing with Consumptions, and Hectick-Fevers. But
as for those that are torn of a sudden out of gross Bodies,
they bring a great Deal of corpulent Substance along with
them; such as are sent hither by Apoplexies, Quinseys,
Pestilences, and especially by War.

Al. I don't think the *French* or *Spaniards* bring much
Weight along with them.

Ch. Much less than the rest; but for all that, their Ghosts
are not altogether so light as Feathers neither. But as for
the *Englishmen* and *Germans* that feed well, they come
sometimes in such Case, that I was lately in Danger of
going to the Bottom in carrying only ten; and unless I had
thrown some of my Lading over-Board, I had been lost,
Boat, Passengers, and Boat-Hire, all together.

Al. You were in great Danger then indeed.

Ch. But what do you think I must do, when so many
fat Lords, Hectors, and Bullies, shall come to us?

Al. As for those that die in a just War, I suppose none
of them will come to you; for they say, they fly bolt upright into Heaven.

Ch. I can't tell where they fly to; but this I am sure of,
as often as there is a War, there come so many Wounded
and Cripples to me, that I admire that there should be one

Soul left above Ground; and they come over-charg'd, not only with Surfeits and Paunch-Bellies, but with Bulls, Benefices, and a great many other Things.

Al. But they don't bring these Things along with them, but come naked to you.

Ch. True; but at their first coming, they bring the Dreams of all these Things along with them.

Al. Are Dreams so heavy then?

Ch. They load my Boat; load it, did I say? nay, they have sunk it before now. And, in the last Place, do you think so many Halfpence don't weigh any Thing?

Al. Yes, I believe they do, if they bring Brass ones.

Ch. Therefore I am resolv'd to look out for a Vessel, that shall be fit for my Cargo.

Al. You're a happy Fellow.

Ch. Wherein?

Al. Because you'll get an Estate in a Trice.

Ch. What, out of a Multitude of Ghosts?

Al. Yes, indeed.

Ch. Ay, if they did but bring their Wealth along with them. But now they sit in my Boat, bewailing themselves for the Kingdoms, and Dignities, and Abbacies, and the innumerable Talents of Gold they have left behind them, and bring me nothing but a poor Halfpenny: So that all I have been scraping together for these three thousand Years, will go for the Purchase of a new Boat.

Al. They that expect Gain, must be at some Charge.

Ch. But the People in the World have better Trading, I hear; for, if Fortune favour them, they can get an Estate in three Years Time.

Al. Ay, and sometimes turn Bankrupts too; tho' your Gain is less, it is more certain.

Ch. I can't tell how certain it is, if any Deity should start up, and make Peace among the Princes, all this goodly Expectation of mine is knock'd on the Head at once.

Al. As to that Matter, I'll take upon me to be your Security, so that you may set your Heart at Rest. You have no Reason to fear a Peace for these ten Years: The Pope is the only Man that persuades them to come to an Agreement among themselves; but he had as good *keep his Breath to cool his Porridge*. The Cities murmur at the Load of Calamities they lie under; and some there are, I can't tell who, that whisper it about, that it is an unreasonable Thing, that the whole World should be turned upside down, for the private Piques and Ambition of two or three Persons. But for all this, take my Word for it, the Furies will get the better of it, let these Attempts be as promising as they will. But what Occasion had you to come into this World to get a Boat? han't we Workmen enough among ourselves? We have *Vulcan*,[7] have we not?

Ch. Ay, right, if I wanted a Boat of Brass.

Al. Or, you may send for a Workman for a small Matter.

Ch. I might do that, but I want Materials.

Al. What say you? Are there no Woods in this Country?

Ch. All the Woods in the *Elysian* Fields are destroy'd.

Al. In doing what?

Ch. In burning Hereticks Ghosts, so that of late, for Fuel we have been forc'd to dig for Coals in the Bowels of the Earth.

Al. What, could not Ghosts be punish'd at a less Charge than that?

Ch. Rhadamanthus[8] would have it so.

Al. If it be so, when you have got a Boat, where will you get Oars?

Ch. It is my Business to steer, let the Ghosts row themselves, if they have a Mind to get over.

Al. But some of them never learned to row.

Ch. I have no Respect for Persons, Kings and Cardinals row with me; every one takes his Turn, as much as the poorest Peasant, whether they have learned to row or not.

Al. Well, do you see and get a Boat as cheap as you can, I won't detain you any longer, I'll away to Hell with my good News: But, soho, soho, *Charon*.

Ch. What's the Matter?

Al. Make Haste, and get back as soon as you can, lest you be smothered in the Crowd.

Ch. Nay, you'll find at least Two hundred thousand upon the Bank already, besides those that are paddling in the Lake. I'll make what Haste I can; and do you tell them I shall be there presently.

[7]Roman god of fire and metalworking.
[8]One of the judges of the dead.

8.
A Critique of Royal Absolutism*

Victor Hugo's assertion that the France of Louis XIV (r. 1643–1715) was "queen of the world and slave of a man" is not far from the truth. Under the "Sun King's" leadership France was perhaps the most active and influential country in the world. La grande nation achieved a political ascendancy in Europe greater than anything known since Charlemagne. And though the other peoples of Europe deplored the aggressive wars which led to that ascendancy, they nevertheless paid homage to France's cultural superiority. French literature, manners, fashions, art, and architecture were everywhere imitated.

To a very great degree Louis himself was the conscious embodiment of French greatness as well as of the idea of divine-right monarchy. His countrymen—many of whom apparently believed that he had been divinely appointed as the instrument of God's wrath on earth—accorded him a veneration which is difficult for twentieth-century Americans to comprehend. In no other nation was the cult of the monarch carried to such lengths. Princes and dukes actually vied for the honor of handing Louis his underwear and other garments when he rose from his bed in the morning.

An exception to the almost unanimous praise showered upon Louis by his subjects is found in a letter addressed to him by Archbishop Fénelon of Cambrai (1651–1715).

*A. Caron and J. Gosselin, eds., Oeuvres de Fénelon, Archévêque de Cambrai (Paris: A. Le Clere et cie, 1827), Vol. XXIV, pp. 334–35, 338. Translated by the editors.

*Written in 1694, after Fénelon's growing concern with the
direction of affairs caused his retirement into the country,
it is one of the most unqualified denunciations of the "Sun
King's" rule ever penned by one of his contemporaries.
Two excerpts from the letter are reprinted below. As they
clearly demonstrate, Fénelon considered the record of the
reign to be lacking in every respect.*

. . . For thirty years, your chief ministers have shaken
and overthrown all the ancient maxims of the state in
order to increase your authority beyond all bounds, because this authority had become theirs since it was in their
hands. They no longer spoke of the state or the rules;
they spoke only of the king and his pleasure. They steadily
increased your revenues and your expenses. They exalted
you to the heavens, in order to efface, they said, the
grandeur of all your predecessors together, that is to say,
in order to impoverish all of France so as to introduce a
monstrous and incurable extravagance into the court. They
wished to raise you above the ruins of all the social classes
in the state—as if you might become great by ruining all
your subjects on whom your greatness is founded. It is
true that you have been overly jealous of your authority,
but essentially each minister has been master within his
administrative area. You believed that you were governing
because you regulated the limits of power among those
who governed. They paraded their power before the public,
and it was felt only too well. They have been harsh,
haughty, unjust, violent, and dishonest. They have known
no other rule of conduct, either in domestic or foreign
affairs, except to threaten, crush, and annihilate all who
opposed them. They consulted you only in order to dispel
any feelings on your part which might later cause resentment. They accustomed you to receiving endless, extrava-
gant praise approaching idolatry, which you, for the sake
of your honor, should have rejected with indignation.
They have rendered your name odious and the French

nation insufferable to all our neighbors. They have not retained a single of our ancient allies, since they only desired slaves. They have caused more than twenty years of bloody wars. . . .

In the meantime, your people, whom you should love as your children and who up until now have been so enamored of you, are dying of hunger. Agriculture is almost abandoned; the cities and the countryside are depopulated; all crafts languish and no longer support the workers. Commerce has been decimated. You have consequently destroyed half of the real power within your state in order to win and defend vain conquests abroad. Instead of squeezing money from the poor people, you ought to give them alms and sustenance. All France is but a great poorhouse without provisions. The magistrates are demeaned and overworked. The nobility, whose entire wealth depends on royal decrees, live solely on grants from the state. You are annoyed by a mob of people who beg and grumble. It is you, Sire, who have called down upon yourself all these difficulties; for, since the realm is in ruins, you have everything in your own hands, and no one can live without gifts from you. Such is the state of affairs in this great realm, so flourishing under a king who daily is described to us as the delight of the people, and who would be this in reality if flattering advice had not corrupted him. . . .

9.

Corruption and Depravity
through Progress: Rousseau's Discourse
on the Arts and Sciences*

Historians have always found it necessary to set Jean Jacques Rousseau (1712–1778) apart from other philosophes when evaluating the French Enlightenment. Unlike most of his fellow polemicists, Rousseau was never satisfied that reason alone could serve man adequately in the search for truth. He believed that if man is to find true happiness it must be in association with the heart, not merely the mind, and that such a quest must necessarily lead back to the simple instinctive virtue which all men by nature possess, rather than up any ladder of methodical progress. For Rousseau sought for man two conditions which the human experience had rarely recorded as reconcilable: liberty and equality.

In viewing the society around him, Rousseau concluded that man was neither free nor properly governed. And he was convinced that the remedy to this dilemma could not be found in organized religion, sophisticated governmental systems, or cultivation of the arts and sciences. What had come to be called progress in his day was to Rousseau no more than a refinement of the techniques by which the many were subjected to the corrupt control of a few. As he saw it, no amount of material productivity or cultural excellence would improve the condition of man's happiness or free him from moral depravity. Only if man returned to his natural state, close to the soil (which must be held, utilized, and defended in common), could he approach

---

*Jean Jacques Rousseau, *The Cultivation of the Arts and Sciences*. Translated by Henry Smithers (Brussels: British Press, 1818), pp. 1–3, 4–14, 16–20, 22–25, 30.

*happiness. Then and only then could the moral rectitude
and essential goodness of man's nature govern human relationships, a state in which values would reflect pure love
and freedom.*

*In 1749, after fifteen years of scholarly association with
other eighteenth-century philosophes, Rousseau penned his
first discourse, which has proved to be his most eloquent
statement of dissent. It was written for an essay contest
held by the Academy of Dijon in which the participants
were asked to write on the topic "Whether the revival of
the arts and sciences has improved morals and manners."
Whether it was Rousseau's own idea to take the negative
side of the question, or whether he did so at Diderot's
suggestion, as has been claimed, is open to conjecture. In
any event, alone among the dozens of entrants, he wrote
on the degree to which the sciences and arts had served
to corrupt mankind. By his strong words Rousseau took
issue not only with the entire social structure of the ancien
régime, but with all the heralded greatness of earlier epochs
which historian and poet have lauded.*

It has been doubted whether the re-establishment of the
Arts and Sciences, have operated most to purify or to corrupt the manners. Which part shall I take in this question?
That which becomes an honest man, who is of no party,
and who does not value himself the less for that.

I feel it difficult to adapt what I have to observe to the
tribunal which I address. How shall I dare to contemn
the sciences before one of the most learned societies of
Europe; to praise ignorance in a celebrated academy, and
reconcile a contempt of study with a respect for the truly
wise. I have foreseen these contrarieties, but they have not
deterred me. It is not science that I arraign—it is virtue
which I defend before virtuous men. Truth is more dear
to such men, than learning to the learned. . . .

. . . Europe had sunk into the barbarism of the earliest
ages. The inhabitants of this part of the world, now so

enlightened, lived for several centuries in *a state worse* than that of ignorance. I know not how to describe the scientific jargon more contemptible, even, than ignorance, that had usurped the name of knowledge, and opposed an almost invincible obstacle to its advancement. A revolution became necessary to awaken mankind to the exercise of common sense. It appeared, at length, where it was least expected. It was the stupid Mussulman, the eternal enemy of science, who gave it new birth. The fall of Constantine from the throne, transported into Italy the ruins of ancient Greece. France, in her turn, enriched herself with the precious spoils. The sciences soon followed the introduction of letters—the art of writing connected itself with the art of printing—an union which, however it may appear strange, is nevertheless, natural; and men began to experience that the principal advantage of an intercourse with the muses, was to render them more sociable, and to inspire them with the desire to please each other by works worthy of approbation.

The mind has its wants as well as the body, the one becomes the foundation of society, the other constitutes its charms. Whilst laws and government, afford safety and happiness to men when associated together—letters, arts and sciences, less despotic, but perhaps more powerful, entwine garlands of flowers amongst the iron chains with which they are loaded, stifling in them that original sentiment of freedom to which they appear to have been destined, teaching them to hug their chains, and forcing them into what is denominated a well regulated people. Necessity raised thrones, the arts and the sciences have strengthened them, and a well governed population cultivate them. Happy slaves, you are indebted to them for that delicate taste and ingenuity on which you pique yourselves, that docility and that urbanity of manners which makes the intercourses between you so binding and so easy, in a word, the semblance of the virtues, without the possession of any of them.

It was this sort of politeness, so much the more amiable as it affects the least to exhibit itself, that formerly distinguished Athens and Rome, in the boasted days of their magnificence and glory. By it also our own nation excels all other people, and all other times. A philosophic character without pedantry, natural manners equally distant from the rusticity of the Teutonic, and from Italian pantomime. These are the fruits of a taste acquired by excellent study and perfected by intercourse with mankind.

How delightful would it be to live among you, if the exterior countenance was ever the true image of the heart, if decency was virtue, if our maxims became the rules of our conduct, if true philosophy was inseparable from pretensions. But these things are seldom found united, and virtue does not long march forward in such triumph. The richness of his attire may announce an opulent man, and elegance of dress a man of taste. Man, healthy and robust, acknowledges no other token of honour, it is under the rustic garb of a labourer, and not under that of a courtier, that we find strength and vigour of body. Finery is not less foreign to virtue than to strength and vigour of soul. A vigorous man, in strong health, is a champion who can fight naked if he please. He despises all the false ornaments which restrains the use of his strength, and of which the greater part have been invented, only to conceal some deformity.

Before art had regulated our intercourses, and taught our passions to speak a language prepared for them, our manners were rustic, but they were natural, and the difference in behaviour announced at the first sight the diversity of character. Human nature, indeed, was not really better, but men founded their safety in a facility to penetrate each other's intentions, and this advantage, of which we no longer know the value, spared them many vices.

Now, indeed, researches more subtle, and a more refined taste, has reduced the art of pleasing to principles, there is found amongst us a shameful and deceitful uniformity, and all minds seem to have been cast in the same mould. Politeness incessantly rules—convenience orders —we follow custom, but never our own inclinations. We dare not appear what we really are, and in this perpetual constraint mankind compose what we denominate society, placed in the same situations, doing the same things, if more powerful motives do not forbid. We can never know those with whom we have to do; it is necessary, therefore, to know a friend—to wait for great occasions—that is to say, to wait until there is no longer time so to do; since, for these very occasions themselves, it is essential to know him.

What a train of vices is to be found in this uncertainty, no more sincere friendships, no more real esteem, no more well grounded confidence, suspicions, jealousies, fears, coolness, reserve, hatred, deceit, conceal themselves incessantly under this constraint; a veil of perfidious politeness under this boasted urbanity, for which we are indebted to this enlightened age. We no longer profane the name of the Creator of the universe, but we insult him by our blasphemies, without offence to our scrupulous ears. We boast not of our own merit, but we derogate from that of others. We do not grossly outrage our enemy, but we calumniate him with great address. National hatreds will be extinguished, but it will be by a love of country; a dangerous scepticism is substituted for a despised ignorance—some excesses are forbidden, some vices are proscribed, but others are adorned with the name of virtues, it is necessary to have them, or to exhibit an affectation of having them. Boast who will, of the sobriety of the philosophers of modern times, for my part I see nothing amongst them but a refinement in intemperance, as unworthy of my praise as of their artificial simplicity.

Such is the purity which our manners have acquired—it is thus that we are become good people, it is for literature, the sciences, and the arts, to claim that which belongs to them in this valuable work. I shall add only one observation more, it is that an inhabitant of some distant countries, who would be desirous to form an idea of European manners, of the state of the sciences amongst us, of the perfection of the arts, of the decency of our spectacles, the politeness of our manners, the affability of our conversation, our perpetual offers of service, and the great concourse of persons of all ages, and of all ranks, who seem eager from the rising until the setting of the sun, reciprocally to oblige each other. This stranger, I say, would form an opinion of our manners, the contrary of what they really are. . . .

. . . Contemplate Egypt, that first school of the world, that climate so fertile under a brazen sky, that celebrated country whence Seostris set out to conquer the world. It became the mother of philosophy and of the fine arts, and soon after was conquered by Cambysses, then by the Greeks, the Romans, the Arabs, and finally by the Turks.

Turn to Greece, formerly peopled by heroes, who twice conquered Asia, once before Troy, and afterwards on their own hearths. The birth of letters had not yet spread corruption into the hearts of the inhabitants, but the progress of the arts, the dissoluteness of the public manners, and the Macedonian yoke followed each other closely. And Greece, ever learned, ever voluptuous, and ever enslaved, amidst its several revolutions, experienced nothing but a change of masters. All the eloquence of Demosthenes could never re-animate a body which luxury and the arts had never enervated.

It was in the times of the Ennius' and the Terence's, that Rome, which was founded by a goatherd, and illustrious by its labours, began to degenerate. It was after the Ovids, the Catullus's, the Martials, and that crowd of obscene authors, whose very names put modesty to the blush, that Rome, once the temple of the virtues, became the theatre of crimes, the shame of nations, and the sport of barbarians. This capital of the world soon fell under a yoke which they had imposed on so many other nations, and the day of her fall was the eve of that, which gave to one of its citizens the title of arbiter of fine taste.

But wherefore seek in times that are past, proofs of a truth of which we have sufficient evidences under our own eyes. In Asia, that immense country, literature is so esteemed, that it conducts to the first honours of the state; if the sciences tend to purify the manners, if they teach men to shed their blood for their country, if they inspire courage, the inhabitants of China ought to be wise, free and invincible. But if it should appear that there is not a vice which does not prevail there, not a species of crime but is there familiarized. If the instructions of ministers of religion, nor the pretended wisdom of their laws, nor the extensive population of this vast empire, is unable to protect them from the yoke of the ignorant, but hardy Tartar race—of what advantage is all their learning—what benefit have they derived from the honours with which they are loaded—except that of being an enslaved and a vicious people. . . .

. . . Can I forget that it was in the heart of that same Greece where we saw arise that city, celebrated as much for its happy ignorance, as for the wisdom of its laws; that republic of demi-gods, rather than of men; their virtues seemed to elevate them so much above humanity. Oh Sparta! the eternal opprobrium of a false doctrine, whilst vice introduced by the fine arts, advanced hand in hand into Athens, whilst a tyrant encouraged there with so much care the works of the prince of poets, you effaced from your walls the arts and the artists, the sciences and the learned.

The event corresponded with this difference, Athens became the seat of politeness and of good taste, the country of orators and of philosophers. The elegance of its architecture corresponded with that of its language; on every side were the embroidered linens, and the marbles made animate by the hands of the most able masters. It was from Athens that sprung those surprising works which have served as models in the future corrupt ages. The records of Lacedemon are less brilliant indeed; there said the other Grecians—men are born virtuous, and the air of the country seems to inspire virtue. There has come down to us, from that people, the memoirs of their heroic actions. But have these memorials done less for us than the curious marbles which Athens has left behind her . . . .

. . . Thus Socrates, the wisest of men, in the judgment of the Gods, and the most learned of the Athenians in the opinion of all Greece, is the eulogist of ignorance. Can we believe that if he was to come again and dwell among us, that our learned men and artists would induce him to change his opinion.—No, Sirs, this upright man would continue to despise our boasted knowledge. He would not help to increase the multitude of books, which inundate us on every side, and would only leave to his disciples and to posterity, as he has done, his example, and the memory of his virtues. This mode of instructing mankind is truly beautiful.

Socrates commenced in Athens, the elder Cato remained at Rome, inveighing against the artful and subtil Greeks, who ensnared virtue, and subdued the courage of its citizens. But the sciences, the arts and logic, still prevailed, Rome supplied herself with philosophers and orators, she neglected military discipline, contemned agriculture, became the partizans of sects, and patriotism was forgotten. To a sacred reverence for liberty, disinterestedness and obedience to the laws, succeeded the names of Epicurus, Zeno and Arcesilaus. Since, said their own philosophers, that learned men began to appear among us—good men are thrown into shade. Until then the Romans were contented to practise virtue, all was lost when she began to study.

Oh Fabricius! what would have been the sentiment of your noble soul, if you had been so unhappy as to have been called to life, and beheld the pompous face of that Rome which your respectable name had honoured more than all her conquests. "Ye Gods," ye would have said, "what is become of those straw-built sheds, and those rustic hearths, where moderation and the virtues ever dwelt? What fatal splendour is this which has banished Roman simplicity? What foreign language is this? Whence these effeminate manners? What mean these statues, these pictures, these edifices? Thoughtless people, what have you done? You, the conquerors of nations, you are become slaves of the frivolous men whom you have conquered. They are the masters of eloquence who govern you. Was it to enrich architects, painters, statuaries and historians, that you watered Greece and Asia with your best blood? The spoils of Carthage are become the prey of a music master. Romans, hasten to overturn these amphitheatres, destroy those marbles, burn those pictures, drive away the slaves that have subdued you, and whose fatal arts have corrupted you. Let others employ themselves in these empty arts, the only talent worthy of Rome is to conquer the world and to bid virtue triumph. . . .

. . . Examine how luxury, dissipation and slavery, have at all times chastised the proud attempts which we have made to depart from that happy state of ignorance where eternal wisdom has placed us. The thick veil which conceals all his operations, seems to admonish us sufficiently that he has not designed us for vain researches. But is it one of these lessons of which we have failed to profit, or which we have neglected with impunity? Learn then mortals for once, that nature is desirous to preserve you from science, as a mother wards off the stroke of danger from her beloved infant. That all the secrets which she withholds are as many evils from which she defends, and that the difficulties we meet with in prying into them, are not the least of her blessings. Men are perverse, they would be still more so if they had the misfortune to be born learned. . . .

. . . It was an ancient tradition, which passed from Egypt into Greece, that some God inimical to the peace of mankind had invented the sciences. What opinion had the Egyptians themselves of them, amongst whom they were invented.

In short whether it is on the records of the annals of the world, or whether supplied by the uncertain chronicles of philosophical research, we find not in human science an origin which corresponds with the idea which we wish to form of it. Astronomy is the child of superstition, eloquence of ambition, of hatred, of flattery, of lies. Geometry of avarice, physics of vain curiosity; all, even morality itself, of human pride. The arts and the sciences owe their birth to our vices, we should be less in doubt respecting their advantages, if they contributed to our virtues.

The defect in their origin is but too strongly marked in their objects. What shall we do with the arts, without the luxury which nourishes them. If men were not unjust,

what necessity of jurisprudence—what would become of
history if we had no tyrants, no wars, no conspirators.
Who, in a word, would pass his life in barren contemplations, if every one consulted only the duties of men, and
the wants of nature, and had no time but for his country,
for the unhappy, and for his friends. Are we then appointed to die, fastened upon the borders of those pits
where truth has concealed herself. This reflection alone
should check in the first step all men who seriously seek to
instruct themselves by the study of philosophy. . . .

. . . There is a greater evil than even the waste of time.
Other evils, yet worse, follow literature and the arts. *Such
is luxury, engendered by them of indolence and human
vanity.* Luxury is rarely seen without the sciences, and the
arts and they are *never seen* without it. I know that our
philosophy, ever fruitful in singular maxims, pretends contrary to the experience of all ages, that luxury constitutes
the splendour of states. But after having forgotten the
necessity of sumptuary laws, dare they still to deny that
morality is not essential to the welfare of empires, and that
luxury is not diametrically opposed thereto. Admit that
luxury is a certain sign of wealth, that it serves at the same
time to increase it. What shall we conclude from this
paradox so worthy of our time, and what will become of
virtue when it is necessary to enrich itself, at whatever
price it may be. Ancient politicians speak without ceasing
of manners and of virtue, ours speak only of trade and
of money. . . .

. . . We cannot reflect upon the manners of former
times, without recalling to recollection the pleasing images
of their simplicity. It is a beautiful bank of a river, adorned
solely by the hand of nature, towards which we turn our
eyes incessantly, and from which we feel our distance with
regret. When men, innocent and virtuous, loved to have
the Gods to witness their actions, they dwelt together in
the same cottages; but soon becoming corrupted, they
quitted these troublesome spectators, and banished them to
magnificent temples. They drove them thence, to establish
themselves in their stead, or at least the altars of the gods
no longer distinguished the houses of the citizens. It was
then the height of depravity, and the vices were never
carried to greater extremity, than when they saw themselves, so to say, supported at the entrance of the palaces
of the great, and graven upon Corinthian capitals.

As the conveniences of life multiplied, the arts obtained
perfection and luxury was extended. True courage became

enfeebled, the military virtues vanished, and the powerful effects of all the arts still display themselves in the secrets of the cabinet. When the Goths ravished Greece, all the libraries would have been burnt had it not been suggested by one among them, that it was necessary to leave to their enemies what was so adapted to turn them from military exercises, and to amuse them with idle and sedentary occupations. Charles VIII became master of Tuscany, and of the kingdom of Naples, without drawing his sword and all around him, attributed this unhoped for facility to the princes and nobility of Italy, amusing themselves more to become ingenious and learned than to qualify themselves to become vigorous and warlike. Thus all history teaches that in this martial policy, and in all like states, the study of the sciences is more proper to soften and subdue courage, than to confirm and animate it. . . .

. . . If the culture of the sciences is prejudicial to the qualification of warriors, it is still more so to morality. It is in our earliest years that education insensibly adorns our minds and corrupts our judgment. *I see on all sides immense establishments where they bring up youth at great cost, and teach them all things except their duties.* Your children are ignorant of their mother tongue, but they speak others which are not in use any where; they can compose verses, which with difficulty they comprehend, without being able to distinguish error from truth. They possess the art of rendering themselves unintelligible to others by specious arguments. But magnanimity, equity, temperance, humanity, courage, they know not what they mean. The blandishments of patriotism now meet their ears, and if they hear God spoken of, it is rather to fear him, than to have him in reverence. I should prefer, said a sage, that my scholar should pass his time in a game of tennis—his body would at least be well formed. I know that it is necessary to employ children, and that *idleness is for them of all things most dangerous.* What then ought they to learn? This is the grand question. *Let them learn that which they ought to do when men, and not that which they ought to forget.* . . .

. . . For us, who are of common mould, to whom heaven has not imparted eminent talents, and whom he has not destined to enjoy distinguished honours, let us remain contented in our obscurity; nor pursue a reputation which flies us, and which in the present state of things will not render us back what it has cost us, when we shall be entitled to obtain it. To what end shall we seek our happiness in the opinion of others, if we cannot find it in ourselves? Let us leave to others the care of instructing mankind in their duty, and confine ourselves to fulfil our own, we want no other knowledge.

10.

The Conspiracy of the Equals*

Let the ax fall, for I am ready. There is no better
way for a man to die than to offer his life for the
sake of justice.

—"Gracchus" Babeuf before
the High Court of Vendôme

*During the bitter winter of 1795–1796—the most severe
of the entire century—the economic situation in France
was going from bad to worse. Markets were empty of food,
private profiteering was rife, and hospitals and almshouses
were overcrowded with the sick and the destitute. To add
to the country's difficulties, the members of the government of the Directory (1795–1799) appeared to be more
interested in opportunities for personal profit than in the
plight of the citizenry.*

*It was against this background that François Émile
Babeuf (1760–1797), an idealistic ex-Jacobin who called
himself "Gracchus" in emulation of the Roman agrarian
reformer, launched the first attempt in history to establish
a communist society by political means. Together with a
group of his followers, he organized a "Society of Equals"
and plotted to overthrow the Directory and replace it with
a regime based on full political and economic equality.*

*Despite careful planning, the conspiracy was crushed
without difficulty by the police. One hundred thirty-one
of the conspirators were arrested and thirty shot out of
hand; and early in 1797, after public opinion had been
sufficiently prepared, Babeuf and his chief associates were
guillotined.*

*Although it ended in failure, the "Conspiracy of the
Equals" has been singled out by later generations of socialists as one of those first acts out of which the militantly*

*Ernest Belfort Bax, *The Last Episode of the French Revolution*
(London: Grant Richards Ltd., 1911), pp. 107–13. Reprinted by
permission of The Richards Press.

*revolutionary variety of modern socialism has developed.
The manifesto distributed by its leaders is reprinted below.*

People of France! During fifteen centuries you have
lived as slaves, and in consequence unhappily. It is scarcely
six years that you have begun to breathe, in the expectation of independence, happiness, equality! The first demand
of nature, the first need of man, and the chief knot binding
together all legitimate association! People of France! you
have not been more favoured than other nations who
vegetate on this unfortunate growth! Always and everywhere the poor human race, delivered over to more or
less adroit cannibals, has served as a plaything for all
ambitions, as a pasture for all tyrannies. Always and
everywhere men have been lulled by fine words; never and
nowhere have they obtained the thing with the word.
From time immemorial it has been repeated, with hypocrisy, that *men are equal*; and from time immemorial the
most degrading and the most monstrous inequality cease-
lessly weighs on the human race. Since the dawn of civil
society this noblest appanage of man has been recognised
without contradiction, but has on no single occasion been
realised; equality has never been anything but a beautiful
and sterile fiction of the law. To-day, when it is demanded
with a stronger voice, they reply to us: "Be silent, wretches!
Equality of fact is nought but a chimera; be contented
with conditional equality; you are all equal before the law.
Canaille, what do you want more?" What do we want
more? Legislators, governors, rich proprietors, listen, in
your turn! We are all equal, are we not? This principle
remains uncontested. For, unless attacked by madness, no
one could seriously say that it was night when it was day.

Well! we demand henceforth to live and to die equal, as
we have been born equal. We demand real equality or
death; that is what we want.

And we shall have it, this real equality, it matters not
at what price! Woe betide those who place themselves

between us and it! Woe betide him who offers resistance to a vow thus pronounced!

The French Revolution is but the precursor of another, and a greater and more solemn revolution, and which will be the last!

The People has marched over the bodies of kings and priests who coalesced against it: it will be the same with the new tyrants, with the new political hypocrites, seated in the place of the old ones! What do we want more than equality of rights? We want not only the equality transcribed in the declaration of the Rights of Man and the citizen; we will have it in the midst of us, under the roof of our houses. We consent to everything for its sake; to make a clear board, that we may hold to it alone. Perish, if it must be, all the arts, provided real equality be left us! Legislators and governors, who have neither genius nor good faith; rich proprietors without bowels of compassion, you will try in vain to neutralise our holy enterprise by saying that it does no more than reproduce that agrarian law already demanded more than once before! Calumniators! be silent in your turn, and, in the silence of confusion, listen to our demands, dictated by nature and based upon justice!

The agrarian law, or the partition of lands, was the immediate aim of certain soldiers without principles, of certain peoples moved by their instinct rather than by reason. We aim at something more sublime and more equitable—the common good, or the community of goods. No more individual property in land; the land belongs to no one. We demand, we would have, the communal enjoyment of the fruits of the earth, fruits which are for everyone!

We declare that we can no longer suffer, with the enormous majority of men, labour and sweat in the service and for the good pleasure of a small minority! Enough and too long have less than a million of individuals disposed of that which belongs to more than twenty millions of their kind!

Let this great scandal, that our grandchildren will hardly be willing to believe in, cease!

Let disappear, once for all, the revolting distinction of rich and poor, of great and small, of masters and valets, of governors and governed!

Let there be no other difference between human beings than those of age and sex. Since all have the same needs and the same faculties, let there be one education for all, one food for all. We are contented with one sun and one air for all. Why should the same portion and the same quality of nourishment not suffice for each of us? But already the enemies of an order of things the most natural that can be imagined, declaim against us. Disorganisers and factious persons, say they, you only seek massacre and plunder. People of France! we shall not waste our time in replying to them, but we shall tell you: the holy enterprise which we organise has no other aim than to put an end to civil dissensions and to the public misery.

Never has a vaster design been conceived or put into execution. From time to time some men of genius, some sages, have spoken of it in a low and trembling voice. Not one of them has had the courage to tell the whole truth.

The moment for great measures has come. The evil is at its height. It covers the face of the earth. Chaos, under the name of politics, reigns there throughout too many centuries. Let everything return once more to order, and reassume its just place!

At the voice of equality, let the elements of justice and well-being organise themselves. The moment has arrived for founding the Republic of the Equals, that grand refuge open for all men. The days of general restitution have come. Families groaning in misery, come and seat yourselves at the common table prepared by nature for all her children! People of France! the purest form of all glory has been reserved for thee! Yes, it is you who may first offer to the world this touching spectacle!

Ancient customs, antiquated conventions, would anew raise an obstacle to the establishment of the Republic of the Equals. The organisation of real equality, the only kind that answers all needs without making victims, without costing sacrifices, will not perhaps please everybody at first. The egoist, the ambitious man, will tremble with rage. Those who possess unjustly will cry aloud against its injustice. Exclusive enjoyments, solitary pleasures, personal ease, will cause sharp regrets on the part of individuals who have fattened on the labour of others. The lovers of absolute power, the vile supporters of arbitrary authority, will scarcely bend their arrogant chiefs to the level of real equality. Their narrow view will penetrate with difficulty, it may be, the near future of common well-being. But what can a few thousand malcontents do against a mass of men, all of them happy, and surprised to have sought so long for a happiness which they had beneath their hand?

The day after this veritable revolution they will say, with astonishment, What? the common well-being was to be had for so little? We had only to will it. Ah! why did we not will it sooner? Why had we to be told about it so many times? Yes, doubtless, with one man on earth richer, more powerful than his neighbours, than his equals, the equilibrium is broken, crime and misery are already in the world. People of France! by what sign ought you henceforward to recognise the excellence of a constitution? That which rests entirely on an equality of fact is the only one that can benefit you and satisfy all your wants. . . .

. . . People of France! open your eyes and your heart to the fulness of happiness. Recognise and proclaim with us the "Republic of the Equals"!

11.

Class Conflict
and "Enlightened Despotism":
The Pugachev Rebellion*

It is often claimed that the Russian Empress Catherine the Great (1762–1796) was an "enlightened despot," a benevolent ruler whose chief aim was the well-being of her subjects. How far this claim is justified is open to question. Though Catherine made a point of expressing her interest in Western liberal thought, the conclusion is inescapable that the lofty maxims which she borrowed from Montesquieu, Voltaire, and other intellectual friends abroad were not the expression of deep convictions to be translated into practical policies, but rather were intended to obtain applause and international publicity. Her position on the throne was too precarious, her liberalism too shallow and confused, and the obstacles confronting any enlightened policy in the Russia of her day too formidable to permit any major changes in the political, social, and economic structure.

It is difficult to find a more striking contrast than that offered by Catherine's glorification of the ideas of the Enlightenment and her practical policies with regard to the peasantry. At the end of her thirty-four-year reign the institution of serfdom was more firmly entrenched than it had ever been before. As the result of a decree issued in 1767, it was even forbidden for serfs to complain against cruel treatment by their masters.

Not surprisingly, one effect of the increased rigor of

*Basil Dmytryshyn, ed., *Imperial Russia: A Source Book, 1700–1917* (New York: Holt, Rinehart and Winston, 1967), p. 97. Reprinted by permission.

serfdom was agrarian discontent. During the years 1762–1769 alone, there took place seventy-three peasant uprisings. And at the beginning of Catherine's second decade of rule Russia experienced the Pugachev rebellion, the greatest outburst of social protest anywhere in Europe during this period.

Emelian Pugachev (1730–1775) was a Cossack of the Don who had seen military service in Poland and in Turkey and whose career as a soldier had been punctuated by frequent conflicts with authority, followed by spells of imprisonment. In 1773 he raised the standard of a rebellion which swiftly spread to take in peasants and non-Russian peoples east of the Volga. Posing as Emperor Peter III, Catherine's late husband and predecessor, he seized control of vast areas in the Volga basin and led his forces (at one point numbering nearly thirty thousand) dangerously close to Moscow. Though a capable and inspiring leader, he had no real program beyond that of removing the burdens which weighed so heavily on the peasantry.

Having portrayed Russia to her foreign admirers as a benevolent despotism where happy rustics basked in idyllic pastoral conditions, Catherine at first attempted to suppress all information about the uprising. As the situation became more threatening, however, she was forced to abandon her policy of secrecy. She issued a strongly worded manifesto expressing her contempt for Pugachev and his "troop of vagabonds" and appointed one of her trusted advisers to command the forces dispatched to restore "public tranquillity."

Late in 1774 the insurrection was crushed and Pugachev was captured and brought in an iron cage to Moscow, where he suffered quartering and decapitation. The partisan chief's head was displayed on a pole and his limbs were exhibited on wheels in four suburbs of the city as a grim reminder of the fate in store for those who dared to challenge the autocratic structure.

Pugachev's "Emancipation Decree," issued on July 31, 1774, is reprinted below.

We, Peter III, by the Grace of God Emperor and Autocrat of All-Russia, etc.

This is given for nationwide information.

By this personal decree, with our monarchial and fatherly love, we grant [freedom] to everyone who formerly was in serfdom or in any other obligation to the nobility; and we transfer these to be faithful personal subjects of our crown; [to the Old Believers] we grant the right to use the ancient sign of the Cross, and to pray, and to wear beards; while to the Cossacks [we restore] for eternity their freedoms and liberties; we [hereby] terminate the recruiting system, cancel personal and other monetary taxes, abolish without compensation the ownership of land, forest, pastures, fisheries and salt deposits; and [finally] we free everyone from all taxes and obligations which the thievish nobles and extortionist city judges have imposed on the peasantry and the rest of the population. We pray for the salvation of your souls and wish you a happy and peaceful life here [on earth] where we have suffered and experienced much from the above-mentioned thievish nobles. Now since our name, thanks to the hand of Providence, flourishes throughout Russia, we make hereby known by this personal decree the following: all nobles who have owned either *pomesties* [estates granted by the state] or *votchinas* [inherited estates], who have opposed our rule, who have rebelled against the empire, and who have ruined the peasantry should be seized, arrested, and hanged; that is, treated in the same manner as these unchristians have treated you, the peasantry. After the extermination of these opponents and thievish nobles everyone will live in a peace and happiness that shall continue to eternity.

Given July 31, 1774   Peter

12.

The Peterloo Massacre*

I met Murder on the way—
He had a mask like Castlereagh—
Very smooth he looked, yet grim;
Seven bloodhounds followed him:

All were fat; and well they might
Be in admirable plight.
For one by one, and two by two,
He tossed them human hearts to chew
Which from his wide cloak he drew.

*"Mask of Anarchy," Percy Bysshe
Shelley's reaction to news of the
Massacre of Peterloo, in 1819.*

During the years immediately following the close of the
Napoleonic Wars (1815), English town and country life
witnessed sporadic outbreaks of violence, radical agitation
for Parliamentary reform (wider representation), and constant demands for removal of the tariff, especially on grain.
In addition, serious economic contractions, aggravated by
increased use of machinery, resulted in the destruction of
certain classes of labor. Often those directly affected responded by burning hay ricks, smashing machines, and
parading in demonstrations led by self-appointed and militant political spokesmen.

The government, understandably nervous in an age
which boasted no police force or standing army, chose to

*Samuel Bamford, *Passages in the Life of a Radical* (London:
Simpkin, Marshall and Co., 1844), Vol. I. pp. 176–77, 197, 200,
206–210.

look upon the many incidents as part of a great conspiracy, much like the one believed to have been responsible for the extremes of French Jacobinism. The Tory Ministry at first responded with measures which further widened the gap between government and governed and which obstructed the lines of communication essential for peaceful constitutional change. While the practice of petitioning Parliament was as old as that august body itself, the government rendered the petition vehicle near useless both by applying the Seditious Societies Act, which made it illegal for any society to organize branches, and by resurrecting an old statute which prohibited more than twenty signatures on a petition concerned with laws affecting Church and State.

Finding themselves thus largely outmaneuvered in the political sense, radicals took to open-air meetings to sell their ideas—in much the same fashion that John Wesley had spread Methodism. Unfortunately, this not only provided greater influence for those prone to violence, but also cost the movement the stabilizing support of sympathetic intellectuals and members of Parliament. When outbreaks of violence increased in size and number, frightened magistrates invoked the Riot Act, the government suspended the Habeas Corpus Act and passed a Seditious Meetings Act, and the hangman's noose came to have a political connotation. Hence a movement whose original style and intent lay within the constitutional customs of English society was driven into a dissenting posture outside that framework.

In August of 1819 a mass meeting of more than fifty thousand Blanketeers (a derisive term for participants in such open-air meetings) was held at St. Peter's Field, Manchester, to hear a notorious political demagogue, Henry "Orator" Hunt. The local magistrates, alarmed by the size of the crowd and by the knowledge that sporadic violence had erupted at similar gatherings, ordered the arrest of some speakers who were addressing the crowd. When the chief constable and the local yeomanry were unable to break through the throng, a troop of hussars was ordered to clear the way. The sight of the approaching hussars, sabres flashing, caused a panic, which resulted in eleven people being trampled to death and four hundred others being injured. In all it was a hopelessly bungled affair which furnished ample material for anti-government cartoonists and pamphleteers.

AMONGST the meetings for reform held in the early part of the summer of 1819 were the one which took place on Spa Fields, London, at which Mr. Hunt was chairman, and another held at Birmingham, at which Major Cartwright and Sir Charles Wolseley were elected to act as legislatorial attornies for that town in Parliament.

It would seem that these movements in the country induced our friends at Manchester to adopt a course similar to that at Birmingham, and it was accordingly arranged that a meeting for that purpose should be held on St. Peter's Field on the 9th of August. But the object of that meeting having been declared illegal by the authorities, it was countermanded, and another was appointed to be held on the 16th of the same month.

It was deemed expedient that this meeting should be as morally effective as possible, and that it should exhibit a spectacle such as had never before been witnessed in England. We had frequently been taunted by the press with our ragged, dirty appearance at these assemblages; with the confusion of our proceedings, and the mob-like crowds in which our numbers were mustered; and we determined that, for once at least, these reflections should not be deserved—that we would disarm the bitterness of our political opponents by a display of cleanliness, sobriety, and decorum, such as we never before had exhibited. In short, we would deserve their respect by showing that we respected ourselves, and knew how to exercise our rights of meeting, as it were well Englishmen always should do, in a spirit of sober thoughtfulness, respectful, at the same time, to the opinions of others.

"Cleanliness," "sobriety," "order," were the first injunctions issued by the committee, to which, on the suggestion of Mr. Hunt, was subsequently added that of "peace." The fulfilment of the two first was left to the good sense of those who intended to join our procession to this "grand meeting"; the observance of the third and of the last injunctions—order, peace—were provided for by general regulations. Order in our movements was obtained by drilling; and peace, on our parts, was secured by a prohibition of all weapons of offence or defence, and by the strictest discipline, of silence, steadiness, and obedience to the directions of the conductors. Thus our arrangements, by constant practice and an alert willingness, were soon rendered perfect, and ten thousand men moved with the regularity of ten score. . . .

By eight o'clock on the morning of Monday, the 16th

of August, 1819, the whole town of Middleton might be said to be on the alert: some to go to the meeting, and others to see the procession, the like of which, for such a purpose, had never before taken place in that neighborhood. . . .

Our whole column, with the Rochdale people, would probably consist of six thousand men. At our head were a hundred or two of women, mostly young wives, and mine own was amongst them. A hundred or two of our handsomest girls, sweethearts to the lads who were with us, danced to the music, or sung snatches of popular songs; a score or two of children were sent back, though some went forward; whilst on each side of our line walked some thousands of stragglers. And thus, accompanied by our friends and our dearest and most tender connections, we went slowly towards Manchester.

. . . The meeting was indeed a tremendous one. [Hunt] mounted the hustings; the music ceased . . . Mr. Hunt, stepping towards the front of the stage, took off his white hat, and addressed the people.

Whilst he was doing so, I proposed to an acquaintance that, as the speeches and resolutions were not likely to contain anything new to us, and as we could see them in the papers, we should retire awhile and get some refreshment, of which I stood much in need, being not in very robust health. He assented, and we had got to nearly the outside of the crowd, when a noise and strange murmur arose towards the church. Some persons said it was the Blackburn people coming, and I stood on tip-toe and looked in the direction whence the noise proceeded, and saw a party of cavalry in blue and white uniform come trotting, sword in hand, round the corner of a garden-wall, and to the front of a row of new houses, where they reined up in a line.

"The soldiers are here," I said; "we must go back and see what this means." "Oh," some one made reply, "they are only come to be ready if there should be any disturbance in the meeting." "Well, let us go back," I said, and we forced our way towards the colours.

On the cavalry drawing up they were received with a shout of good-will, as I understood it. They shouted again, waving their sabres over their heads; and then, slackening rein, and striking spur into their steeds, they dashed forward and began cutting the people.

"Stand fast," I said, "they are riding upon us; stand fast." And there was a general cry in our quarter of "Stand fast." The cavalry were in confusion: they evidently could not, with all the weight of man and horse, penetrate that compact mass of human beings; and their sabres were plied to hew a way through naked held-up hands and defenceless heads; and then chopped limbs and wound-gaping skulls were seen; and groans and cries were mingled with the din of that horried confusion. "Ah! ah!" "for shame! for shame!" was shouted. Then, "Break! break! they are killing them in front, and they cannot get away;" and there was a general cry of "break! break." For a moment the crowd held back as in a pause; then was a rush, heavy and resistless as a headlong sea, and a sound like low thunder, with screams, prayers, and imprecations from the crowd-moiled and sabre-doomed who could not escape.

By this time Hunt and his companions had disappeared from the hustings, and some of the yeomanry, perhaps less sanguinarily disposed than others, were busied in cutting down the flag-staves and demolishing the flags at the hustings.

On the breaking of the crowd the yeomanry wheeled, and, dashing whenever there was an opening, they followed, pressing and wounding. Many females appeared as the crowd opened; and striplings or mere youths also were found. Their cries were piteous and heart-rending, and would, one might have supposed, have disarmed any human resentment: but here their appeals were in vain. Women, white-vested maids, and tender youths, were indiscriminately sabred or trampled; and we have reason for believing that few were the instances in which that forbearance was vouchsafed which they so earnestly implored.

In ten minutes from the commencement of the havoc the field was an open and almost deserted space. The sun looked down through a sultry and motionless air. The curtains and blinds of the windows within view were all closed. A gentleman or two might occasionally be seen looking out from one of the new houses before mentioned, near the door of which a group of persons (special constables) were collected, and apparently in conversation; others were assisting the wounded or carrying off the dead. The hustings remained, with a few broken and hewed flag-staves erect, and a torn and gashed banner or two dropping; whilst over the whole field were strewed caps, bonnets, hats, shawls, and shoes, and other parts of male and female dress, trampled, torn, and bloody. The yeomanry had dismounted—some were easing their horses' girths, others adjusting their accoutrements, and some were wiping their sabres. Several mounds of human beings still remained where they had fallen, crushed down and smothered. Some of these still groaning, others with staring eyes, were gasping for breath, and others would never breathe more. All were silent save those low sounds, and the occasional snorting and pawing of steeds. Persons might sometimes be noticed peeping from attics and over the tall ridgings of houses, but they quickly withdrew, as if fearful of being observed, or unable to sustain the full gaze of a scene so hideous and abhorrent.

Besides the Manchester yeomanry, who, as I have already shown, did "the duty of the day," there came upon the ground soon after the attack the 15th Hussars and the Cheshire yeomanry; and the latter, as if emulous of the Manchester corps, intercepted the flying masses, and inflicted some severe sabre wounds. The hussars, we have reason for supposing, gave but few wounds, and I am not aware that it has been shown, that one of those brave soldiers dishonoured his sword by using the edge of it. In addition to the cavalry, a strong body of the 88th Foot was stationed at the lower corner of Dickinson Street: with their bayonets at the charge, they wounded several persons, and greatly impeded the escape of the fugitives by that outlet. Almost simultaneously with the hussars, four pieces of Horse artillery appeared from Deansgate, and about two hundred special constables were also in attendance; so that force for a thorough massacre was ready, had it been wanted.

On the first rush of the crowd I called to our men to break their flag-staves and secure their banners, but probably I was not heard or understood, all being then inextricable confusion. He with the blue banner saved it, the cap of liberty was dropped and left behind—indeed, woe to him who stopped, he would never have risen again; and Thomas Redford, who carried the green banner, held it aloft until the staff was cut in his hand, and his shoulder was divided by the sabre of one of the Manchester yeomanry.

A number of our people were driven to some timber which lay at the foot of the wall of the Quakers' meeting house. Being pressed by the yeomanry, a number sprung over the balks and defended themselves with stones which they found there. It was not without difficulty, and after several were wounded, that they were driven out. A heroine, a young married woman of our party, with her face all bloody, her hair streaming about her, her bonnet hanging by the string, and her apron weighed with stones, kept her assailant at bay until she fell backwards and was near being taken; but she got away covered with severe bruises. It was near this place and about this time that one of the yeomanry was dangerously wounded and unhorsed by a blow from a fragment of a brick; and it was supposed to have been flung by this woman.

13.

Revolt Against Autocracy

In December, 1825, a revolt took place in Russia known as the Decembrist uprising. Organized and led by a relatively small group of enlightened liberal aristocrats and young army officers who were disturbed by the monarchy's failure to achieve basic political and social reforms following the Napoleonic Wars, it was the first attempt at a political revolution in modern Russian history. The occasion of the uprising was the accession to the throne of Nicholas I (r. 1825–1855), an arrogant and self-assured reactionary who believed that monarchs were given divine rights to rule their countries without interference.

Badly organized and lacking popular support, the uprising was easily crushed and its participants were severely punished. Of the 121 persons subsequently tried before a specially constituted high criminal court, five were condemned to death by hanging and 102 were sentenced to penal servitude and deportation to Siberia. Yet, even in its failure, the uprising made a very strong impression on public opinion and was regarded by later generations as the first chapter in the history of the Russian revolutionary movement. In the decades that followed, radical politicians and thinkers glorified the Decembrists as the pioneers of Russian freedom and tried, in their own way, to follow in their steps.

The two selections which follow reveal the causes and objectives of the Decembrist uprising. The first is an extract from an undated letter to Nicholas I from A. A. Bestuzhev (1797–1837), a writer and literary critic then confined in Petropavlosk prison. The second is a manifesto drawn up on the eve of the uprising by one of its leaders, Prince

S. P. Trubetskoi (1790–1860). It was to have been issued in the event of the revolt's success.

I

Decembrist A. A. Bestuzhev to Emperor Nicholas I*

Your Imperial Majesty!

Confident that you, the Sovereign, love the truth, I make bold to set before you the historical development of freedom of thought in Russia and, in general, of the many concepts which constitute the moral and political aspects of the events of December 14. I shall speak with complete frankness, without concealing the evil, likewise without toning down my expressions, for the duty of a loyal subject is to tell the monarch the unvarnished truth. I commence.

The beginning of the reign of the Emperor Alexander was marked by the most brilliant hopes for the well-being of Russia. The nobility had recuperated; the merchant class made no complaints about advancing credit; the army served without making trouble; scholars studied what they pleased; everyone said what he thought, and all who were doing well expected to do still better. Unfortunately, circumstances prevented that and hopes faded without fulfillment. The unsuccessful war of 1807[1] and many other things upset the finances; but this was lost sight of during preparations for the War of the Fatherland. Finally, Napoleon invaded Russia, and only then did the Russian people, for the first time, become aware of their strength; only then did there awaken in all hearts a feeling for independence, first political, and later also national. This marked the beginning of freedom of thought in Russia. The government itself uttered the words: "Freedom, Liberation!" It disseminated works about the abuses resulting from the unlimited power of Napoleon; and the cry of the

*Ivar and Marion Spector, *Readings in Russian History and Culture* (Boston: Allyn and Bacon, Inc., 1965), pp. 129–32. Reprinted by permission of Ivar and Marion Spector.
[1]The War of Russia against Napoleon, 1806–1807, in alliance with Prussia, culminated badly for Russia in the Peace of Tilsit.

Russian monarch resounded on the banks of the Rhine and the Seine. The war was not yet over, when the soldiers returning home first spread discontent among the masses. "We have shed our blood," they said, "and yet once again we are forced to sweat under the *barshchina*. We delivered the Fatherland from the tyrant, but once again the gentry tyrannizes over us." The army, from generals down to common soldiers, upon its return harped only on how good things were in foreign lands. The comparison with their own country naturally gave rise to the question: Why are things not the same here? At first, as long as they talked about this freely, their words were wafted away on the wind, for the mind, like gunpowder, is dangerous only under pressure. The ray of hope that the Tsar Emperor would grant a constitution, as he mentioned at the opening of the Seim[2] in Warsaw, and the attempts of some generals to liberate their serfs, still encouraged many. But after 1817 everything was changed. The people who witnessed evil, or who wished for better things, were compelled by the great number of spies to start conversing secretly, and this was the beginning of the secret societies. Oppression of deserving officers by the authorities inflamed men's minds. Then the military began to say: "Did we liberate Europe, only to assume her chains ourselves? Did we grant a constitution to France, only so that we dare not speak about it ourselves, and did we buy with our blood the first place among the nations, only to abase ourselves at home?" The destruction of the model schools and the persecution of education compelled us to think, in despair, about most important measures. And since the grumbling of the people, which stemmed from exhaustion and the abuses by rural and civil authorities, threatened bloody revolution, these societies intended to avert the greater evil by a lesser one, and to begin their activities at the earliest opportunity. Now I shall describe the situation, as we saw it in Russia.

Napoleon's troops, like locusts, for a long time left in their wake the seeds of destruction. Many provinces were impoverished and the dilatory measures or meager assistance given them by the government altogether destroyed them. Rain and drought brought famine to other areas. A system of jerry-built roads covered a third of Russia and grain rotted before it was cut. The abuses of the district police officers became more apparent to the impoverished

---

[2]The representative assembly granted to Poland, and opened by the Tsar in 1818.

peasants, and those of the nobility more perceptible, because they began to understand the rights of the people. Forbidding distillation deprived many provinces of all means of marketing seed and the multiplication of saloons corrupted morals and ruined peasant life. The military colonies paralyzed not only the minds but also all the trade of the places in which they settled, and produced terror in the rest. The frequent marches of the regiments were an infinite burden to the inhabitants; shortage of money led the peasants into arrears that could not be repaid—in brief, everybody pined for the past, all grumbled about the present, and all craved something better than the empty rumor that places are being allotted on the Amu-Darya, which attracted thousands of residents of the Ukraine. Whither? They did not know themselves. Entire villages got under way and wandered at random, and much resentment of the *barshchina* marked the last three years of Alexander's reign.

The petty bourgeoisie [*meshchane*], a respectable and important class in all other countries, is insignificant among us, is reduced to poverty, burdened with obligations, and deprived of the means of subsistence. In other nations, it inhabits the cities; with us, however, cities exist only on the map, and freedom of trade hampers their shops, they roam from place to place like gypsies, and busy themselves with the resale of trifles. The decline of trade is reflected among them even more than among the poor; for, as petty traders or factory workers, they depend on the merchants.

The merchant class [*kypetchestvo*], restricted by the guilds and hampered in making deliveries, suffered a serious decline in 1812. Many colossal fortunes were lost; others were shattered. Doing business with the Treasury brought ruin to the majority of the merchants and contractors, and along with them to their clients and warranters, due to delayed payments, accounts and illegal pressure methods. Extortion made itself felt everywhere. . . . Fraudulent bankruptcies multiplied and confidence collapsed. The instability of the tariff reduced to destitution many manufacturers and frightened others, and both our own and foreign negotiators lost confidence in our government. Consequently, there was a great decline in the value of our money abroad, because of state debts and the general complaint that no cash was available. The illegal system, which enriched the smugglers, did not increase the prices of our products and, as was the fashion, all paid exorbitant prices for so-called confiscated goods. Finally, a decree that the petty bourgeoisie and small traders must either register with the police or pay fines would have inflicted a decisive blow on trade, and the failure to execute it did not stop people from complaining. Even without that, the decline in trade was so great that at the principal fairs and at the ports exchange and exports abroad were reduced by one-third. The merchants also complained justifiably against foreigners, especially the English who, in spite of the law, had their agents in the villages buying at the source raw materials for export abroad, and thereby depriving small traders of business and the state of the circulation of currency.

The nobility [*dvoryanstvo*] was likewise dissatisfied with the poor sale of its products, high prices for luxury items, and protracted legal procedures. It is divided into three categories: the educated, of whom the great part consists of people of rank; the literate, who either torture others as judges or are themselves the victims of one lawsuit after another; and finally, the hicks, who live in villages, serve as church elders, or are already retired, having served, God knows, just as if they were in the army. Of these, however, the small gentry constitutes the ulcer of Russia; always guilty and always grumbling, and desiring to live beyond its means and in accordance with its pretentions, it tortures its poor peasants mercilessly. Others have ruined themselves at the chase, brawling [?], by riotous living in the capital, or by lawsuits. The greater part of the best nobility, which serves in the army or in the capitals, demanding luxury, entrusts its property to hirelings who rob the peasants and defraud their masters, and thus nine-tenths of the estates in Russia are disorganized and mortgaged. The village priesthood is in a sorry plight. Not having any fixed salary, its members are completely at the mercy of the peasants and are compelled to cater to them; and by so doing they lapse into vice, for which the law prescribes their removal. . . .

. . . The soldiers grumbled at exhausting drills, cleaning up, and performing guard duty; the officers, at their meager salaries and excessive discipline; the sailors at unskilled labor, aggravated by abuses; the naval officers at inactivity. People with talents complain that the road to advancement in the service is blocked to them, demanding from them nothing but unquestioning obedience; scholars that they are not allowed to teach; the youth at impediments to study. In brief, dissatisfied faces were to be seen everywhere; on

the streets people shrugged their shoulders, everywhere
they whispered rumors—everyone talked about where this
would lead. All elements were in ferment. The government
alone slumbered lightheartedly on the brink of a volcano;
the tribunal alone was blissfully happy, because only for
it was Russia the promised land. Their extortion reached
an unprecedented degree of shamelessness. Scribes acquired
horses, court clerks bought villages, and only the high cost
of bribes distinguished people in high places, so that in
the capital under the eyes of the police there was conducted an open traffic in justice. It wouldn't be so bad if
payment were made for service, but they took it and did
nothing. In all probability, Your Imperial Majesty is now
familiar with these abuses, but they were concealed from
the late Emperor. Lucrative positions were sold for a fixed
fee and likewise required a kickback. The centralization of
the courts, by luring each trifling matter to the top, encouraged appeals, inquiries, reviews, and decades elapsed
before decisions were made, with the result that both sides
were ruined.

In brief, in the treasury, in the courts, in the commis-
sariats, at the governor's and at the governor-general's—
everywhere, where interest was involved, whoever could,
robbed, whoever lacked the courage, stole. Everywhere
honest people suffered and pettifoggers and knaves rejoiced. . . .

II

Trubetskoi's Manifesto
to the Russian People,
*December 13, 1825**

The Manifesto of the Senate should proclaim:
(1) abolition of the former government;
(2) establishment of a Provisional Government until a
permanent one is decided upon by representatives;
(3) freedom of the press, hence abolition of censorship;
(4) religious tolerance to all faiths;

*Anatole G. Mazour, *The First Russian Revolution, 1825*
(Berkeley and Los Angeles, California: University of California
Press, 1937), pp. 283–84. Reprinted by permission of the Regents
of the University of California.

(5) abolition of the right to own men;

(6) equality of all classes before the law and therefore abolition of military courts and all sorts of judicial commissions from which all cases proceed to civil courts;

(7) announcement of rights for every citizen to occupy himself with whatever he wishes and therefore—nobleman, merchant, middle-class man, peasant—all to have equal right to enter military, civil, or clerical service, trade wholesale or retail, paying established taxes for such trade; to acquire all kinds of property such as land, or houses in villages and cities; make all kinds of contracts among themselves, or summon each other for trial;

(8) cancellation of poll tax and arrears;

(9) abolition of monopolies on salt and alcohol; permission for free distillation and for the procuring of salt with payment of tax according to the respective amounts of salt and alcohol produced;

(10) abolition of recruiting and military colonies;

(11) reduction of the term of military service for privates to be followed by equalization of military service of all classes;

(12) retirement without exception of all privates who have served fifteen years;

(13) the creation of Community, County, Gubernia, and Regional administrations, which are to be substituted for all civil service men appointed formerly by the government;

(14) public trials;

(15) introduction of a jury system in criminal and civil courts. There shall be created an administration of two or three persons to which all the highest officers of the government shall be subordinated, such as the Ministry, the Council, the Ministerial Committee, the Army and Navy: in a word, the entire Supreme Executive government, but not the legislative nor judicial. For the latter there remains the Ministry subordinated to the Provisional Government, but for decision of cases not passed upon by the lower courts there will remain a department of the Senate which shall handle civil and criminal cases; its members shall remain in service until a permanent administration is established.

The Provisional Government is instructed to:

(1) equalize all classes;

(2) form all local, Community, County, Gubernia, and Regional administrations;

(3) form a National Guard;

(4) form a judicial branch with a jury;

(5) equalize recruiting obligations among all classes;

(6) abolish a permanent army;

(7) establish a form of election of representatives to the Lower Chamber which will have to ratify the future form of Government.

III

*The Executive Committee to Emperor Alexander III, March 23, 1881**

To you who desire to cross this threshold,
do you know what awaits you?
I know, replied the girl.
Cold, hunger, abhorrence, derision, contempt,
abuse, prison, disease, and death!
I know, I am ready, I shall endure all blows.
Not from enemies alone, but also from relatives,
from friends.
Yes, even from them. . . .
Are you ready even to commit a crime?
I am ready for crime, too.
Do you know that you may be disillusioned in
that which you believe, that you may discover
that you were mistaken, that you ruined your
young life in vain?
I know that, too.
Enter!
The girl crossed the threshold, and a heavy
curtain fell behind her.
Fool! said some one, gnashing his teeth.
Saint! some one uttered in reply.

—Ivan Turgenev's tribute to the Russian
   terrorist Sofia Perovskaia.

The pattern of autocracy and serfdom which had so disturbed the Decembrists was significantly modified under

*Konni Zilliacus, *The Russian Revolutionary Movement* (London: Alston Rivers, 1905), pp. 118–25. Reprinted by permission.

Alexander II (r. 1855–1881). Through a series of "Great Reforms" serfdom was abolished, a more efficient and equitable legal system and a considerable measure of rural and urban self-government were introduced, and an end was put to the cruelty and injustice that had equated military service with punishment. Yet these liberal reforms, leaving as they did the institution of autocracy intact, failed to satisfy many groups of the Russian intelligentsia, particularly the university youth—some of whom demanded the complete destruction of the existing order.

In 1879 a group of terrorists formed a clandestine organization known as the People's Will and embarked on a series of fantastic adventures, even gaining entrance to the Winter Palace and blowing up the imperial dining room, killing or wounding soldiers who were on guard. On March 13, 1881, they succeeded in killing Alexander II, thus eliminating a man who had done more to improve the lot of the Russian people than any other ruler in their history. Just hours before his assassination, Alexander had signed a decree which seemed to point the way to a constitutional system by associating elected representatives with the business of legislation.

Shortly after the "tsar-liberator's" death, the executive committee of the People's Will addressed an open letter to the new ruler, Alexander III (r. 1881–1894), explaining to him the reason for his father's assassination and setting forth the conditions that might end political terror and restore public order.

Your Majesty,

The executive committee quite understands the mental depression from which you are suffering, but does not think that a feeling of sympathy should release it from the duty of making the following declaration. There is something still higher than even the most justifiable feelings of humanity. It is the duty to our country, a duty which commands every fellow-citizen to sacrifice himself, his own feelings, and even those of others. Impelled by this imperious duty, we turn unhesitatingly to you, because the development of events which threaten us in the future with terrible struggles and torrents of blood will brook no delay.

The bloody tragedy enacted on the Catherine Canal[1] was not the work of chance, and should have astonished no one. Considering what has happened during the past ten years, it appeared inevitable, and therein lies its deep significance, which should be thoroughly grasped by those whom fate has placed at the head of the State.

Only those who are quite incapable of understanding the life of the people, of seeing through it, can stigmatise such events as a crime committed by individuals or a "band" of individuals. During a whole decade we have seen the revolutionary movement, in spite of the most zealous persecution, in spite of the fact that the Government of the late Tsar had sacrificed everything, the freedom, the interests of all classes of the people, their work, aye and their own dignity—in a word, in the face of all the measures adopted to destroy it, we have seen this revolutionary movement increase and expand; the best forces of the country, the most energetic and most self-sacrificing men in Russia, have come forward to enroll themselves in its ranks, and during three whole years a desperate struggle has been going on between the revolution and the Government.

Your Majesty must admit that the Government of the late Tsar cannot be accused of want of energy. The innocent and guilty were hanged without distinction, the prisons of the remotest provinces were filled to overflowing, and the so-called leaders were executed by the dozen.

They died peacefully and with the calm of martyrs; but this did not put a stop to the movement. On the contrary, it increased and acquired more and more strength. A revolutionary movement, your Majesty, does not depend on individuals. It is a process of the social organism, and with regard to it the gallows, erected for the most energetic representatives of this process, are just as impotent to save the existing order of state as was the crucifixion of the Nazarene to preserve the crumbling ancient world from the triumph of reforming Christianity.

The Government may go on with its hanging and arresting as long as it chooses; it may, perhaps, succeed in

[1] Location of the assassination of Alexander II.

crushing a few revolutionary associations; it might, by some possibility, succeed in destroying the very organisation of the revolution; but it will never be able to prevent the further development of events. The revolutionists are born of this development of the people, of the development of Russia in the direction of new social forms.

A whole nation cannot be crushed; still less can the discontent of a nation be removed by measures of severity. Such measures will, on the contrary, not only augment the volume of discontent, but also its energy and strength. These will be better organised exactly in the same proportion as advantage is taken to utilise the experiences previously acquired. This being the case, the revolutionary organisations cannot but increase in numbers and gain in strength with the lapse of time. This was exactly what happened in our case. What advantage did the Government secure by suppressing the "Dolgutschintski" and "Tschaikovski" circles and the propagandists of 1874? Their places were taken by other more active leaders.

The severity of the Government after 1878 and 1879 gave birth to terrorism. In vain did the Government execute Kowalsky, Dubrovin, Osinsky, and Lisogub, and abolish dozens of revolutionary associations. In the place of these incomplete organisations other and more stable associations came together by a process of natural selection. Finally the executive committee came into being, against which the Government still wages its hopeless fight.

If we contemplate with an impartial mind the last melancholy decade, we can easily and infallibly gauge the future of the revolutionary movement if the Government does not alter its policy. It will advance and expand; the deeds of the terrorists will make a deeper impression, and the revolutionary organisations will assume a more perfect and potent form. At the same time, new causes will create still further discontent; the trust of the people in its Government will dwindle more and more; and the idea of revolution, the conviction of its possibility and inevitableness, will gain ground in a corresponding degree.

A frightful outbreak, a bloody revolution, a spasmodic convulsion embracing all Russia, will complete the destruction of the old order of the State.

Your Majesty, this is a sorrowful and terrible prospect, aye, sorrowful and terrible indeed. Think not, your Majesty, that these are empty words. We know better than anyone what a disaster the loss of so much talent, so much energy, will be in the time of destruction and bloody conflict, when, under other circumstances, the same forces could be applied to productive labour, to educating the people, and to the welfare of all.

But why should such a sanguinary struggle be necessary?

For the reason, your Majesty, that we have no Government in the right meaning of the word. A Government, to be true to the principle of its being, should exist merely to give expression to the people's efforts and execute the people's will. With us, on the contrary—pardon our saying it—the Government is nothing but a cabal, a clique, much more deserving to be called "a gang of usurpers" than the executive committee.

Whatever the intentions of the Emperor may be, the actions of the Government have nothing in common with the hopes and the welfare of the people.

The Imperial Government has long since robbed the people of its personal freedom and placed it in a state of slavery to the nobility. Now it is creating a pernicious class of speculators and usurpers. All reforms result in making the condition of the people worse than before. The Government of Russia has gone so far, has plunged the masses into such poverty and misery, that they have not even the liberty to look after their common well-being, that they are not even safe from the lowest prying, not even in their own homes.

It is only the bloodsucking officials, whose rascally extortions go unpunished, who enjoy the protection of the Government and the laws.

On the other hand, what a terrible fate befalls the honest man who works for the welfare of all! Your Majesty knows well that it is not only socialists who are persecuted and exiled.

What kind of Government can that be which upholds such a state of things? Is it not in reality a gang of usurpers?

This is the reason why the Government in Russia has no moral influence over the people, why Russia produces so many revolutionists, why even such an event as the assassination of the Tsar excites sympathy among a large portion of the people. Your Majesty, do not listen to sycophants. Regicide is very popular in Russia.

There are only two ways out of such a situation. The one is a revolution which cannot be avoided or hindered by sentences of death; the other is the transfer of power to the people and its participation in the Government.

In the interest of the country and to avoid the destruction of talent and energy and the terrible calamities which always follow in the track of a revolution, the executive committee appeals to your Majesty and advises that the latter remedy be adopted. Be assured that as soon as the highest power in the land ceases to be despotic, as soon as it gives proofs of its firm determination to execute that which is demanded by the will and conscience of the people, then you may dismiss your spies, who are the disgrace of the Government, send your Life Guards back to their quarters, and burn the gallows which demoralise the people.

When these things are done, the executive committee will, on its own initiative, cease its action; its organised forces will be disbanded and employed in productive work on behalf of the civilisation, education, and welfare of the people.

A peaceful contest between ideas will take the place of acts of violence, which are far more repugnant to us than to your servants, and which nothing but absolute necessity compels us to adopt.

We appeal to your Majesty to lay aside all prejudices and distrust caused in the past. We will forget that you represent the power which has misled the people and inflicted so much wrong on it. We appeal to your Majesty as a fellow-citizen and an honourable man.

We hope that personal bitterness will not destroy in you the feeling of duty or the wish to hear the truth.

We also have reason to be bitter. Your Majesty has lost your father; we also have lost not only our fathers, but our brothers, wives, sons, and best friends. We are, however, none the less willing to forget all personal feelings of vengeance when the welfare of Russia requires it; we expect the same from you.

We do not put to you terms of any kind. Do not, therefore, take offence at our proposals. The conditions which must be fulfilled to enable the revolutionary movement to give place to a peaceful development of affairs are not made by us, but are the outcome of events. We simply indicate them. These conditions should, in our opinion, be embodied under two principal heads:

First, a general amnesty for all political offenders, because they have committed no crime, but have simply done their duty as citizens;

Secondly, the convocation of representatives of the whole people for the discussion and regulation of matters relating to social and political life in accordance with the wishes and necessities of the people.

We consider it necessary, however, to point out that the Government can only be said to be legalised by popular representation if the elections are absolutely free. The latter must, therefore, take place under the following conditions:

1. The representatives must be chosen from all classes without distinction, according to the statistics of population.
2. No restrictions of any kind must be put upon the voters and representatives.
3. The elections and electoral proceedings must be absolutely free. The Government must therefore sanction the following by way of temporary provisions until convocation of the National Assembly:
   (*a*) Full liberty of the press;
   (*b*) Full liberty of speech;
   (*c*) Full liberty of meeting;
   (*d*) Full liberty to address electoral meetings.

These are the only means by whose help Russia can enter on the path of peaceful and regular development. To our country and before the whole world we solemnly declare that our party will subordinate itself absolutely to a National Assembly called together under the said conditions. It will not display any opposition to the Government acknowledged by the National Assembly.

It is now for your Majesty to decide. The choice rests with you. We, on our part, can only express the hope that your intelligence and conscience will inspire you with the only decision compatible with the welfare of Russia, your own dignity, and duty to your country.

14.

Proudhon:
Opposing Private Property
and the Oppressive State

The nineteenth century witnessed an almost constant acceleration in the tempo of economic and political centralization. Rapid increase in industrialization, accompanied by wider application of machinery, expanding urban populations, and a growing use of applied science all rendered a tremendous impact on Western European states. By the time of the 1848 revolutions and the appearance of the Communist Manifesto, *the socialist thought of Robert Owen, Saint-Simon, and Fourier was two decades old. The twenty years which followed the* Manifesto *saw the first rounds in the long struggles between church and nation-state, centralism and federalism, big capital and the working classes. In each there were both sociological trials and ultimately verdicts which had the tendency of dwarfing the individual.*

Well within the long tradition of French moralists, the anarchist Pierre Joseph Proudhon (1808–1865) believed the threat to freedom and individuality posed by both laissez-faire capitalism and scientific socialism was foremost among human problems. For Proudhon the French Revolution, followed by the Code Napoleon, had brought a concept of property which produced oppression of the worker on a unique scale. The socialist alternative, which might well be brought on by the revolution against capitalist excesses, presented no less than a nightmare of collective tyranny. Nor could full-blown political democracy provide a solution to the dilemma. Under a centralized democracy the people would only reign but not rule.

Proudhon believed that much of man's social misery

*stemmed from two sources, the system of private property
and the regulation of life by government. Both obstructed
true freedom and happiness. What man needed was a
liberated society characterized by voluntary cooperation,
a worker's society imbued with the inherent goodness of
the workingman's morality. He described it as "order in
anarchy."*

I

What is Property?*

If I were asked to answer the following question: *What
is slavery?* and I should answer in one word, *It is murder,*
my meaning would be understood at once. No extended
argument would be required to show that the power to
take from a man his thought, his will, his personality, is
a power of life and death; and that to enslave a man is to
kill him. Why, then, to this other question: *What is
property?* may I not likewise answer, *It is robbery,* without the certainty of being misunderstood; the second
proposition being no other than a transformation of the
first? . . .

. . . But murmurs arise!

Property is robbery! That is the war-cry of '93! That is
the signal of revolutions!

Reader, calm yourself: I am no agent of discord, no
firebrand of sedition. I anticipate history by a few days;
I disclose a truth whose development we may try in vain
to arrest; I write the preamble of our future constitution.
This proposition which seems to you blasphemous—
property is robbery—would, if our prejudices allowed us
to consider it, be recognized as the lightning-rod to shield
us from the coming thunderbolt; but too many interests
stand in the way! . . . Alas! philosophy will not change
the course of events: destiny will fulfill itself regardless of

*Pierre Joseph Proudhon, *What Is Property?* Translated by
Benjamin R. Tucker (New York: Humbolt Publishing Co., 1890),
pp. 11–12, 92, 94–95, 209–10, 247–49, 279–80.

prophecy. Besides, must not justice be done and our education be finished? . . .

. . . From whatever point we view this question of property—provided we go to the bottom of it—we reach equality. I will not insist farther on the distinction between things which can, and things which cannot, be appropriated. On this point, economists and legists talk worse than nonsense. . . .

. . . The right of property was the origin of evil on the earth, the first link in the long chain of crimes and misfortunes which the human race has endured since its birth. The delusion of prescription is the fatal charm thrown over the intellect, the death sentence breathed into the conscience, to arrest man's progress towards truth, and bolster up the worship of error.

The Code defines prescription thus: "The process of gaining and losing through the lapse of time." In applying this definition to ideas and beliefs, we may use the word *prescription* to denote the everlasting prejudice in favor of old superstitions, whatever be their object; the opposition, often furious and bloody, with which new light has always been received, and which makes the sage a martyr. Not a principle, not a discovery, not a generous thought but has met, at its entrance into the world, with a formidable barrier of preconceived opinions, seeming like a conspiracy of all old prejudices. Prescriptions against reason, prescriptions against facts, prescriptions against every truth hitherto unknown—that is the sum and substance of the *statu quo* philosophy, the watchword of conservatives throughout the centuries. . . .

. . . *Property is impossible, because, in consuming its Receipts, it loses them; in hoarding them, it nullifies them; and in using them as Capital, it turns them against Production.*

I. If, with the economists, we consider the laborer as a living machine, we must regard the wages paid to him as the amount necessary to support this machine, and keep it in repair. The head of a manufacturing establishment—who employs laborers at three, five, ten, and fifteen francs per day, and who charges twenty francs for his superintendence—does not regard his disbursements as losses, because he knows they will return to him in the form of products. Consequently, *labor* and *reproductive consumption* are identical.

What is the proprietor? He is a machine which does not

work; or, which working for its own pleasure, and only when it sees fit, produces nothing.

What is it to consume as a proprietor? It is to consume without working, to consume without reproducing. For, once more, that which the proprietor consumes as a laborer comes back to him; he does not give his labor in exchange for his property, since, if he did, he would thereby cease to be a proprietor. In consuming as a laborer, the proprietor gains, or at least does not lose, since he recovers that which he consumes; in consuming as a proprietor, he impoverishes himself. To enjoy property, then, it is necessary to destroy it; to be a real proprietor, one must cease to be a proprietor.

The laborer who consumes his wages is a machine which destroys and reproduces; the proprietor who consumes his income is a bottomless gulf—sand which we water, a stone which we sow. So true is this, that the proprietor —neither wishing nor knowing how to produce, and perceiving that as fast as he uses his property he destroys it for ever—has taken the precaution to make some one produce in his place. That is what political economy, speaking in the name of eternal justice, calls *producing by his capital—producing by his tools.* And that is what ought to be called *producing by a slave—producing as a thief and as a tyrant.* He, the proprietor, produce! . . . The robber might say, as well: "I produce." . . .

. . . Equality of conditions has never been realized, thanks to our passions and our ignorance; but our opposition to this law has made it all the more a necessity. To that fact history bears perpetual testimony, and the course of events reveals it to us. Society advances from equation to equation. To the eyes of the economist, the revolutions of empires seem now like the reduction of algebraical quantities, which are inter-deducible; now like the discovery of unknown quantities, induced by the inevitable influence of time. Figures are the providence of history. Undoubtedly there are other elements in human progress; but in the multitude of hidden causes which agitate nations, there is none more powerful or constant, none less obscure, than the periodical explosions of the proletariat against property. Property, acting by exclusion and encroachment, while population was increasing, has been the life-principle and definitive cause of all revolutions. Religious wars, and wars of conquest, when they have stopped short of the extermination of races, have been only accidental disturbances, soon repaired by the mathematical progression of the life of nations. The downfall and death of societies are due to the power of accumulation possessed by property. . . .

. . . Here my task should end. I have proved the right of the poor; I have shown the usurpation of the rich. I demand justice; it is not my business to execute the sentence. If it should be argued—in order to prolong for a few years an illegitimate privilege—that it is not enough to demonstrate equality, that it is necessary also to organize it, and above all to establish it peacefully, I might reply: The welfare of the oppressed is of more importance than official composure. Equality of conditions is a natural law upon which public economy and jurisprudence are based. The right to labor, and the principle of equal distribution of wealth, cannot give way to the anxieties of power. It is not for the proletaire to reconcile the contradictions of the codes, still less to suffer for the errors of the government. On the contrary, it is the duty of the civil and administrative power to reconstruct itself on the basis of political equality. An evil, when known, should be condemned and destroyed. The legislator cannot plead ignorance as an excuse for upholding a glaring iniquity. Restitution should not be delayed. Justice, justice! recognition of right! reinstatement of the proletaire!— when these results are accomplished, then, judges and consuls, you may attend to your police, and provide a government for the Republic! . . .

. . . Now, property necessarily engenders despotism— the government of caprice, the reign of libidinous pleasure. That is so clearly the essence of property that, to be convinced of it, one need but remember what it is, and observe what happens around him. Property is the right to *use* and *abuse*. If, then, government is economy—if its object is production and consumption, and the distribution of labor and products—how is government possible while property exists? And if goods are property, why should not the proprietors be kings, and despotic kings—kings in proportion to their *facultés bonitaires*? And if each proprietor is sovereign lord within the sphere of his property, absolute king throughout his own domain, how could a government of proprietors be any thing but chaos and confusion?

II

General Idea of the Revolution in the Nineteenth Century*

Through the land the plundering of man began, and in the land it has rooted its foundations. The land is the fortress of the modern capitalist, as it was the citadel of feudalism, and of the ancient patriciate. Finally, it is the land which gives authority to the governmental principle, an ever-renewed strength, whenever the popular Hercules overthrows the giant.

To-day the stronghold, attacked upon all the secret points of its bastions, is about to fall before us, as fell, at the sound of Joshua's trumpets, the walls of Jericho. The machine which is able to overthrow the ramparts has been found; it is not my invention; it has been invented by property itself. . . .

. . . From the origin of societies, the spirit of man, confined and enveloped by the theologico-political system, shut up in a hermetically closed box, of which Government is the bottom and Religion the top, has taken the limits of this narrow horizon for the limits of a rational society. God and King, Church and State, twisted in every way, worked over to infinity, have been his Universe. For a long time he has known nothing, imagined nothing beyond. At last, the circle has been traversed; the excitement of the systems suggested by this has exhausted him; philosophy, history, political economy, have completed the triangulation of this inner world; the map of it has been drawn; and it is known that the supernatural scheme which humanity contemplates as its horizon, and its limit, is but itself; that, far as humanity may look into the depths of its consciousness, it sees but itself; that this God, source of all power, origin of all causality, of which humanity makes its sun, is a lamp in a cavern, and all these govern-

*Pierre Joseph Proudhon, *General Idea of the Revolution in the Nineteenth Century.* Translated by John Beverley Robinson (London: Freedom Press, 1923), pp. 195, 290-92, 294. Reprinted by permission.

ments made in his image are but grains of sand that reflect the faint light.

These religions, these legislations, these empires, these Governments, this wisdom of State, this virtue of Pontiffs, all are but a dream and a lie, which all hang upon one another and converge toward a central point, which itself has no reality. If we want to get a more correct idea of things, we must burst this crust and get out of this inferno, in which man's reason will be lost, and he will become an idiot. . . .

. . . When society has turned from within to without, all relations are overturned. Yesterday we were walking with our heads downwards: to-day we hold them erect, without any interruption to our life. Without losing our personality, we change our existence. Such is the nineteenth century Revolution.

The fundamental, decisive idea of this Revolution is it not this: NO MORE AUTHORITY, neither in the Church, nor in the State, nor in land, nor in money?

No more Authority! That means something we have never seen, something we have never understood; the harmony of the interest of one with the interest of all; the identity of collective sovereignty and individual sovereignty.

No more Authority! That means debts paid, servitude abolished, mortgages lifted, rents reimbursed, the expense of worship, justice, and the State suppressed; free credit, equal exchange, free association, regulated value, education, work, property, domicile, low price, guaranteed: no more antagonism, no more war, no more centralization, no more governments, no more priests. Is not that Society emerged from its shell and walking upright?

No more Authority! That is to say further: free contract in place of arbitrary law; voluntary transactions in place of the control of the State; equitable and reciprocal justice in place of sovereign and distributive justice; rational instead of revealed morals; equilibrium of forces instead of equilibrium of powers; economic unity in place of political centralization. Once more, I ask, is not this what I may venture to call a complete reversal, a turn-over, a Revolution? . . .

. . . O, personality of man! Can it be that for sixty centuries you have grovelled in this abjection? You call yourself holy and sacred, but you are only the prostitute, the unwearied and unpaid prostitute of your servants, of your monks, and of your soldiers. You know it, and you permit it. To be GOVERNED is to be kept in sight, inspected, spied upon, directed, law-driven, numbered, enrolled, indoctrinated, preached at, controlled, estimated, valued, censured, commanded, by creatures who have neither the right, nor the wisdom, nor the virtue to do so. . . . To be GOVERNED is to be at every operation, at every transaction, noted, registered, enrolled, taxed, stamped, measured, numbered, assessed, licensed, authorized, admonished, forbidden, reformed, corrected, punished. It is, under pretext of public utility, and in the name of the general interest, to be placed under contribution, trained, ransomed, exploited, monopolized, extorted, squeezed, mystified, robbed; then, at the slightest resistance, the first word of complaint, to be repressed, fined, despised, harassed, tracked, abused, clubbed, disarmed, choked, imprisoned, judged, condemned, shot, deported, sacrificed, sold, betrayed; and, to crown all, mocked, ridiculed, outraged, dishonored. That is government; that is its justice; that is its morality. And to think that there are democrats among us who pretend that there is any good in government; Socialists who support this ignominy, in the name of Liberty, Equality and Fraternity; proletarians who proclaim their candidacy for the Presidency of the Republic! Hypocrisy! . . .

15.

Thoreau:

Dissent as a Duty*

> Let every soul be subject unto the higher
> powers. For there is no power but of God: the
> powers that be are ordained by God.
>
> Whosoever therefore resisteth the power, re-
> sisteth the ordinance of God: and they that resist
> shall receive to themselves damnation.
>
> —St. Paul's Epistle to the Romans, 13:1–2.

*There are two alternatives open to an individual whose
conscience is outraged by a given law or the whole system
of laws. He may obey the law until such time as it can
be changed, or he may decline to obey. The American
writer Henry David Thoreau (1817–1862) chose the latter
course. A trenchant critic of existing institutions and a
supreme individualist who regarded the organized state
as a threat to true independence, he assisted the "under-
ground railway" in transporting runaway slaves to Canada
and, in 1846, went to jail rather than pay taxes in support of a government that had launched an unjust war
against Mexico in order to extend slave territory into the
Southwest.*

*Born in Concord, Massachusetts, Thoreau was graduated
from Harvard at the age of twenty. He taught school for
some years, did odd jobs in the household of Ralph Waldo
Emerson, and spent two years in a hut on the edge of*

*Henry David Thoreau, *A Yankee in Canada, with Anti-Slavery
and Reform Papers* (Boston: Ticknor and Fields, 1866), pp. 123–28,
130–35.

Walden Pond near Concord, where he wrote the well-known Walden; or, Life in the Woods.

The selection here is from Thoreau's essay "Civil Disobedience" (1849), one of the chief bases for Mahatma Gandhi's doctrine of passive resistance. The essay is both a fervent protest against governments that do not conduct themselves in accordance with higher moral principle and a reasoned assertion of the individual's duty to deny support or allegiance to a government that he believes to be wrong.

I heartily accept the motto—"That government is best which governs least"; and I should like to see it acted up to more rapidly and systematically. Carried out, it finally amounts to this, which also I believe—"That government is best which governs not at all"; and when men are prepared for it, that will be the kind of government which they will have. Government is at best but an expedient; but most governments are usually, and all governments are sometimes, inexpedient. The objections which have been brought against a standing army, and they are many and weighty, and deserve to prevail, may also at last be brought against a standing government. The standing army is only an arm of the standing government. The government itself, which is only the mode which the people have chosen to execute their will, is equally liable to be abused and perverted before the people can act through it. Witness the present Mexican war, the work of comparatively a few individuals using the standing government as their tool; for, in the outset, the people would not have consented to this measure.

This American government—what is it but a tradition, though a recent one, endeavoring to transmit itself unimpaired to posterity, but each instant losing some of its integrity? It has not the vitality and force of a single living man; for a single man can bend it to his will. It is a sort of wooden gun to the people themselves. But it is not the less necessary for this; for the people must have some complicated machinery or other, and hear its din, to satisfy that idea of government which they have. Governments show thus how successfully men can be imposed on, even impose on themselves, for their own advantage. It is excellent, we must all allow. Yet this government never of itself furthered any enterprise, but by the alacrity with which it got out of its way. *It* does not keep the country free. *It* does not settle the West. *It* does not educate. The character inherent in the American people has done all that has been accomplished; and it would have done somewhat more, if the government had not sometimes got in its way. For government is an expedient by which men would fain succeed in letting one another alone; and, as has been said, when it is most expedient, the governed are most let alone by it. Trade and commerce, if they were not made of India-rubber, would never manage to bounce over the obstacles which legislators are continually putting in their way; and, if one were to judge these men wholly by the effects of their actions and not partly by their intentions, they would deserve to be classed and punished with those mischievous persons who put obstructions on the railroads.

But, to speak practically and as a citizen, unlike those who call themselves no-government men, I ask for, not at once no government, but *at once* a better government. Let every man make known what kind of government would command his respect, and that will be one step toward obtaining it.

After all, the practical reason why, when the power is once in the hands of the people, a majority are permitted, and for a long period continue, to rule, is not because they are most likely to be in the right, nor because this seems fairest to the minority, but because they are physically the strongest. But a government in which the majority rule in all cases cannot be based on justice, even as far as men understand it. Can there not be a government in which majorities do not virtually decide right and wrong, but conscience?—in which majorities decide only those questions to which the rule of expediency is applicable? Must the citizen ever for a moment, or in the least degree, resign his conscience to the legislator? Why has every man a conscience, then? I think that we should be men first, and subjects afterward. It is not desirable to cultivate a respect for the law, so much as for the right. The only obligation which I have a right to assume, is to do at any time what I think right. It is truly enough said, that a corporation has no conscience; but a corporation of conscientious men is a corporation *with* a conscience. Law never made men a whit more just; and, by means of their respect for it, even the well-disposed are daily made the agents of injustice. A common and natural result of an undue respect for law is, that you may see a file of soldiers, colonel, captain, corporal, privates, powder-monkeys, and all, marching in admirable order over hill and dale to the wars, against their wills, ay, against their common sense and consciences, which makes it very steep marching indeed, and produces a palpitation of the heart. They have no doubt that it is a damnable business in which they are concerned; they are all peaceably inclined. Now, what are they? Men at all? or small movable forts and magazines, at the service of some unscrupulous man in power? Visit the Navy-Yard, and behold a marine, such a man as an American government can make, or such as it can make a man with its black arts—a mere shadow and reminiscence of humanity, a man laid out alive and standing, and already, as one may say, buried under arms with funeral accompaniments, though it may be—

> Not a drum was heard, not a funeral note,
> As his corse to the rampart we hurried;
> Not a soldier discharged his farewell shot
> O'er the grave where our hero we buried.

The mass of men serve the state thus, not as men mainly, but as machines, with their bodies. They are the standing army, and the militia, jailers, constables, posse comitatus, &c. In most cases there is no free exercise whatever of the judgment or of the moral sense; but they put themselves on a level with wood and earth and stones; and wooden men can perhaps be manufactured that will serve the purpose as well. Such command no more respect than men of straw or a lump of dirt. They have the same sort of worth only as horses and dogs. Yet such as these even are commonly esteemed good citizens. Others—as most legislators, politicians, lawyers, ministers, and office-holders—serve the state chiefly with their heads; and, as they rarely make any moral distinctions, they are as likely to serve the Devil, without *intending* it, as God. A very few, as heroes, patriots, martyrs, reformers in the great sense, and *men*, serve the state with their consciences also, and so necessarily resist it for the most part; and they are commonly treated as enemies by it. A wise man will only be useful as a man, and will not submit to be "clay," and "stop a hole to keep the wind away," but leave that office to his dust at least—

> I am too high-born to be propertied,
> To be a secondary at control,
> Or useful serving-man and instrument
> To any sovereign state throughout the world.

He who gives himself entirely to his fellow-men appears to them useless and selfish; but he who gives himself partially to them is pronounced a benefactor and philanthropist.

How does it become a man to behave toward this American government to-day? I answer, that he cannot without disgrace be associated with it. I cannot for an instant recognize that political organization as *my* government which is the *slave's* government also.

All men recognize the right of revolution; that is, the right to refuse allegiance to, and to resist, the government, when its tyranny or its inefficiency are great and unendurable. But almost all say that such is not the case now. But such was the case, they think, in the Revolution of '75. If one were to tell me that this was a bad government because it taxed certain foreign commodities brought to its ports, it is most probable that I should not make an ado about it, for I can do without them. All machines have their friction; and possibly this does enough good to counterbalance the evil. At any rate, it is a great evil to make a stir about it. But when the friction comes to have its machine, and oppression and robbery are organized, I say, let us not have such a machine any longer. In other words, when a sixth of the population of a nation which has undertaken to be the refuge of liberty are slaves, and a whole country is unjustly overrun and conquered by a foreign army, and subjected to military law, I think that it is not too soon for honest men to rebel and revolutionize. What makes this duty the more urgent is the fact, that the country so overrun is not our own, but ours is the invading army.

Paley, a common authority with many on moral questions, in his chapter on the "Duty of Submission to Civil Government," resolves all civil obligation into expediency; and he proceeds to say, "that so long as the interest of the whole society requires it, that is, so long as the established government cannot be resisted or changed without public inconveniency, it is the will of God that the established government be obeyed, and no longer. . . . This principle being admitted, the justice of every particular case of resistance is reduced to a computation of the quantity of the danger and grievance on the one side, and of the probability and expense of redressing it on the other." Of this, he says, every man shall judge for himself. But Paley appears never to have contemplated those cases to which the rule of expediency does not apply, in which a people, as well as an individual, must do justice, cost what it may. If I have unjustly wrested a plank from a drowning man, I must restore it to him though I drown myself. This, according to Paley, would be inconvenient. But he that would save his life, in such a case, shall lose it. This people must cease to hold slaves, and to make war on Mexico, though it cost them their existence as a people.

In their practice, nations agree with Paley; but does any one think that Massachusetts does exactly what is right at the present crisis? . . .

. . . All voting is a sort of gaming, like checkers or backgammon, with a slight moral tinge to it, a playing with right and wrong, with moral questions; and betting naturally accompanies it. The character of the voters is not staked. I cast my vote, perchance, as I think right; but I am not vitally concerned that that right should prevail. I am willing to leave it to the majority. Its obligation, therefore, never exceeds that of expediency. Even voting *for the right* is *doing* nothing for it. It is only expressing to men feebly your desire that it should prevail. A wise man will not leave the right to the mercy of chance, nor wish it to prevail through the power of the majority. There is but little virtue in the action of masses of men. When the majority shall at length vote for the abolition of slavery, it will be because they are indifferent to slavery, or because there is but little slavery left to be abolished by their vote. *They* will then be the only slaves. Only *his* vote can hasten the abolition of slavery who asserts his own freedom by his vote. . . .

. . . It is not a man's duty, as a matter of course, to devote himself to the eradication of any, even the most enormous wrong; he may still properly have other concerns to engage him; but it is his duty, at least, to wash his hands of it, and, if he gives it no thought longer, not to give it practically his support. If I devote myself to other pursuits and contemplations, I must first see, at least, that

I do not pursue them sitting upon another man's shoulders. I must get off him first, that he may pursue his contemplations too. See what gross inconsistency is tolerated. I have heard some of my townsmen say, "I should like to have them order me out to help put down an insurrection of the slaves, or to march to Mexico—see if I would go"; and yet these very men have each, directly by their allegiance, and so indirectly, at least, by their money, furnished a substitute. The soldier is applauded who refuses to serve in an unjust war by those who do not refuse to sustain the unjust government which makes the war; is applauded by those whose own act and authority he disregards and sets at naught; as if the State were penitent to that degree that it hired one to scourge it while it sinned, but not to that degree that it left off sinning for a moment. Thus, under the name of Order and Civil Government, we are all made at last to pay homage to and support our own meanness. After the first blush of sin comes its indifference; and from immoral it becomes, as it were, *un*moral, and not quite unnecessary to that life which we have made. . . .

. . . Unjust laws exist: shall we be content to obey them, or shall we endeavor to amend them, and obey them until we have succeeded, or shall we transgress them at once? Men generally, under such a government as this, think that they ought to wait until they have persuaded the majority to alter them. They think that, if they should resist, the remedy would be worse than the evil. But it is the fault of the government itself that the remedy *is* worse than the evil. *It* makes it worse. Why is it not more apt to anticipate and provide for reform? Why does it not cherish its wise minority? Why does it cry and resist before it is hurt? Why does it not encourage its citizens to be on the alert to point out its faults, and *do* better than it would have them? Why does it always crucify Christ, and excommunicate Copernicus and Luther, and pronounce Washington and Franklin rebels?

One would think, that a deliberate and practical denial of its authority was the only offence never contemplated by government; else, why has it not assigned its definite, its suitable and proportionate penalty? If a man who has no property refuses but once to earn nine shillings for the State, he is put in prison for a period unlimited by any law that I know, and determined only by the discretion of those who placed him there; but if he should steal ninety times nine shillings from the State, he is soon permitted to go at large again.

If the injustice is part of the necessary friction of the machine of government, let it go, let it go: perchance it will wear smooth—certainly the machine will wear out. If the injustice has a spring, or a pulley, or a rope, or a crank, exclusively for itself, then perhaps you may consider whether the remedy will not be worse than the evil; but if it is of such a nature that it requires you to be the agent of injustice to another, then, I say, break the law. Let your life be a counter friction to stop the machine. What I have to do is to see, at any rate, that I do not lend myself to the wrong which I condemn.

As for adopting the ways which the State has provided for remedying the evil, I know not of such ways. They take too much time, and a man's life will be gone. I have other affairs to attend to. I came into this world, not chiefly to make this a good place to live in, but to live in it, be it good or bad. A man has not everything to do, but something; and because he cannot do *everything,* it is not necessary that he should do *something* wrong. It is not my business to be petitioning the Governor or the Legislature any more than it is theirs to petition me; and, if they should not hear my petition, what should I do then? But in this case the State has provided no way: its very Constitution is the evil. This may seem to be harsh and stubborn and unconciliatory; but it is to treat with the utmost kindness and consideration the only spirit that can appreciate or deserves it. So is all change for the better, like birth and death, which convulse the body.

I do not hesitate to say, that those who call themselves Abolitionists should at once effectually withdraw their support both in person and property, from the government of Massachusetts, and not wait till they constitute a majority of one, before they suffer the right to prevail through them. I think that it is enough if they have God on their side, without waiting for that other one. Moreover, any man more right than his neighbors constitutes a majority of one already.

I meet this American government, or its representative, the State government, directly, and face to face, once a year—no more—in the person of its tax-gatherer; this is the only mode in which a man situated as I am necessarily meets it; and it then says distinctly, Recognize me; and the simplest, the most effectual, and, in the present posture of affairs, the indispensablest mode of treating with it on this head, of expressing your little satisfaction with and love for it, is to deny it then. My civil neighbor, the tax-gatherer, is the very man I have to deal with—for it is, after all, with men and not with parchment that I quarrel —and he has voluntarily chosen to be an agent of the government.

16.
Collectivist Anarchism:
Bakunin and Kropotkin

*The development of anarchism into an organized move-
ment with a popular following was due primarily to the
ideas and activities of two Russian intellectuals, Mikhail
Bakunin (1814–1876) and Pëtr Kropotkin (1842–1921).*

*Bakunin, the eldest son of an aristocratic family, re-
nounced a promising military career in 1841 to travel in
Germany, France, and Switzerland, where he collaborated
with radical groups interested in overthrowing the Russian
and other oppressive governments. In 1849, following the
collapse of a brief but violent revolution in Dresden, he
was arrested and handed over to the Russian atuhorities.
From 1851 to 1857 he was in prison in Russia; and in
1857 was banished to Siberia. He escaped from Siberia
four years later and fled to Western Europe, where he
became the leader of exiled anarchists from many lands.
In 1868 he joined the First International and engaged the
Marxists in an unsuccessful struggle for its control. When
the International split in 1872, the Bakuninists continued
as a separate organization. He withdrew from the movement in 1874 after the abortive insurrection in Bologna.*

*Bakunin's social and political ideal was an organization
of society based on a free federation of workers' associations modeled on the Russian peasant commune. He was
convinced that any state, regardless of its political form,
was simply systematized oppression, and he saw the "path
of combat and rebellion" as the only means for the complete emancipation of the masses. More than any of his
contemporaries, he derived from the revolutionary movements of Russia and Europe a belief in the virtue of
violence for its own sake and a confidence in the technique*

*of terrorism which would influence many other revolu-
tionaries besides anarchists.*

*Like all anarchists, Bakunin viewed religion as a form
of superstition, the chief function of which was to teach
submission to authority. In* God and the State, *excerpted
below, he denounced belief in God as "the negation of
human liberty" and described the manner in which religions
"debase and corrupt the people."*

*Bakunin's successor as the world's leading protagonist
of anarchism was Pëtr Kropotkin, a prince by birth and a
geographer and naturalist by profession. Whereas Bakunin
was an agitator and conspirator, Kropotkin was a theoretician. Convinced that the rise of the centralized state
from the sixteenth through the nineteenth centuries was
merely a transitory aberration from the normal pattern
of Western civilization, he saw the predominant trends of
modern history pointing back toward decentralized co-
operative societies, or collectives, in which the individual
could develop his creative faculties freely. The collectives would operate on the principle "from each according
to his means, to each according to his need." There would
be no private property. Instead, the collectives would have
ownership of every material object and each person would
be given his food and other requirements from the common stock.*

*Kropotkin published at least five books on the subject
of anarchism, the best known of which are* Fields, Factories, and Workshops *(1899) and* Mutual Aid *(1902). Por-
tions of two of his revolutionary pamphlets are reprinted
below as the second and third selections.*

I

God and the State*

. . . Nothing is more natural than that the belief in God,
the creator, regulator, judge, master, curser, saviour, and
benefactor of the world, should still prevail among the

*Michael Bakunin, *God and the State*. Translated by B. R. Tucker
(Boston: Benjamin R. Tucker, 1883), pp. 10, 14–16, 17.

people, especially in the rural districts, where it is even more widespread than among the proletariat of the cities. The people unfortunately are still very ignorant, and are kept in ignorance by the systematic efforts of all the governments, who consider them, not without good reason, as one of the essential conditions of their own power. Weighted down by their daily labor, deprived of leisure, of intellectual intercourse, of reading, in short, of all the means and a good portion of the stimulants that develop thought in men, the people generally accept religious traditions without criticism and in a lump. These traditions surround them from infancy in all the situations of life, and, artificially sustained in their minds by a multitude of official poisoners of all sorts, priests and laymen, are transformed therein into a sort of mental habit, too often more powerful than even their natural good sense.

There is another reason which explains and in some sort justifies the absurd beliefs of the people—namely, the wretched situation to which they find themselves fatally condemned by the economic organization of society in the most civilized countries of Europe. Reduced, intellectually and morally as well as materially, to the minimum of human existence, confined in their life like a prisoner in his prison, without horizon, without outlet, without even a future if we may believe the economists, the people would have the singularly narrow souls and blunted instincts of the *bourgeois* if they did not feel a desire to escape: but of escape there are but three methods—two chimerical and a third real. The first two are the dramshop and the church, debauchery of the body or debauchery of the mind; the third is social revolution. This last will be much more potent than all the theological propagandism of the free-thinkers to destroy the religious beliefs and dissolute habits of the people, beliefs and habits much more intimately connected than is generally supposed. In substituting for the at once illusory and brutal enjoyments of bodily and spiritual licentiousness the enjoyments, as refined as they are abundant, of humanity developed in each and all, the social revolution alone will have the power to close at the same time all the dram-shops and all the churches.

Till then the people, taken as a whole, will believe; and, if they have no reason to believe, they will have at least the right.

There is a class of people who, if they do not believe, must at least make a semblance of believing. This class

comprises all the tormentors, all the oppressors, and all
the exploiters of humanity: priests, monarchs, statesmen,
soldiers, public and private financiers, officials of all sorts,
policemen, *gendarmes,* jailers and executioners, monopolists, capitalists, tax-leeches, contractors and proprietors,
lawyers, economists, politicians of all shades, down to the
smallest vender of sweetmeats, all will repeat in unison
these words of Voltaire:

If God did not exist, it would be necessary to invent him.

For, you understand, "the people must have a religion."
That is the safety-valve. . . .

. . . I have stated the chief practical reason of the power
still exercised today over the masses by religious beliefs.
These mystical tendencies do not signify in man so much
an aberration of mind as a deep discontent at heart. They
are the instinctive and passionate protest of the human
being against the narrownesses, the platitudes, the sorrows,
and the shames of a wretched existence. For this malady,
I have already said, there is but one remedy—social Revolution.

In other writings I have endeavored to show the causes
responsible for the birth and historical development of
religious hallucinations in the human conscience. Here it
is my purpose to treat this question of the existence of a
God, or of the divine origin of the world or of man, solely
from the standpoint of its moral and social utility, and I
shall say only a few words, to better explain my thought,
regarding the theoretical grounds of this belief.

All religions, with their gods, their demigods and their
prophets, their messiahs and their saints, were created by
the credulous fancy of men who had not attained the
full development and full possession of their intellectual
faculties. Consequently, the religious heaven is nothing
but a mirage in which man, exalted by ignorance and
faith, discovers his own image, but enlarged and reversed
—that is, *divinized.* The history of religions, of the birth,
grandeur, and decline of the gods who have succeeded one
another in human belief, is nothing, therefore, but the
development of the collective intelligence and conscience
of mankind. As fast as they discovered, in the course of
their historically progressive advance, either in themselves
or in external nature, a power, a quality, or even any
great defect whatever, they attributed them to their gods,
after having exaggerated and enlarged them beyond mea-

sure, after the manner of children, by an act of their religious fancy. Thanks to this modesty and pious generosity of believing and credulous men, heaven has grown rich with the spoils of the earth, and, by a necessary consequence, the richer heaven became, the more wretched became humanity and the earth. God once installed, he was naturally proclaimed the cause, reason, arbiter, and absolute disposer of all things: the world thenceforth was nothing, God was all; and man, his real creator, after having extracted him from the void, bowed down before him, worshipped him, and avowed himself his creature and his slave.

Christianity is precisely the religion *par excellence,* because it exhibits and manifests, to the fullest extent, the very nature and essence of every religious system, which is *the impoverishment, enslavement, and annihilation of humanity for the benefit of divinity.*

God being everything, the real world and man are nothing. God being truth, justice, goodness, beauty, power, and life, man is falsehood, iniquity, evil, ugliness, impotence and death. God being master, man is the slave. Incapable of finding justice, truth, and eternal life by his own effort, he can attain them only through a divine revelation. But whoever says revelation says revealers, messiahs, prophets, priests, and legislators inspired by God himself; and these, once recognized as the representatives of divinity on earth, as the holy instructors of humanity, chosen by God himself to direct it in the path of salvation, necessarily exercise absolute power. All men owe them passive and unlimited obedience; for against the divine reason there is no human reason, and against the justice of God no terrestrial justice holds. Slaves of God, men must be slaves also of Church and State, *in so far as the State is consecrated by the Church.* This truth Christianity, better than all other religions that exist or have existed, has understood, not excepting even the majority of the old Oriental religions, which included only distinct and privileged nations, while Christianity aspires to embrace entire humanity; and this truth Roman Catholicism, alone among all the Christian sects, has proclaimed and realized with rigorous logic. That is why Christianity is the absolute religion, the final religion; why the Apostolic and Roman Church is the only consistent, legitimate, and divine church.

With all due respect, then, to the metaphysicians and religious idealists, philosophers, politicians, or poets: *The*

*idea of God implies the abdication of human reason and
justice; it is the most decisive negation of human liberty,
and necessarily ends in the enslavement of mankind, both
in theory and practice.*

Unless, then, we desire the enslavement and degradation
of mankind, as the Jesuits desire it, as the *mômiers*, pietists,
or Protestant Methodists desire it, we may not, must not
make the slightest concession either to the God of theology
or to the God of metaphysics. He who, in this mystical
alphabet, begins with God will inevitably end with God;
he who desires to worship God must harbor no childish
illusions about the matter, but bravely renounce his liberty
and humanity.

If God is, man is a slave; now, man can and must be
free; then, God does not exist.

I defy any one whomsoever to avoid this circle; now,
therefore, let all choose.

Is it necessary to point out to what extent and in what
manner religions debase and corrupt the people? They
destroy their reason, the principal instrument of human
emancipation, and reduce them to imbecility, the essential
condition of slavery. They dishonor human labor, and
make it a sign and source of servitude. They kill the idea
and sentiment of human justice, ever tipping the balance to
the side of triumphant knaves, privileged objects of divine
indulgence. They kill human pride and dignity, protecting
only the cringing and humble. They stifle in the heart of
nations every feeling of human fraternity, filling it with
cruelty instead.

All religions are cruel, all founded on blood; for all
rest principally on the idea of sacrifice—that is, on the
perpetual immolation of humanity to the insatiable vengeance of divinity. In this bloody mystery man is always the
victim, and the priest—a man also, but a man privileged
by grace—is the divine executioner. That explains why the
priests of all religions, the best, the most humane, the
gentlest, almost always have at the bottom of their hearts
—and, if not in their hearts, in their imaginations, in their
minds—something cruel and sanguinary. . . .

. . . A jealous lover of human liberty, and deeming it
the absolute condition of all that we admire and respect in
humanity, I reverse the phrase of Voltaire, and say that,
if God existed, it would be necessary to abolish him. . . .

II

Anarchism, Its Philosophy and Ideal*

... It was by massacre, the wheel, the gibbet, the sword, and the fire that church and State established their domination, and that they succeeded henceforth to reign over an incoherent agglomeration of "subjects" who had no more direct union among themselves. ...

... Educated men tremble at the idea that society might some day be without judges, police or jailers.

But frankly, do you need them as much as you have been told in musty books? Books written, be it noted, by scientists who generally know well what has been written before them, but, for the most part, absolutely ignore the people and their everyday life.

If we can wander, without fear, not only in the streets of Paris, which bristle with police, but especially in rustic walks where you rarely meet passers-by, is it to the police that we owe this security? or rather to the absence of people who care to rob or murder us? I am evidently not speaking of the one who carries millions about him. That one—a recent trial tells us—is soon robbed, by preference in places where there are as many policemen as lamp-posts. No, I speak of the man who fears for his life and not for his purse filled with ill-gotten sovereigns. Are his fears real?

Besides, has not experience demonstrated quite recently that Jack the Ripper performed his exploits under the eye of the London police—a most active force—and that he only left off killing when the population of Whitechapel itself began to give chase to him?

And in our everyday relations with our fellow-citizens, do you think that it is really judges, jailers, and police that hinder anti-social acts from multiplying? The judge, ever ferocious, because he is a maniac of law, the accuser, the informer, the police spy, all those interlopers that live from

*Roger Baldwin, ed., *Kropotkin's Revolutionary Pamphlets* (New York: Benjamin Blom, 1927), pp. 132, 133–35. Reprinted by permission.

hand to mouth around the law courts, do they not scatter demoralization far and wide into society? Read the trials, glance behind the scenes, push your analysis further than the exterior façade of law courts, and you will come out sickened.

Have not prisons—which kill all will and force of character in man, which enclose within their walls more vices than are met with on any other spot of the globe—always been universities of crime? Is not the court of a tribunal a school of ferocity? And so on.

When we ask for the abolition of the State and its organs we are always told that we dream of a society composed of men better than they are in reality. But no; a thousand times, no. All we ask is that men should not be made worse than they are, by such institutions!

If by following the very old advice given by Bentham you begin to think of the fatal consequences—direct, and especially indirect—of legal coercion, then, like Tolstoy, like us, you will begin to hate the use of coercion, and you will begin to say that society possesses a thousand other means for preventing anti-social acts. If it neglects those means today, it is because, being educated by church and State, our cowardice and apathy of spirit hinder our seeing clearly on this point. When a child has committed a fault, it is so easy to punish it: that puts an end to all discussions! It is so easy to hang a man—especially when there is an executioner who is paid so much for each execution—and it relieves us of thinking of the cause of crimes.

It is often said that anarchists live in a world of dreams to come, and do not see the things which happen today. We see them only too well, and in their true colors, and that is what makes us carry the hatchet into the forest of prejudices that besets us.

Far from living in a world of visions and imagining men better than they are, we see them as they are; and that is why we affirm that the best of men is made essentially bad by the exercise of authority, and that the theory of the "balancing of powers" and "control of authorities" is a hypocritical formula, invented by those who have seized power, to make the "sovereign people," whom they despise, believe that the people themselves are governing. It is because we know men that we say to those who imagine that men would devour one another without those governors: "You reason like the king, who, being sent across the frontier, called out, 'What will become of my poor subjects without me?' " . . .

III

Law and Authority*

"When ignorance reigns in society and disorder in the minds of men, laws are multiplied, legislation is expected to do everything, and each fresh law being a fresh miscalculation, men are continually led to demand from it what can proceed only from themselves, from their own education and their own morality." It is no revolutionist who says this, not even a reformer. It is the jurist, Dalloy, author of the collection of French law known as *Répertoire de la Législation*. And yet, though these lines were written by a man who was himself a maker and admirer of law, they perfectly represent the abnormal condition of our society.

In existing States a fresh law is looked upon as a remedy for evil. Instead of themselves altering what is bad, people begin by demanding a *law* to alter it. If the road between two villages is impassable, the peasant says: "There should be a law about parish roads. If a park-keeper takes advantage of the want of spirit in those who follow him with servile observance and insults one of them, the insulted man says, "There should be a law to enjoin more politeness upon park-keepers." If there is stagnation in agriculture or commerce, the husbandman, cattle-breeder, or corn speculator argues, "It is protective legislation that we require." Down to the old clothesman there is not one who does not demand a law to protect his own little trade. If the employer lowers wages or increases the hours of labor, the politician in embryo exclaims, "We must have a law to put all that to rights." In short, a law everywhere and for everything! A law about fashions, a law about mad dogs, a law about virtue, a law to put a stop to all the vices and all the evils which result from human indolence and cowardice.

We are so perverted by an education which from in-

*Roger Baldwin, ed., *Kropotkin's Revolutionary Pamphlets* (New York: Benjamin Blom, 1927), pp. 196–99, 204–206, 212–13, 216–18. Reprinted by permission.

fancy seeks to kill in us the spirit of revolt, and to develop that of submission to authority; we are so perverted by this existence under the ferrule of a law, which regulates every event in life—our birth, our education, our development, our love, our friendship—that, if this state of things continues, we shall lose all initiative, all habit of thinking for ourselves. Our society seems no longer able to understand that it is possible to exist otherwise than under the reign of law, elaborated by a representative government and administered by a handful of rulers. And even when it has gone so far as to emancipate itself from the thraldom, its first care has been to reconstitute it immediately. "The Year I of Liberty" has never lasted more than a day, for after proclaiming it men put themselves the very next morning under the yoke of law and authority.

Indeed, for some thousands of years, those who govern us have done nothing but ring the changes upon "Respect for law, obedience to authority." This is the moral atmosphere in which parents bring up their children, and school only serves to confirm the impression. Cleverly assorted scraps of spurious science are inculcated upon the children to prove necessity of law; obedience to the law is made a religion; moral goodness and the law of the masters are fused into one and the same divinity. The historical hero of the schoolroom is the man who obeys the law, and defends it against rebels.

Later when we enter upon public life, society and literature, impressing us day by day and hour by hour as the water-drop hollows the stone, continue to inculcate the same prejudice. Books of history, of political science, of social economy, are stuffed with this respect for law. Even the physical sciences have been pressed into the service by introducing artificial modes of expression, borrowed from theology and arbitrary power, into knowledge which is purely the result of observation. Thus our intelligence is successfully befogged, and always to maintain our respect for law. The same work is done by newspapers. They have not an article which does not preach respect for law, even where the third page proves every day the imbecility of that law, and shows how it is dragged through every variety of mud and filth by those charged with its administration. Servility before the law has become a virtue, and I doubt if there was ever even a revolutionist who did not begin in his youth as the defender of law against what are generally called "abuses," although these last are inevitable consequences of the law itself.

Art pipes in unison with would-be science. The hero of the sculptor, the painter, the musician, shields Law beneath his buckler, and with flashing eyes and distended nostrils stands ever ready to strike down the man who would lay hands upon her. Temples are raised to her; revolutionists themselves hesitate to touch the high priests consecrated to her service, and when revolution is about to sweep away some ancient institution, it is still by law that it endeavors to sanctify the deed.

The confused mass of rules of conduct called law, which has been bequeathed to us by slavery, serfdom, feudalism, and royalty, has taken the place of those stone monsters, before whom human victims used to be immolated, and whom slavish savages dared not even touch lest they should be slain by the thunderbolts of heaven.

This new worship has been established with especial success since the rise to supreme power of the middle class —since the great French Revolution. Under the ancien régime, men spoke little of laws; unless, indeed, it were, with Montesquieu, Rousseau, and Voltaire, to oppose them to royal caprice. Obedience to the good pleasure of the king and his lackeys was compulsory on pain of hanging or imprisonment. But during and after the revolutions, when the lawyers rose to power, they did their best to strengthen the principle upon which their ascendancy depended. The middle class at once accepted it as a dyke to dam up the popular torrent. The priestly crew hastened to sanctify it, to save their bark from foundering amid the breakers. Finally the people received it as an improvement upon the arbitrary authority and violence of the past.

To understand this, we must transport ourselves in imagination into the eighteenth century. Our hearts must have ached at the story of the atrocities committed by the all-powerful nobles of that time upon the men and women of the people before we can understand what must have been the magic influence upon the peasant's mind of the words, "Equality before the law, obedience to the law without distinction of birth or fortune." He who until then had been treated more cruelly than a beast, he who had never had any rights, he who had never obtained justice against the most revolting actions on the part of a noble, unless in revenge he killed him and was hanged—he saw himself recognized by this maxim, at least in theory, at least with regard to his personal rights, as the equal of his lord. Whatever this law might be, it promised to affect lord and peasant alike; it proclaimed the equality of rich and poor before the judge. The promise was a lie, and to-day we know it; but at that period it was an advance, a homage to justice, as hypocrisy is a homage rendered to truth. This is the reason that when the saviors of the men-aced middle class (the Robespierres and the Dantons) took their stand upon the writings of the Rousseaus and the Voltaires, and proclaimed "respect for law, the same for every man," the people accepted the compromise; for their revolutionary impetus had already spent its force in the contest with a foe whose ranks drew closer day by day; they bowed their neck beneath the yoke of law to save themselves from the arbitrary power of their lords. . . .

. . . The spirit of routine, originating in superstition, indolence, and cowardice, has in all times been the mainstay of oppression. In primitive human societies it was cleverly turned to account by priests and military chiefs. They perpetuated customs useful only to themselves, and suc-ceeded in imposing them on the whole tribe. So long as this conservative spirit could be exploited so as to assure the chief in his encroachments upon individual liberty, so long as the only inequalities between men were the work of nature, and these were not increased a hundred-fold by the concentration of power and wealth, there was no need for law and the formidable paraphernalia of tribunals and ever-augmenting penalties to enforce it.

But as society became more and more divided into two hostile classes, one seeking to establish its domination, the other struggling to escape, the strife began. Now the con-queror was in a hurry to secure the results of his actions in a permanent form, he tried to place them beyond question, to make them holy and venerable by every means in his power. Law made its appearance under the sanction of the priest, and the warrior's club was placed at its service. Its office was to render immutable such customs as were to the advantage of the dominant minority. Military authority undertook to ensure obedience. This new function was a fresh guarantee to the power of the warrior; now he had not only mere brute force at his service; he was the de-fender of law.

If law, however, presented nothing but a collection of prescriptions serviceable to rulers, it would find some diffi-culty in insuring acceptance and obedience. Well, the legislators confounded in one code the two currents of custom of which we have just been speaking, the maxims which represent principles of morality and social union wrought out as a result of life in common, and the mandates which are meant to ensure external existence to inequality. Customs, absolutely essential to the very being of society, are, in the code, cleverly intermingled with usages imposed by the ruling caste, and both claim equal respect from the crowd. "Do not kill," says the code, and hastens to add, "And pay tithes to the priest." "Do not steal," says the code, and immediately after, "He who refuses to pay taxes, shall have his hand struck off."

Such was law; and it has maintained its two-fold character to this day. Its origin is the desire of the ruling class to give permanence to customs imposed by themselves for their own advantage. Its character is the skilful commingling of customs useful to society, customs which have no need of law to insure respect, with other customs useful only to rulers, injurious to the mass of the people, and maintained only by the fear of punishment.

Like individual capital, which was born of fraud and violence, and developed under the auspices of authority, law has no title to the respect of men. Born of violence and superstition, and established in the interests of consumer, priest, and rich exploiter, it must be utterly destroyed on the day when the people desire to break their chains. . . .

. . . The millions of laws which exist for the regulation of humanity appear upon investigation to be divided into three principal categories: protection of property, protection of persons, protection of government. And by analyzing each of these three categories, we arrive at the same logical and necessary conclusion: *the uselessness and hurtfulness of law*.

Socialists know what is meant by protection of property. Laws on property are not made to guarantee either to the individual or to society the enjoyment of the produce of their own labor. On the contrary, they are made to rob the producer of a part of what he has created, and to secure to certain other people that portion of the produce which they have stolen either from the producer or from society as a whole. When, for example, the law establishes Mr. So-and-So's right to a house, it is not establishing his right to a cottage he has built for himself, or to a house he has erected with the help of some of his friends. In that case no one would have disputed his right. On the contrary, the law is establishing his right to a house which is *not* the product of his labor; first of all because he has had it built for him by others to whom he has not paid the full value of their work, and next because that house represents a social value which he could not have produced for himself. The law is establishing his right to what belongs to everybody in general and to nobody in particular. The same house built in the midst of Siberia would not have the value it possesses in a large town, and, as we know, that value arises from the labor of something like fifty generations of men who have built the town, beautified it, supplied it with water and gas, fine promenades, colleges, theatres, shops, railways, and roads leading in all directions. Thus, by recognizing the right of Mr. So-and-So to a particular house in Paris, London, or Rouen, the law is unjustly appropriating to him a certain portion of the produce of the labor of mankind in general. And it is precisely because this appropriation and all other forms of property bearing the same character are a crying injustice, that a whole arsenal of laws and a whole army of soldiers, police-men, and judges are needed to maintain it against the good sense and just feeling inherent in humanity.

Half our laws—the civil code in each country—serves no other purpose than to maintain this appropriation, this monopoly for the benefit of certain individuals against the whole of mankind. Three-fourths of the causes decided by the tribunals are nothing but quarrels between monopolists —two robbers disputing over their booty. And a great many of our criminal laws have the same object in view, their end being to keep the workman in a subordinate position towards his employer, and thus afford security for exploitation.

As for guaranteeing the product of his labor to the pro-ducer, there are no laws which even attempt such a thing. It is so simple and natural, so much a part of the manners and customs of mankind, that law has not given it so much as a thought. Open brigandage, sword in hand, is no feature of our age. Neither does one workman ever come and dis-pute the produce of his labor with another. If they have a misunderstanding they settle it by calling in a third person, without having recourse to law. The only person who exacts from another what that other has produced, is the proprietor, who comes in and deducts the lion's share. As for humanity in general, it everywhere respects the right of each to what he has created, without the interposition of any special laws.

As all the laws about property which make up thick volumes of codes and are the delight of our lawyers have no other object than to protect the unjust appropriation of human labor by certain monopolists, there is no reason for their existence, and, on the day of the revolution, social revolutionists are thoroughly determined to put an end to them. . . .

. . . We are continually being told of the benefits conferred by law, and the beneficial effect of penalties, but have the speakers ever attempted to strike a balance between the benefits attributed to laws and penalties, and the degrading effect of these penalties upon humanity? Only calculate all the evil passions awakened in mankind by the atrocious punishments formerly inflicted in our streets! Man is the cruelest animal upon earth. And who has pampered and developed the cruel instincts unknown, even among monkeys, if it is not the king, the judge, and the priests, armed with law, who caused flesh to be torn off in strips, boiling pitch to be poured into wounds, limbs to be dislocated, bones to be crushed, men to be sawn asunder to maintain their authority? Only estimate the torrent of depravity let loose in human society by the "informing" which is countenanced by judges, and paid in hard cash by governments, under pretext of assisting in the discovery of "crime." Only go into the jails and study what man becomes when he is deprived of freedom and shut up with other depraved beings, steeped in the vice and corruption which oozes from the very walls of our existing prisons. Only remember that the more these prisons are reformed, the more detestable they become. Our model modern penitentiaries are a hundred-fold more abominable than the dungeons of the middle ages. Finally, consider what corruption, what depravity of mind is kept up among men by the idea of obedience, the very essence of law; of chastisement; of authority having the right to punish, to judge irrespective of our conscience and the esteem of our friends; of the necessity for executioners, jailers, and informers—in a word, by all the attributes of law and authority. Consider all this, and you will assuredly agree with us in saying that a law inflicting penalties is an abomination which should cease to exist.

Peoples without political organization, and therefore less depraved than ourselves, have perfectly understood that the man who is called "criminal" is simply unfortunate; that the remedy is not to flog him, to chain him up, or to kill him on the scaffold or in prison, but to help him by the most brotherly care, by treatment based on equality, by the usages of life among honest men. In the next revolution we hope that this cry will go forth:

"Burn the guillotines; demolish the prisons; drive away

the judges, policemen, and informers—the impurest race upon the face of the earth; treat as a brother the man who has been led by passion to do ill to his fellow; above all, take from the ignoble products of middle-class idleness the possibility of displaying their vices in attractive colors; and be sure that but few crimes will mar our society."

The main supports of crime are idleness, law, and authority; laws about property, laws about government, laws about penalties and misdemeanors; and authority, which takes upon itself to manufacture these laws and to apply them.

No more laws! No more judges! Liberty, equality, and practical human sympathy are the only effectual barriers we can oppose to the anti-social instincts of certain among us.

17.

Emma Goldman:

Testament of an American

Anarchist*

Be of good cheer, good friends and comrades.
We are going to prison with light hearts. To us it
is more satisfactory to stay behind prison bars
than to remain MUZZLED in freedom. Our spirit
will not be daunted, nor our will broken. We will
return to our work in due time.

This is our farewell to you. The light of Liberty
burns low just now. But do not despair, friends.
Keep the spark alive. The night cannot last forever. Soon there will come a rift in the darkness,
and the New Day break even here. May each of
us feel that we have contributed our mite toward
the great Awakening.

*The above is an excerpt from a farewell message[1] by the
Russian-born anarchist Emma Goldman (1869–1940) and
her long-time collaborator Alexander Berkman (1870[?]–
1936), a Polish immigrant who had first gained notoriety
in 1892 when he attempted to kill industrialist Henry
Clay Frick. The message was written at the beginning of
1918 not long after the two radicals were convicted for
draft obstruction and sentenced to two years' imprisonment.*

Prison was no novelty to Miss Goldman. Perhaps the

*Emma Goldman, "What I Believe," New York World, July 19,
1908, p. 3m.
[1]Emma Goldman and Alexander Berkman, "Farewell, Friends
and Comrades," Mother Earth Bulletin, I, No. 4 (January, 1918),
p. 1.

*most active and audacious rebel of her time, she had
already been imprisoned several times (once for urging
women to "keep their minds open and their wombs
closed") before directing her energy toward opposing
America's involvement in World War I. For thirty years
she had been advocating anarchism, practicing free love,
and touring the United States lecturing on subjects rang-
ing from Ibsen to birth control to the evils of patriotism.
Her compassion for the oppressed and her opposition to
economic inequality and political injustice were such that
she had defended Berkman's attack on Frick and had
campaigned on behalf of President McKinley's assassin,
Czolgosz. To radicals like Eugene Debs, who considered
Goldman "one of the sincerest women" he knew, these
were activities worthy of admiration. But they did little to
endear her to the authorities.*

*Miss Goldman wrote the selection which follows in
1908 in an attempt to clear up what she regarded as widespread misconceptions about her views.*

"What I believe" has many times been the target of hack
writers. Such blood-curdling and incoherent stories have
been circulated about me, it is no wonder that the average
human being has palpitation of the heart at the very
mention of the name Emma Goldman. It is too bad that
we no longer live in the times when witches were burned
at the stake or tortured to drive the evil spirit out of them.
For, indeed, Emma Goldman is a witch! True, she does
not eat little children, but she does many worse things.
She manufactures bombs and gambles in crowned heads.
B-r-r-r!

Such is the impression the public has of myself and my
beliefs. It is therefore very much to the credit of *The
World* that it gives its readers at least an opportunity to
learn what my beliefs really are.

The student of the history of progressive thought is well
aware that every idea in its early stages has been mis-

represented and the adherents of such ideas have been maligned and persecuted. One need not go back two thousand years to the time when those who believed in the gospel of Jesus were thrown into the arena or hunted into dungeons to realize how little great beliefs or earnest believers are understood. The history of progress is written in the blood of men and women who have dared to espouse an unpopular cause, as, for instance, the black man's right to his body, or woman's right to her soul. If, then, from time immemorial, the New has met with opposition and condemnation, why should my beliefs be exempt from a crown of thorns?

"What I believe" is a process rather than a finality. Finalities are for gods and governments, not for the human intellect. While it may be true that Herbert Spencer's formulation of liberty is the most important on the subject, as a political basis of society, yet life is something more than formulas. In the battle for freedom, as Ibsen has so well pointed out, it is the struggle for, not so much the attainment of, liberty, that develops all that is strongest, sturdiest and finest in human character.

Anarchism is not only a process, however, that marches on with "sombre steps," coloring all that is positive and constructive in organic development. It is a conspicuous protest of the most militant type. It is so absolutely uncompromising, insisting and permeating a force as to overcome the most stubborn assault and to withstand the criticism of those who really constitute the last trumpets of a decaying age.

Anarchists are by no means passive spectators in the theatre of social development; on the contrary, they have some very positive notions as regards aims and methods.

That I may make myself as clear as possible without using too much space, permit me to adopt the topical mode of treatment of "What I Believe."

I. As to Property

"Property" means dominion over things and the denial to others of the use of those things. So long as production was not equal to the normal demand, institutional property may have had some *raison d'être*. One has only to consult economics, however, to know that the productivity of labor within the last few decades has increased so tremendously as to exceed normal demand a hundred-fold, and to make property not only a hindrance to human well-being, but an obstacle, a deadly barrier, to all progress. It is the private dominion over things that condemns millions of people to be mere nonentities, living corpses without originality or power of initiative, human machines of flesh and blood, who pile up mountains of wealth for others and pay for it with a gray, dull and wretched existence for themselves. I believe that there can be no real wealth, social wealth, so long as it rests on human lives—young lives, old lives and lives in the making.

It is conceded by all radical thinkers that the fundamental cause of this terrible state of affairs is (1) that man must sell his labor; (2) that his inclination and judgment are subordinated to the will of a master.

Anarchism is the only philosophy that can and will do away with this humiliating and degrading situation. It differs from all other theories inasmuch as it points out that man's development, his physical well-being, his latent qualities and innate disposition alone must determine the character and conditions of his work. Similarly will one's physical and mental appreciations and his soul cravings decide how much he shall consume. To make this a reality will, I believe, be possible only in a society based on voluntary co-operation of productive groups, communities and societies loosely federated together, eventually developing into a free communism, actuated by a solidarity of interests. There can be no freedom in the large sense of the word, no harmonious development, so long as mercenary and commercial considerations play an important part in the determination of personal conduct.

II. As to Government

I believe Government, organized authority, or the State, is necessary only to maintain or protect property and monopoly. It has proven efficient in that function only. As a promoter of individual liberty, human well-being and social harmony, which alone constitute real order, government stands condemned by all the great men of the world.

I therefore believe, with my fellow-Anarchists, that the statutory regulations, legislative enactments, constitutional provisions, are invasive. They never yet induced man to do anything he could and would not do by virtue of his intellect or temperament, nor prevented anything that man was impelled to do by the same dictates. Millet's pictorial description of "The Man with the Hoe," Meunter's masterpieces of the miners that have aided in lifting labor from its degrading position, Gorki's descriptions of the underworld, Ibsen's psychological analysis of human life, could never have been induced by government any more than the spirit which impels a man to save a drowning child or a crippled woman from a burning building has ever been called into operation by statutory regulations or the policeman's club. I believe—indeed, I know—that whatever is fine and beautiful in the human, expresses and asserts itself in spite of government, and not because of it.

The Anarchists are therefore justified in assuming that anarchism—the absence of government—will insure the widest and greatest scope for unhampered human development, the cornerstone of true social progress and harmony.

As to the stereotyped argument that government acts as a check on crime and vice, even the makers of law no longer believe it. This country spends millions of dollars for the maintenance of her "criminals" behind prison bars, yet crime is on the increase. Surely this state of affairs is not owing to an insufficiency of laws! Ninety per cent of all crimes are property crimes, which have their root in our economic iniquities. So long as these latter continue to exist we might convert every lamp-post into a gibbet without having the least effect on the crime in our midst. Crimes resulting from heredity can certainly never be cured by law. Surely we are learning even today that such crimes can effectively be treated only by the best modern medical methods at our command, and, above all, by the spirit of a deeper sense of fellowship, kindness and understanding.

III   As to Militarism

I should not treat of this subject separately since it belongs to the paraphernalia of government, if it were not for the fact that those who are most vigorously opposed to my beliefs on the ground that the latter stand for force are the advocates of militarism.

The fact is that Anarchists are the only true advocates of peace, the only people who call a halt to the growing tendency of militarism, which is fast making of this erstwhile free country an imperialistic and despotic power.

The military spirit is the most merciless, heartless and brutal in existence. It fosters an institution for which there is not even a pretense of justification. The soldier, to quote Tolstoi, is a professional man-killer. He does not kill for the love of it, like a savage, or in a passion, like a homicide. He is a cold-blooded, mechanical, obedient tool of his military superiors. He is ready to cut throats or scuttle a ship at the command of his ranking officer, without knowing or, perhaps, caring how, why or wherefore. I am supported in this contention by no less a military light than General Funston. I quote from the latter's communication to *The New York Evening Post* of June 30 [1908], dealing with the case of Private William Buwalda, which caused such a stir all through the Northwest. "The first duty of an officer or enlisted man," says our noble warrior, "is unquestioning obedience and loyalty to the Government to which he has sworn allegiance; it makes no difference whether he approves of that Government or not."

How can we harmonize the principle of "unquestioning obedience" with the principle of "life, liberty and the pursuit of happiness"? The deadly power of militarism has never before been so effectually demonstrated in this country as in the recent condemnation by court-martial of William Buwalda, of San Francisco, Company A, Engineers, to five years in military prison. Here was a man who had a record of fifteen years of continuous service. "His character and conduct were unimpeachable," we are told by General Funston, who, in consideration of it, reduced Buwalda's sentence to three years. Yet the man is thrown suddenly out of the army, dishonored, robbed of his chances of a pension and sent to prison. What was his crime? Just listen, ye free-born Americans! William Buwalda attended a public meeting, and after the lecture he shook hands with the speaker. General Funston, in his letter to *The Post*, to which I have already referred above, asserts that Buwalda's action was a "great military offense, infinitely worse than desertion." In another public statement, which the General made in Portland, Oregon, he said that "Buwalda's was a serious crime, equal to treason."

It is quite true that the meeting had been arranged by Anarchists. Had the Socialists issued the call, General Funston informs us, there would have been no objection to Buwalda's presence. Indeed, the General says, "I would not have the slightest hesitancy about attending a Socialist meeting myself." But to attend an Anarchist meeting with Emma Goldman as speaker—could there be anything more "treasonable"?

For this horrible crime a man, a free-born American citizen, who has given this country the best fifteen years of his life, and whose character and conduct during that time were "unimpeachable," is now languishing in a prison, dishonored, disgraced and robbed of a livelihood.

Can there be anything more destructive of the true genius of liberty than the spirit that made Buwalda's sentence possible—the spirit of unquestioning obedience? Is it for this that the American people have in the last few years sacrificed four hundred million dollars and their hearts' blood?

I believe that militarism—a standing army and navy in any country—is indicative of the decay of liberty and of the destruction of all that is best and finest in our nation. The steadily growing clamor for more battleships and an increased army on the ground that these guarantee us peace is as absurd as the argument that the peaceful man is he who goes well armed.

The same lack of consistency is displayed by those peace pretenders who oppose anarchism because it supposedly teaches violence, and who would yet be delighted over the possibility of the American nation soon being able to hurl dynamite bombs upon defenseless enemies from flying machines.

I believe that militarism will cease when the liberty-loving spirits of the world say to their masters: "Go and do your own killing. We have sacrificed ourselves and our loved ones long enough fighting your battles. In return you have made parasites and criminals of us in times of peace and brutalized us in times of war. You have separated us from our brothers and have made of the world a human slaughterhouse. No, we will not do your killing or fight for the country that you have stolen from us."

Oh, I believe with all my heart that human brotherhood and solidarity will clear the horizon from the terrible red streak of war and destruction.

IV. As to Free Speech and Press

The Buwalda case is only one phase of the larger question of free speech, free press and the right of free assembly.

Many good people imagine that the principles of free speech or press can be exercised properly and with safety within the limits of constitutional guarantees. That is the only excuse, it seems to me, for the terrible apathy and indifference to the onslaught upon free speech and press that we have witnessed in this country within the last few months.

I believe that free speech and press means that I may say and write what I please. This right, when regulated by constitutional provisions, legislative enactments, almighty decisions of the Postmaster-General or the policeman's club, becomes a farce. I am well aware that I will be warned of consequences if we remove the chains from speech and press. I believe, however, that the core of consequences resulting from the unlimited exercise of expression is to allow more expression.

Mental shackles have never yet stemmed the tide of progress, whereas premature social explosions have only too often been brought about through a wave of repression.

Will our governors never learn that countries like England, Holland, Norway, Sweden and Denmark, with the largest freedom of expression, have been freest from "consequences"? Whereas Russia, Spain, Italy, France and, alas! even America, have raised these "consequences" to the most pressing political factor. Ours is supposed to be a country ruled by the majority, yet every policeman who is not vested with power by the majority can break up a meeting, drag the lecturer off the platform and club the audience out of the hall in true Russian fashion. The Postmaster-General, who is not an elective officer, has the power to suppress publications and confiscate mail. From his decision there is no more appeal than from that of the Russian Czar. Truly, I believe we need a new Declaration of Independence. Is there no modern Jefferson or Adams?

V. As to the Church

At the recent convention of the political remnants of a once revolutionary idea it was voted that religion and vote getting have nothing to do with each other. Why should they? So long as man is willing to delegate to the devil the care of his soul, he might with the same consistency delegate to the politician the care of his rights. That religion is a private affair has long been settled by the Bis-Marxian Socialists of Germany. Our American Marxians, poor of blood and originality, must needs go to Germany for their wisdom. That wisdom has served as a capital whip to lash the several millions of people into the well disciplined army of Socialism. It might do the same here. For goodness' sake, let's not offend respectability, let's not hurt the religious feelings of the people.

Religion is a superstition that originated in man's

mental inability to solve natural phenomena. The Church is an organized institution that has always been a stumbling block to progress.

Organized churchism has stripped religion of its naiveté and primitiveness. It has turned religion into a nightmare that oppresses the human soul and holds the mind in bondage. "The Dominion of Darkness," as the last true Christian, Leo Tolstoi, calls the Church, has been a foe of human development and free thought, and as such it has no place in the life of a truly free people.

VI. As to Marriage and Love

I believe these are probably the most tabooed subjects in this country. It is almost impossible to talk about them without scandalizing the cherished propriety of a lot of good folk. No wonder so much ignorance prevails relative to these questions. Nothing short of an open, frank and intelligent discussion will purify the air from the hysterical, sentimental rubbish that is shrouding these vital subjects, vital to individual as well as social well-being.

Marriage and love are not synonymous; on the contrary, they are often antagonistic to each other. I am aware of the fact that some marriages are actuated by love, but the narrow, material confines of marriage, as it is, speedily crush the tender flower of affection.

Marriage is an institution which furnishes the State and Church with a tremendous revenue and the means of prying into that phase of life which refined people have long considered their own, their very own most sacred affair. Love is that most powerful factor of human relationship which from time immemorial has defied all manmade laws and broken through the iron bars of conventions in church and morality. Marriage is often an economic arrangement purely, furnishing the woman with a life long insurance policy and the man with a perpetuator of his kind or a pretty toy. That is, marriage, or the training thereto, prepares the woman for the life of a parasite, a dependent, helpless servant, while it furnishes to man the right of a chattel mortgage over a human life.

How can such a condition of affairs have anything in common with love?—with the element that would forego all the wealth of money and power and live in its own world of untrammelled human expression? But this is not the age of romanticism, of Romeo and Juliet, Faust and Marguerite, of moonlight ecstasies, of flowers and songs.

Ours is a practical age. Our first consideration is an income. So much the worse for us if we have reached the era when the soul's highest flights are to be checked. No race can develop without the love element.

But if two people are to worship at the shrine of love, what is to become of the golden calf, marriage? "It is the only security for the woman, for the child, the family, the State." But it is no security to love; and without love no true home can or does exist. Without love no child should be born; without love no true woman can be related to a man. The fear that love is not sufficient material safety for the child is out of date. I believe when woman signs her own emancipation, her first declaration of independence will consist in admiring and loving a man for the qualities of his heart and mind and not for the quantities in his pocket. The second declaration will be that she has the right to follow that love without let or hindrance from the outside world. The third and most important declaration will be the absolute right to free motherhood.

In such a mother and in an equally free father rests the safety of the child. They have the strength, the sturdiness, the harmony to create an atmosphere wherein alone the human plant can grow into an exquisite flower.

VII. As to Acts of Violence

And now I have come to that point in my beliefs about which the greatest misunderstanding prevails in the minds of the American public. "Well, come, now, don't you propagate violence, the killing of crowned heads and Presidents?" Who says that I do? Have you heard me, has any one heard me? Has any one seen it printed in our literature? No, but the papers say so, everybody says so; consequently it must be so. Oh, for the accuracy and logic of the dear public!

I believe that anarchism is the only philosophy of peace, the only theory of a social relationship that values human life above everything else. I know that some Anarchists have committed acts of violence, but it is the terrible economic inequality and great political injustice that prompt such acts, not anarchism. Every institution to-day rests on violence, our very atmosphere is saturated with it. So long as such a state exists we might as well strive to stop the rush of Niagara as hope to do away with violence. I have already stated that countries with some measure of freedom of expression have had few or no acts of violence. What is the moral? Simply this: No act committed by an Anarchist has been for personal gain, aggrandizement or profit, but rather a conscious protest against some repressive, arbitrary, tyrannical measure from above.

President Carnot of France was killed by Caserio in response to Carnot's refusal to commute the death sentence of Vaillant, for whose life the entire literary, scientific and humanitarian world of France had pleaded.

Bresel went to Italy on his own money earned in the silk weaving mills at Paterson to call King Humbert to the bar of justice for his order to shoot defenseless women and children during a bread riot. Angelino executed Prime Minister Canovas for the latter's resurrection of the Spanish inquisition at Montjuich Prison. Alexander Berkman attempted the life of Henry C. Frick during the Homestead strike only because of his intense sympathy for the eleven strikers killed by Pinkertons and for the widows and orphans evicted by Frick from their wretched little homes that were owned by Mr. Carnegie.

Every one of these men not only made their reasons known to the world in spoken or written statements, showing the causes that led to their acts, proving that the unbearable economic and political pressure, the suffering and despair of their fellowmen [sic], women and children prompted their acts, and not the philosophy of anarchism. They came openly, frankly and ready to stand the consequences, ready to give their own lives.

In diagnosing the true nature of our social disease I cannot condemn those who through no fault of their own are suffering from a widespread malady.

I do not believe that these acts can or ever have been intended to bring about the social reconstruction. That can only be done, first, by a broad and wide education as to man's place in society and his proper relation to his fellows; and, second, through example. By example I mean the actual living of a truth once recognized, not the mere theorizing of its life element. Lastly, and the most powerful weapon, is the conscious, intelligent, organized, economic protest of the masses through direct action and the general strike.

It is the harmony of organic growth which produces variety of color and form—the complete whole we admire in the flower. Analogously will the organized activity of free human beings endowed with the spirit of solidarity result in the perfection of social harmony—which is anarchism. Indeed, only anarchism makes non-authoritarian organization a reality, since it abolishes the existing antagonism between individuals and classes.

18.

Sorel:

The Mystique of Violence

and "Direct Action"*

Syndicalism, as an ideology which gained prominence at the end of the nineteenth century, represented a composite of ideas derived from anarchism, Marxism, and the original concepts of its chief theoretician, Georges Sorel (1847–1922). An engineer turned social philosopher, Sorel's most famous work, Reflections on Violence *(1908), remains the classic expression of revolutionary syndicalist thought. As an ex-Marxist who paid tribute to the ideas of Joseph Proudhon and Henry Bergson and believed that the proletariat was the only class still endowed with dynamism, Sorel became an outspoken enemy of bourgeois society, democracy, and the whole spate of rationalist-positivist-scientist rationale that dominated the French intellectual establishment under the Third Republic.*

A radical critic of both traditional liberalism and socialism, Sorel reassessed what Marx called the class struggle and went on to prescribe a syndicalist approach for proletarian victory which was based on three essential ingredients: the idea of the "myth," the use of violence, and the coercive thrust of the "direct-action" general strike. He believed that men, especially in a group and for a social cause, could generate great inspiration and energy only through belief in a myth, a myth imbued with the

*Reprinted with permission of The Macmillan Company and George Allen & Unwin Ltd. from *Reflections on Violence* by Georges Sorel (translated by T. E. Hulme and J. Roth), pp. 76–78, 80, 100–102, 103–107, 136–40, 142–45, 155. Copyright 1950 by The Free Press, a Corporation.

moral fervor one associates with a crusade or holy war. Under such psychological stimulation the working class would be able to sense a special virtue in violence and hence harness its creative and irrational force to carry out a spontaneous general strike that would bring down the modern bourgeois state and its propertied classes.

Though his philosophy was a compound of various streams of thought current in his day, Sorel not only stood at odds with both the bourgeois and the socialist establishments, but also condemned outright the "worthy progressives" who drew on the rationalist and enlightenment tradition. His unqualified enmity toward the "state" removed any grounds for compromise with contemporary social dogmas and emphasized the direct, brutal, and somewhat apocalyptic decisiveness of his prescription for social action. He desired to supplant the bourgeois state with a corporate one, with a structure based on syndicates of workers identified by occupation and, as the only productive class in society, enjoying the rewards of power. Hence, as a dissenter, Sorel placed himself in opposition to anti-collectivists like Friedrich Nietzsche on the one hand and adherents of "Marxism-through-gradualism" on the other. And he castigated with vehemence any approach which called for seizure and control of the existing establishment or for the patient transformation of existing institutions.

The selection which follows, taken from Reflections on Violence, *carries the essence of Sorel's revolutionary views. The reader should ponder whether the French syndicalist made himself more at home with anarchists, nihilists, or Marxists, and whether his radical vituperations represent a complete break with both past and present or offer tragic prophecy of the brutal vitality of fascism.*

A. To most people the class war is the *principle of Socialist tactics.* That means that the Socialist party founds its electoral successes on the clashing of interests which exist in an acute state between certain groups, and that, if need be, it would undertake to make this hostility still more acute; their candidates ask the poorest and most numerous class to look upon themselves as forming a corporation, and they offer to become the advocates of this corporation; they promise to use their influence as representatives to improve the lot of the disinherited. Thus we are not very far from what happened in the Greek states; Parliamentary Socialists are very much akin to the demagogues who clamoured constantly for the abolition of debts, and the division of landed property, who put all public charges upon the rich, and invented plots in order to get large fortunes confiscated. . . .

. . . Nowadays Parliamentary Socialists no longer entertain the idea of insurrection; if they still occasionally speak of it, it is merely to give themselves airs of importance; they teach that the ballot-box has replaced the gun; but the means of acquiring power may have changed without there being any change of mental attitude. Electoral literature seems inspired by the purest demagogic doctrines; Socialism makes its appeal to the discontented without troubling about the place they occupy in the world of production; in a society as complex as ours, and as subject to economic upheavals, there is an enormous number of discontented people in all classes—that is why Socialists are often found in places where one would least expect to meet them. Parliamentary Socialism speaks as many languages as it has types of clients. . . .

. . . Contemporary democracy in France finds itself somewhat bewildered by the tactics of the class war. This explains why Parliamentary Socialism does not mingle with the main body of the parties of the extreme left.

In order to understand this situation, we must remember the important part played by revolutionary war in our history; an enormous number of our political ideas originated from war; war presupposes the union of national forces against the enemy, and our French historians have always severely criticised those insurrections which hampered the defence of the country. It seems that our democracy is harder on its rebels than monarchies are. . . .

Capitalist society is so rich, and the future appears to it in such optimistic colours, that it endures the most frightful burdens without complaining overmuch: in America politicians waste large taxes shamelessly; in Europe, the expenditure in military preparation increases every year; social peace might very well be bought by a few supple-

mentary sacrifices. Experience shows that the middle classes
allow themselves to be plundered quite easily, provided that
a little pressure is brought to bear, and that they are intimidated by the fear of revolution; that party will possess the
future which can most skillfully manipulate the spectre
of revolution; the radical party is beginning to understand
this; but, however clever its clowns may be, it will have
some difficulty in finding any who can dazzle the big Jew
bankers as well as Jaurès and his friends can do.

C. The Syndicalist organisation gives a third value to
the class war. In each branch of industry employers and
workmen form antagonistic groups, which have continual
discussions, which negotiate and make agreements. Socialism brings along its terminology of class war, and thus com-
plicates conflicts which might have remained of a purely
private order; corporative exclusiveness, which resembles
the local or the racial spirit, is thereby consolidated, and
those who represent it like to imagine that they are ac-
complishing a higher duty and are doing excellent work for
Socialism. . . .

. . . According to Marx, capitalism, by reason of the
innate laws of its own nature, is hurrying along a path
which will lead the world of to-day, with the inevitability
of the evolution of organic life, to the doors of the world
of tomorrow. This movement comprises a long period
of capitalistic construction, and it ends by a rapid destruction, which is the work of the proletariat. Capitalism
creates the heritage which Socialism will receive, the men
who will suppress the present régime, and the means of
bringing about this destruction, at the same time that it
preserves the results obtained in production. Capitalism
begets new ways of working; it throws the working class
into revolutionary organisations by the pressure it exercises
on wages; it restricts its own political basis by competition,
which is constantly eliminating industrial leaders. Thus,
after having solved the great problem of the organisation of
labour, to effect which Utopians have brought forward so
many naïve or stupid hypotheses, capitalism provokes the
birth of the cause which will overthrow it, and thus renders
useless everything that Utopians have written to induce
enlightened people to make reforms; and it gradually ruins
the traditional order, against which the critics of the
idealists had proved themselves to be so deplorably incompetent. It might therefore be said that capitalism plays
a part analogous to that attributed by Hartmann to The
Unconscious in nature, since it prepares the coming of

social reforms which it did not intend to produce. Without any co-ordinated plan, without any directive ideas, without any ideal of a future world, it is the cause of an inevitable evolution; it draws from the present all that the present can give towards historical development; it performs in an almost mechanical manner all that is necessary, in order that a new era may appear, and that this new era may break every link with the idealism of the present times, while preserving the acquisitions of the capitalistic economic system.

Socialists should therefore abandon the attempt (initiated by the Utopians) to find a means of inducing the enlightened middle class to prepare the *transition to a more perfect system of legislation;* their sole function is that of explaining to the proletariat the greatness of the revolutionary part they are called upon to play. By ceaseless criticism the proletariat must be brought to perfect their organisations; they must be shown how the embryonic forms which appear in their unions may be developed, so that, finally, they may build up institutions without any parallel in the history of the middle class; that they may form ideas which depend solely on their position as producers in large industries, and which owe nothing to middle-class thought; and that they may acquire *habits of liberty* with which the middle class nowadays are no longer acquainted. . . .

. . . It is often urged, in objection to the people who defend the Marxian conception, that it is impossible for them to stop the movement of degeneration which is dragging both the middle class and the proletariat far from the paths assigned to them by Marx's theory. They can doubtless influence the working classes, and it is hardly to be denied that strike violences do keep the revolutionary spirit alive. . . .

. . . In any case, the separation of classes being more clearly accentuated, the proletarian movement will have some chance of developing with greater regularity than to-day.

The two antagonistic classes therefore influence each other in a partly indirect but decisive manner. Capitalism drives the proletariat into revolt, because in daily life the employers use their force in a direction opposed to the desire of their workers; but the future of the proletariat is not entirely dependent on this revolt; the working classes are organised under the influence of other causes, and Socialism, inculcating in them the revolutionary idea, prepares them to suppress the hostile class. Capitalist force is at the base of all this process, and its action is automatic and inevitable. Marx supposed that the middle class had no need to be incited to employ force, but we are to-day faced with a new and very unforeseen fact—a middle-class which seeks to weaken its own strength. Must we believe that the Marxian conception is dead? By no means, for proletarian violence comes upon the scene just at the moment when the conception of social peace is being held up as a means of moderating disputes; proletarian violence confines employers to their rôle of producers, and tends to restore the separation of the classes, just when they seemed on the point of intermingling in the democratic marsh.

Proletarian violence not only makes the future revolution certain, but it seems also to be the only means by which the European nations—at present stupefied by humanitarianism—can recover their former energy. This kind of violence compels capitalism to restrict its attentions solely to its material rôle and tends to restore to it the warlike qualities which it formerly possessed. A growing and solidly organised working class can compel the capitalist class to remain firm in the industrial war; if a united and revolutionary proletariat confronts a rich middle class, eager for conquest, capitalist society will have reached its historical perfection.

Thus proletarian violence has become an essential factor of Marxism. Let us add once more that, if properly conducted, it will suppress the Parliamentary Socialists, who will no longer be able to pose as the leaders of the working classes and the guardians of order. . . .

. . . Every time that we attempt to obtain an exact conception of the ideas behind proletarian violence we are forced to go back to the notion of the general strike; and this same conception may render many other services, and throw an unexpected light on all the obscure parts of Socialism. In the last pages of the first chapter I compared the general strike to the Napoleonic battle which definitely crushes an adversary; this comparison will help us to understand the part played by the general strike in the world of ideas.

Military writers of to-day, when discussing the new methods of war necessitated by the employment of troops infinitely more numerous than those of Napoleon, equipped with arms much more deadly than those of his time, do not for all that imagine that wars will be decided in any other way than that of the Napoleonic battle. The new tactics proposed must fit into the drama Napoleon had conceived; the detailed development of the combat will doubtless be quite different from what it used to be, but the end must always be the catastrophic defeat of the enemy. The methods of military instruction are intended to prepare the soldier for this great and terrible action, in which everybody must be ready to take part at the first signal. From the highest to the lowest, the members of a really solid army have always in mind this catastrophic issue of international conflicts.

The revolutionary Syndicates argue about Socialist action exactly in the same manner as military writers argue about war; they restrict the whole of Socialism to the general strike; they look upon every combination as one that should culminate in this catastrophe; they see in each strike a reduced facsimile, an essay, a preparation for the great final upheaval.

The *new school*, which calls itself Marxist, Syndicalist, and revolutionary, declared in favour of the idea of the general strike as soon as it became clearly conscious of the true sense of its own doctrine, of the consequences of its activity, and of its own originality. It was thus led to leave the old official, Utopian, and political tabernacles, which hold the general strike in horror, and to launch itself into the true current of the proletarian revolutionary movement; for a long time past the proletariat had made adherence to the principle of the general strike the *test* by means of which the Socialism of the workers was distinguished from that of the amateur revolutionaries.

Parliamentary Socialists can only obtain great influence if they can manage, by the use of a very confused language, to impose themselves on very diverse groups; for example, they must have working-men constituents simple enough to allow themselves to be duped by high-sounding phrases about future collectivism; they are compelled to represent themselves as profound philosophers to stupid middle-class people who wish to appear to be well informed about social questions; it is very necessary also for them to be able to exploit rich people who think that they are earning the gratitude of humanity by taking shares in the enterprises of Socialist politicians. This influence is founded on balderdash, and our bigwigs endeavour—sometimes only too successfully—to spread confusion among the ideas of their readers; they detest the general strike because all propaganda carried on from that point of view is too socialistic to please philanthropists.

In the mouths of these self-styled representatives of the proletariat all socialistic formulas lose their real sense. The class war still remains the great principle, but it must be subordinated to national solidarity. Internationalism is an article of faith about which the most moderate declare themselves ready to take the most solemn oaths; but patriotism also imposes sacred duties. The emancipation of the workers must be the work of the workers themselves—their newspapers repeat this every day—but real emancipation consists in voting for a professional politician, in securing for him the means of obtaining a comfortable situation in the world, in subjecting oneself to a leader. In the end the State must disappear—and they are very careful not to dispute what Engels has written on this subject—but this disappearance will take place only in a future so far distant that you must prepare yourself for it by using the State meanwhile as a means of providing the politicians with tidbits; and the best means of bringing about the disappearance of the State consists in strengthening meanwhile the Governmental machine. This method of reasoning resembles that of Gribouille, who threw himself into the water in order to escape getting wet in the rain.

Whole pages could be filled with the bare outlines of the contradictory, comical, and quack arguments which form the substance of the harangues of our great men; nothing embarrasses them, and they know how to combine, in pompous, impetuous, and nebulous speeches, the most absolute irreconcilability with the must supple opportunism. A learned exponent of Socialism has said that the art of reconciling opposites by means of nonsense is the most obvious result which he had got from the study of the works of Marx. I confess my extreme incompetence in these difficult matters; moreover, I make no claim whatever to be counted among the people upon whom politicians confer the title of learned; yet I cannot easily bring myself to admit that this is the sum and substance of the Marxian philosophy. . . .

. . . Against this noisy, garrulous, and lying Socialism, which is exploited by ambitious people of every description, which amuses a few buffoons, and which is admired by decadents—revolutionary Syndicalism takes its stand, and endeavours, on the contrary, to leave nothing in a state of indecision; its ideas are honestly expressed, without trickery and without mental reservations; no attempt is made to dilute doctrines by a stream of confused commentaries. Syndicalism endeavours to employ methods of expression which throw a full light on things, which put them exactly in the place assigned to them by their nature, and which bring out the whole value of the forces in play. Oppositions, instead of being glozed over, must be thrown into sharp relief if we desire to obtain a clear idea of the Syndicalist movement; the groups which are struggling one against the other must be shown as separate and as compact as possible; in short, the movements of the revolted masses must be represented in such a way that the soul of the revolutionaries may receive a deep and lasting impression.

These results could not be produced in any very certain manner by the use of ordinary language; use must be made of a body of images which, *by intuition alone,* and before any considered analyses are made, is capable of evoking as an undivided whole the mass of sentiments which corresponds to the different manifestations of the war undertaken by Socialism against modern society. The Syndicalists solve this problem perfectly, by concentrating the whole of Socialism in the drama of the general strike; there is thus no longer any place for the reconciliation of contraries in the equivocations of the professors; everything is clearly mapped out, so that only one interpretation of Socialism is possible. This method has all the advantages which "integral" knowledge has over analysis, according to the doctrine of Bergson; and perhaps it would not be possible to cite another example which would so perfectly demonstrate the value of the famous professor's doctrines. . . .

. . . And yet without leaving the present, without reasoning about this future, which seems for ever condemned to escape our reason, we should be unable to act at all. Experience shows that the *framing of a future, in some indeterminate time,* may, when it is done in a certain way, be very effective, and have very few inconveniences; this happens when the anticipations of the future take the form of those myths, which enclose with them, all the strongest inclinations of a people, of a party or of a class, inclinations which recur to the mind with the insistence of instincts in all the circumstances of life; and which give an aspect of complete reality to the hopes of immediate action by which, more easily than by any other method, men can reform their desires, passions, and mental activity. We know, moreover, that these social myths in no way prevent a man profiting by the observations which he makes in the course of his life, and form no obstacle to the pursuit of his normal occupations.

The truth of this may be shown by numerous examples.

The first Christians expected the return of Christ and the total ruin of the pagan world, with the inauguration of the kingdom of the saints, at the end of the first generation. The catastrophe did not come to pass, but Christian thought profited so greatly from the apocalyptic myth that certain contemporary scholars maintain that the whole preaching of Christ referred solely to this one point. The hopes which Luther and Calvin had formed of the religious exaltation of Europe were by no means realised; these fathers of the Reformation very soon seemed men of a past era; for present-day Protestants they belong rather to the Middle Ages than to modern times, and the problems which troubled them most occupy very little place in contemporary Protestantism. Must we for that reason deny the immense result which came from their dreams of Christian renovation? It must be admitted that the real developments of the Revolution did not in any way resemble the enchanting pictures which created the enthusiasm at its first adepts; but without those pictures would the Revolution have been victorious? Many Utopias were mixed up with the Revolutionary myth, because it had been formed by a society passionately fond of imaginative literature, full of confidence in the "science," and very little acquainted with the economic history of the past. These Utopias came to nothing; but it may be asked whether the Revolution was not a much more profound transformation than those dreamed of by the people who in the eighteenth century had invented social Utopias. In our own times Mazzini pursued what the wiseacres of his time called a mad chimera; but it can no longer be denied that, without Mazzini, Italy would never have become a great power, and that he did more for Italian unity than Cavour and all the politicians of his school.

. . . We have to question men who take a very active part in the real revolutionary movement amidst the proletariat, men who do not aspire to climb into the middle class and whose mind is not dominated by corporative prejudices. . . .

Thanks to these men, we know that the general strike is indeed what I have said: the *myth* in which Socialism is wholly comprised, *i.e.* a body of images capable of evoking instinctively all the sentiments which correspond to the different manifestations of the war undertaken by Socialism against modern society. Strikes have engendered in the proletariat the noblest, deepest, and most moving sentiments that they possess; the general strike groups them all in a co-ordinated picture, and, by bringing them together, gives to each one of them its maximum of intensity; appealing to their painful memories of particular conflicts, it colours with an intense life all the details of the composition presented to consciousness. We thus obtain that intuition of Socialism which language cannot give us with perfect clearness—and we obtain it as a whole, perceived instantaneously. . . .

. . . I have already called attention to the danger for the future of civilisation presented by revolutions which take place in a period of economic decadence; many Marxists do not seem to have formed a clear idea of Marx's thought on this subject. The latter believed that the great catastrophe would be preceded by an enormous economic crisis, but the crisis Marx had in mind must not be confused with an economic decadence; crises appeared to him as the result of a too risky venture on the part of production, which creates productive forces out of proportion to the means of regulation which the capitlalistic system automatically brings into play. Such a venture supposes that the future was looked upon as favourable to very large enterprises, and that the conception of economic progress prevailed absolutely at the time. In order that the lower middle classes, who are still able to find tolerable conditions of existence under the capitalist régime, may join hands with the proletariat, it is essential that they shall be able to picture the future of production as bright with hope, just as the conquest of America formerly appeared to the English peasants, who left Europe to throw themselves into a life of adventure.

The general strike leads to the same conclusions. The workers are accustomed to seeing their revolts against the restrictions imposed by capitalism succeed during periods of prosperity; so that it may be said that if you once identify revolution and general strike it then becomes impossible to conceive this of an essential transformation of the world taking place in a time of economic decadence. The workers are equally well aware that the peasants and the artisans will not join hands with them unless the future appears so rosy-coloured that industrialism will be able to ameliorate the lot not only of the producers, but that of everybody.

19.
Nietzsche:
Transvaluation
of Western Values*

*The philosophy of Friedrich Nietzsche (1844–1900) has
had an appeal, if somewhat episodic, for several generations of European and American students. Many have
been impressed with the German philosopher's frequent
intellectual coalescence with Darwinian evolutionary concepts, others with his sharp agnostic attacks on the religious establishment in an age of heated secularist-
spiritualist debate, and still others with the seeming
antecedents in his views for the energetic thrusts of
twentieth-century fascism. But nearly all who come to
grips with Nietzsche's thought agree that his voice was
one of unqualified dissent against the trends of the later
nineteenth century as well as those of the several decades
which followed.*

*In truth, Nietzsche not only opposed Christian ethics,
the leveling trends of industrial democracy, and bourgeois
individualism, but the basic formula of Social Darwinism
as well. He saw no gradual process the result of which
would be a noble creature, but rather a perpetuation and
standardization of the norm, inevitably leading to bland
mediocrity. Hence, Nietzsche attacked and condemned the*

*Friedrich Nietzsche, *The Will to Power*. Translated by Anthony
M. Ludovici (2 vols.; London: George Allen and Unwin Ltd.,
1924), Vol. I, pp. 228–29, 231, 236, 237, 291; Vol. II, pp. 110,
124, 130–31, 184–86, 204–207, 224–27, 295–99, 312–13, 361–65.
Reprinted by permission. Acknowledgment is also made to Russell
& Russell Publishers, for Friedrich Nietzsche, *The Complete Works
of Friedrich Nietzsche*. Translated under the general editorship of
Oscar Levy (18 vols.) [1909–1911], New York: Russell & Russell,
1964.

foundation, development, and contemporaneous system of European values. Not only were the premises upon which Western civilization rested false, but if they were permitted continued existence the result would be stagnation, a kind of dull purgatory preventing man from progression to a higher state of being.

In order to prevent such a demeaning of man's development, two things were required: a prolonged period of voluntary sacrifice and suffering, and a complete "transvaluation of all values." Only by these methods could man shake the yoke of the "herd" mentality, only then could man save himself from the sociologically paralyzing effects of Socratic, Christian, liberal, and democratic diseases which crippled him with values such as charity, toleration, pity for the suffering, and equality. If man were able to rid himself of his shackles, there was hope for the development of a higher being, one Neitzsche called a superman, one who would be as superior to the Europeans of his century as were the latter to Neanderthal man. This, not comfort or a higher standard of living, should be the true goal of civilization.

The whole of the morality of Europe is based upon the values *which are useful to the herd:* the sorrow of all higher and exceptional men is explained by the fact that everything which distinguishes them from others reaches their consciousness in the form of a feeling of their own smallness and egregiousness. It is the *virtues* of modern men which are the causes of pessimistic gloominess; the mediocre, like the herd, are not troubled much with questions or with conscience—they are cheerful. . . .

The more dangerous a quality seems to the herd, the more completely it is condemned. . . .

. . . The instinct of the herd values the *juste milieu* and the *average* as the highest and most precious of all things: the spot where the majority is to be found, and the air that it breathes there. In this way it is the opponent of all order of rank; it regards a climb from the level to the heights in the same light as a descent from the majority to the minority. The herd regards the *exception,* whether it be above or beneath its general level, as something which is antagonistic and dangerous to itself. Their trick in dealing with the exceptions above them, the strong, the mighty, the wise, and the fruitful, is to persuade them to become guardians, herdsmen, and watchmen—in fact, to become their *head-servants:* thus they convert a danger into a thing which is useful. . . .

. . . The mortal enmity of the herd towards all *order of rank:* its instinct is in favour of the *leveller (Christ).* Towards all *strong individuals (the sovereigns)* it is hostile, unfair, intemperate, arrogant, cheeky, disrespectful, cowardly, false, lying, pitiless, deceitful, envious, revengeful.

My teaching is this, that the herd seeks to maintain and preserve one type of man, and that it defends itself on two sides—that is to say, against those which are decadents from its ranks (criminals, etc.), and against those who rise superior to its dead level. The instincts of the herd tend to a stationary state of society; they merely preserve. They have no creative power. . . .

. . . My philosophy aims at a new *order of rank: not* at an individualistic morality. The spirit of the herd should rule within the herd—but not beyond it: the leaders of the herd require a fundamentally different valuation for their actions, as do also the independent ones or the beasts of prey, etc. . . .

. . . I have declared war against the anæmic Christian ideal (together with what is closely related to it), not because I want to annihilate it, but only to put an end to its *tyranny* and clear the way for other *ideals,* for *more robust* ideals. . . . The *continuance* of the Christian ideal belongs to the most desirable of desiderata: if only for the sake of the ideas which wish to take their stand beside it and perhaps above it—they must have opponents, and strong ones too, in order to grow *strong* themselves. That is why we immoralists require the *power* of *morality:* our instinct of self-preservation insists upon our opponents maintaining their strength—all it requires is to *become master of them.* . . .

. . . The triumphant concept *"energy,"* with which our physicists created God and the world, needs yet to be completed: it must be given an inner will which I characterise as the *"Will to Power"*—that is to say, as an insatiable desire to manifest power; or the application and exercise of power as a creative instinct, etc. Physicists cannot get rid of the *"actio in distans"* in their principles; any more than they can a repelling force (or an attracting one). There is no help for it, all movements, all "appearances," all "laws" must be understood as *symptoms* of an *inner* phenomenon, and the analogy of man must be used for this purpose. It is possible to trace all the instincts of an animal to the will to power; as also all the functions of organic life to this one source. . . .

. . . The Will to Power *interprets* (an organ in the process of formation has to be interpreted): it defines, it determines gradations, differences of power. Mere differences of power could not be aware of each other as such: something must be there which *will* grow, and which interprets all other things that would do the same, according to the value of the latter. . . .

. . . The will to power can manifest itself only against *obstacles;* it therefore goes in search of what resists it—this is the primitive tendency of the protoplasm when it extends its *pseudopodia* and feels about it. The act of appropriation and assimilation is, above all, the result of a desire to overpower, a process of forming, of additional building and rebuilding, until at last the subjected creature has become completely a part of the superior creature's sphere of power, and has increased the latter.—If this process of incorporation does not succeed, then the whole organism falls to pieces; and the *separation* occurs as the result of the will to power: in order to prevent the escape of that which has been subjected, the will to power falls into two wills (under some circumstances without even abandoning completely its relation to the two).

"Hunger" is only a more narrow adaptation, once the fundamental instinct of power has won power of a more abstract kind. . . .

. . . The State, or *unmorality* organised, is from within —the police, the penal code, status, commerce, and the family; and from without, the will to war, to power, to conquest and revenge.

A multitude will do things an individual will not, because of the division of responsibility, of command and execution; because the virtues of obedience, duty, patriotism, and local sentiment are all introduced; because feelings of pride, severity, strength, hate, and revenge—in short, all typical traits are upheld, and these are characteristics utterly alien to the herd-man.

You haven't, any of you, the courage either to kill or to flog a man. But the huge machinery of the State quells the individual and makes him decline to be answerable for his own deed (obedience, loyalty, etc.).

Everything that a man does in the service of the State is against his own nature. Similarly, everything he learns in view of future service of the State. This result is obtained through division of labour (so that responsibility is subdivided too):

The legislator—and he who fulfils the law.

The teacher of discipline—and those who have grown hard and severe under discipline....

... Man has one terrible and fundamental wish; he desires power, and this impulse, which is called freedom, must be the longest restrained. Hence ethics has instinctively aimed at such an education as shall restrain the desire for power; thus our morality slanders the would-be tyrant, and glorifies charity, patriotism, and the ambition of the herd....

... The princes of Europe should really consider whether as a matter of fact they can dispense with our services—with us, the immoralists. We are to-day the only power which can win a victory without allies: and we are therefore far and away the strongest of the strong. We can even do without lying, and let me ask what other power can dispense with this weapon? A strong temptation fights for us; the strongest, perhaps, that exists—the temptation of truth. ... Truth? How do I come by this word? I must withdraw it: I must repudiate this proud word. But no. We do not even want it—we shall be quite able to achieve our victory of power without its help. The real charm which fights for us, the eye of Venus which our opponents themselves deaden and blind—this charm is the magic of the extreme. The fascination which everything extreme exercises: we immoralists—we are in every way the extremists.

The corrupted ruling classes have brought ruling into evil odour. The State administration of justice is a piece of cowardice, because the great man who can serve as a standard is lacking. At last the feeling of insecurity becomes so great that men fall in the dust before any sort of will-power that commands.

"The will to power" is so loathed in democratic ages that the whole of the psychology of these ages seems directed towards its belittlement and slander. The types of men who sought the highest honours are said to have been Napoleon! Cæsar! and Alexander!—as if these had not been precisely the greatest *scorners* of honour. . . .

. . . According as to whether a people feels: "the rights, the keenness of vision, and the gifts of leading, etc., are with the few" or "with the many"—it constitutes an oligarchic or a democratic community.

Monarchy represents the belief in a man who is completely superior—a leader, a saviour, a demigod.

Aristocracy represents the belief in a chosen few—in a higher caste.

Democracy represents the disbelief in all great men and in all élite societies: everybody is everybody else's equal. "At bottom we are all herd and mob."

I am opposed to Socialism because it dreams ingenuously of "goodness, truth, beauty, and equal rights" (anarchy pursues the same ideal, but in a more brutal fashion).

I am opposed to parliamentary government and the power of the press, because they are the means whereby cattle become masters.

The arming of the people means in the end the arming of the mob.

Socialists are particularly ridiculous in my eyes, because of their absurd optimism concerning the "good man" who is supposed to be waiting in their cupboard, and who will come into being when the present order of society has been overturned and has made way for natural instincts. But the opposing party is quite as ludicrous, because it will not see the act of violence which lies beneath every law, the severity and egoism inherent in every kind of authority. "I and my kind will rule and prevail. Whoever degenerates will be either expelled or annihilated."—This was the fundamental feeling of all ancient legislation. The idea of a higher order of man is hated much more profoundly than monarchs themselves. Hatred of aristocracy always uses hatred of monarchy as a mask. . . .

. . . Preoccupations concerning one's self and one's eternal salvation are not expressive either of a rich or of a self-confident nature, for the latter lets all questions of eternal bliss go to the devil—it is not interested in such matters of happiness; it is all power, deeds, desires; it imposes itself upon things; it even violates things. The

Christian is a romantic hypochondriac who does not stand firmly on his legs.

Whenever hedonistic views come to the front, one can always presuppose the existence of pain and a certain ill-constitutedness. . . .

. . . The two traits which characterise the modern European are apparently antagonistic—*individualism and the demand for equal rights:* this I am at last beginning to understand. The individual is an extremely vulnerable piece of vanity: this vanity, when it is conscious of its high degree of susceptibility to pain, demands that every one should be made equal; that the individual should only stand *inter pares.* But in this way a social race is depicted in which, as a matter of fact, gifts and powers are on the whole equally distributed. The pride which would have loneliness and but few appreciators is quite beyond comprehension: really "great" successes are only attained through the masses—indeed, we scarcely understand yet that a mob success is in reality only a small success. . . .

No morality will countenance order of rank among men, and the jurists know nothing of a communal conscience. The principle of individualism rejects *really great* men, and demands the most delicate vision for, and the speediest discovery of, a talent among people who are almost equal; and inasmuch as every one has some modicum of talent in such late and civilised cultures (and can, therefore, expect to receive his share of honour), there is a more general buttering-up of modest merits to-day than there has ever been. This gives the age the appearance of *unlimited justice.* Its want of justice is to be found not in its unbounded hatred of tyrants and demagogues, even in the arts; but in its detestation of noble natures who scorn the praise of the many. The demand for equal rights (that is to say, the privilege of sitting in judgment on everything and everybody) is anti-aristocratic.

This age knows just as little concerning the absorption of the individual, of his mergence into a great type of men who do not want to be personalities. It was this that formerly constituted the distinction and the zeal of many lofty natures (the greatest poets among them); or of the desire to be a *polis,* as in Greece; or of Jesuitism, or of the Prussian Staff Corps, and bureaucracy; or of apprenticeship and a continuation of the tradition of great masters: to all of which things, non-social conditions and the absence of *petty vanity* are necessary.

Individualism is a modest and still unconscious form of will to power; with it a single human unit seems to think it sufficient to free himself from the preponderating power of society (or of the State or Church). He does not set himself up in opposition as a *personality,* but merely as a unit; he represents the rights of all other individuals as against the whole. That is to say, he instinctively places himself on a level with every other unit: what he combats he does not combat as a person, but as a representative of units against a mass. . . .

In this age of universal suffrage, in which everybody is allowed to sit in judgment upon everything and everybody, I feel compelled to re-establish the order of rank.

Quanta of power alone determine rank and distinguish rank: nothing else does.

The will to power.—How must those men be constituted who would undertake this transvaluation? The order of rank as the order of power: war and danger are the prerequisites which allow of a rank maintaining its conditions. The prodigious example: man in Nature—the weakest and shrewdest creature making himself master, and putting a yoke upon all less intelligent forces.

I distinguish between the type which represents ascending life and that which represents decay, decomposition and weakness. Ought one to suppose that the question of rank between these two types can be at all doubtful? . . .

The modicum of power which you represent decides your rank; all the rest is cowardice.

The advantages of standing detached from one's age.— Detached from the two movements, that of individualism and that of collectivist morality; for even the first does not recognise the order of rank, and would give one individual the same freedom as another. My thoughts are not concerned with the degree of freedom which should be granted to the one or to the other or to all, but with the degree of power which the one or the other should exercise over his neighbour or over all; and more especially with the question to what extent a sacrifice of freedom, or even enslavement, may afford the basis for the cultivation of a *superior* type. In plain words: *how could one sacrifice the development of mankind* in order to assist a higher species than man to come into being.

Concerning rank.—The terrible consequences of "equality"—in the end everybody thinks he has the right to every problem. All order of rank has vanished.

It is necessary for *higher* men to declare war upon the masses! In all directions mediocre people are joining hands in order to make themselves masters. Everything that pampers, that softens, and that brings the "people" or "woman" to the front, operates in favour of universal suffrage—that is to say, the dominion of *inferior* men. But we must make reprisals, and draw the whole state of affairs (which commenced in Europe with Christianity) to the light of day and to judgment.

A teaching is needed which is strong enough to work in a *disciplinary* manner; it should operate in such a way as to strengthen the strong and to paralyse and smash up the world-weary.

The annihilation of declining races. The decay of Europe. The annihilation of slave-tainted valuations. The dominion of the world as a means to the rearing of a higher type. The annihilation of the humbug which is called morality (Christianity as a hysterical kind of honesty in this regard: Augustine, Bunyan). The annihilation of universal suffrage—that is to say, that system by means of which the lowest natures prescribe themselves as a law for higher natures. The annihilation of mediocrity and its prevalence. (The one-sided, the individuals—peoples; constitutional plenitude should be aimed at by means of the coupling of opposites; to this end race-combinations should be tried.) The new kind of courage—no *a priori* truths (those who were accustomed to believe in something sought such truths!), but *free* submission to a ruling thought, which has its time; for instance, time conceived as the quality of space, etc.

The notion, "strong and weak man," resolves itself into this, that in the first place much strength is inherited—the man is a total sum: in the other, *not yet enough* (inadequate inheritance, subdivision of the inherited qualities). Weakness may be a *starting* phenomenon: *not yet enough*; or a final phenomenon: "no more."

The determining point is there where great strength is present, or where a great amount of strength can be discharged. The mass, as the sum-total of the *weak,* reacts *slowly*; it defends itself against much for which it is too weak—against that for which it has no use; it *never* creates, it *never* takes a step forward. This is opposed to the theory which denies the strong individual and would maintain that the "masses do everything." The difference is similar to that which obtains between separated generations: four or even five generations may lie between the masses and him who is the moving spirit—it is a *chronological* difference.

The *values of the weak* are in the van, because the strong have adopted them in order to *lead* with them. . . .

. . . *The degeneration of the ruler and of the ruling classes* has been the cause of all the great disorders in history! Without the Roman Cæsars and Roman society, Christianity would never have prevailed.

When it occurs to inferior men to doubt whether higher men exist, then the danger is great! It is then that men finally discover that there are virtues even among inferior, suppressed, and poor-spirited men, and that everybody is equal before God: which is the *non plus ultra* of all confounded nonsense that has ever appeared on earth! For in the end higher men begin to measure themselves according to the standard of virtues upheld by the slaves—and discover that they are "proud," etc., and that all their *higher* qualities should be condemned.

When Nero and Caracalla stood at the helm, it was then that the paradox arose: "The lowest man is of more value than that one on the throne!" And thus the path was prepared for an *image of God* which was as remote as possible from the image of the mightiest—God on the Cross! . . .

. . . The aspect of the European of to-day makes me very hopeful. A daring and ruling race is here building itself up upon the foundation of an extremely intelligent, gregarious mass. It is obvious that the educational movements for the latter are not alone prominent nowadays. . . .

. . . The question, and at the same time the task, is approaching with hesitation, terrible as Fate, but nevertheless inevitable: how shall the earth as a whole be ruled? And to what end shall man as a whole—no longer as a people or as a race—be reared and trained?

Legislative moralities are the principal means by which one can form mankind, according to the fancy of a creative and profound will: provided, of course, that such an artistic will of the first order gets the power into its own hands, and can make its creative will prevail over long periods in the form of legislation, religions, and morals. At present, and probably for some time to come, one will seek such colossally creative men, such really great men, as I understand them, in vain: they will be lacking, until, after many disappointments, we are forced to begin to understand why it is they are lacking, and that nothing bars with greater hostility their rise and development, at present and for some time to come, than that which is now called *the* morality in Europe. Just as if there were no other kind of morality, and could be no other kind, than the one we have already characterised as herd-morality. It is this morality which is now striving with all its power to attain to that green-meadow happiness on earth, which consists in security, absence of danger, ease, facilities for livelihood, and, last but not least, "if all goes well," even hopes to dispense with all kinds of shepherds and bell-wethers. The two doctrines which it preaches most universally are "equality of rights" and "pity for all sufferers" —and it even regards suffering itself as something which must be got rid of absolutely. That such ideas may be modern leads one to think very poorly of modernity. He, however, who has reflected deeply concerning the question, how and where the plant man has hitherto grown most vigorously, is forced to believe that this has always taken place under the opposite conditions; that to this end the danger of the situation has to increase enormously, his inventive faculty and dissembling powers have to fight their way up under long oppression and compulsion, and his will to life has to be increased to the unconditioned will to power, to over-power: he believes that danger, severity, violence, peril in the street and in the heart, inequality of rights, secrecy, stoicism, seductive art, and devilry of every kind—in short, the opposite of all gregarious desiderata— are necessary for the elevation of man. Such a morality with opposite designs, which would rear man upwards instead of to comfort and mediocrity; such a morality, with the intention of producing a ruling caste—the future lords of the earth—must, in order to be taught at all, introduce itself as if it were in some way correlated to the prevailing moral law, and must come forward under the cover of the latter's words and forms. But seeing that, to this end, a host of transitionary and deceptive measures must be discovered, and that the life of a single individual stands for almost nothing in view of the accomplishment of such lengthy tasks and aims, the first thing that must be done is to rear *a new kind* of man in whom the duration of the necessary will and the necessary instincts is guaranteed for many generations. This must be a new kind of ruling species and caste—this ought to be quite as clear as the somewhat lengthy and not easily expressed consequences of this thought. The aim should be to prepare a *transvaluation of values* for a particularly strong kind of man, most highly gifted in intellect and will, and, to this end, slowly and cautiously to liberate in him a whole host of slandered instincts hitherto held in check: whoever meditates about this problem belongs to us, the free spirits—certainly not to that kind of "free spirit" which has existed hitherto: for these desired practically the reverse. To this order, it seems to me, belong, above all, the pessimists of Europe, the poets and thinkers of a revolted idealism, in so far as their discontent with existence in general must *consistently* at least have led them to be dissatisfied with the man of the present; the same applies to certain insatiably ambitious artists who courageously and unconditionally fight against the gregarious animal for the special rights of higher men, and subdue all herd-instincts and precautions of more exceptional minds by their seductive art. Thirdly and lastly, we should include in this group all those critics and historians by whom the discovery of the Old World, which has begun so happily—this was the work of the *new* Columbus, of German intellect—will be courageously *continued* (for we still stand in the very first stages of this conquest). For in the Old World, as a matter of fact, a different and more lordly morality ruled than that of to-day; and the man of antiquity, under the educational ban of his morality, was a stronger and deeper man than the man of to-day—up to the present he has been the only well-constituted man. The temptation, however, which from antiquity to the present day has always exercised its power on such lucky strokes of Nature, *i.e.* on strong and enterprising souls, is, even at the present day, the most subtle and most effective of anti-democratic and anti-Christian powers, just as it was in the time of the Renaissance.

I am writing for a race of men which does not yet exist: for "the lords of the earth."

In Plato's *Theages* the following passage will be found: "Every one of us would like if possible to be master of mankind; if possible, a *God*." *This* attitude of mind must be reinstated in our midst.

Englishmen, Americans, and Russians.

That primeval forest-plant "Man" always appears where the struggle for power has been waged longest. *Great* men. Primeval forest creatures, the *Romans*.

From now henceforward there will be such favourable first conditions for greater ruling powers as have never yet been found on earth. And this is by no means the most important point. The establishment has been made possible of international race unions which will set themselves the task of rearing a ruling race, the future "lords of the earth." ...

20.

Pobedonostsev's Indictment
of Democracy*

Konstantin Pobedonostsev (1827–1907) was a significant political leader in Russia in the last third of the nineteenth century. An arch-reactionary, he is known to historians as the man most responsible for the repressive policies of Czar Alexander III.

Although Pobedonostsev served during his sixty years in the central Russian state bureaucracy as tutor of the last two czars, as a senator, and as a member of both the Council of State and the Council of Ministers, his reputation rests primarily on his actions as Director General of the Most Holy Synod of the Russian Orthodox Church. For twenty-five years—from 1880 until 1905—he was in effect Minister for Religious Affairs in a state which recognized and supported a national church and in which the Church's range of responsibility and authority had always been great.

A plain, humorless man, Pobedonostsev believed that religion was the foundation of civilized life—the homogenizing cement of society—and that modern civilization, especially the rise of parliamentary government, democracy, and the various freedoms associated with liberal political institutions, posed a dreadful threat to the institutions and values all should cherish. Convinced that autocracy was the best form of government and the only conceivable one for Russia, he thought the reign of Czar Nicholas I (creator of the notorious Third Section, or

*K. P. Pobedonostsev, *Reflections of a Russian Statesman*. Translated by Robert Crozier Long (London: Grant Richards, 1898), pp. 26–30, 32–38, 44–47.

*Higher Police) one of the "most clear and brilliant periods"
of Russian history.*

*Pobedonostsev left the imprint of his beliefs on nearly
every aspect of Russian life. A friend of Fëdor Dostoevsky,
many of whose views were close to his own, and a determined enemy and tormentor of Leo Tolstoy, whom he
considered a talented but dangerous lunatic out to destroy
the very bases of the Russian state, Pobedonostsev's un-
stinting opposition to moderate reform thwarted early
efforts at constitutional government and helped prepare the
climate for revolution.*

*In the selection below, reprinted from a volume which
was translated into English, French, German, and Italian,
Pobedonostsev comments on the "falsehood" of democracy.
It should be kept in mind that he was writing at a time
when political life in Europe was increasingly marked by
movements toward constitutional government, representative assemblies, the guarantee of individual liberties, and,
most notably, the adoption of universal manhood suffrage.*

THE NEW DEMOCRACY

What is this freedom by which so many minds are agi-
tated, which inspires so many insensate actions, so many
wild speeches, which leads the people so often to misfortune? In the democratic sense of the word, freedom is
the right of political power, or, to express it otherwise,
the right to participate in the government of the State.
This universal aspiration for a share in government has no
constant limitations. . . . For ever extending its base, the
new Democracy now aspires to universal suffrage—a fatal
error, and one of the most remarkable in the history of
mankind. By this means, the political power so passionately
demanded by Democracy would be shattered into a number
of infinitesimal bits, of which each citizen acquires a single
one. What will he do with it, then? how will he employ it?
In the result it has undoubtedly been shown that in the
attainment of this aim Democracy violates its sacred
formula of "Freedom indissolubly joined with Equality."
It is shown that this apparently equal distribution of
"freedom" among all involves the total destruction of
equality. Each vote, representing an inconsiderable fragment of power, by itself signifies nothing; an aggregation
of votes alone has a relative value. The result may be
likened to the general meetings of shareholders in public

companies. By themselves individuals are ineffective, but he who controls a number of these fragmentary forces is master of all power, and directs all decisions and dispositions. We may well ask in what consists the superiority of Democracy. Everywhere the strongest man becomes master of the State; sometimes a fortunate and resolute general, sometimes a monarch or administrator with knowledge, dexterity, a clear plan of action, and a determined will. In a Democracy, the real rulers are the dexterous manipulators of votes, with their placemen, the mechanics who so skilfully operate the hidden springs which move the puppets in the arena of democratic elections. Men of this kind are ever ready with loud speeches lauding equality; in reality, they rule the people as any despot or military dictator might rule it. The extension of the right to participate in elections is regarded as progress and as the conquest of freedom by democratic theorists, who hold that the more numerous the participants in political rights, the greater is the probability that all will employ this right in the interests of the public welfare, and for the increase of the freedom of the people. Experience proves a very different thing. The history of mankind bears witness that the most necessary and fruitful reforms—the most durable measures—emanated from the supreme will of statesmen, or from a minority enlightened by lofty ideas and deep knowledge, and that, on the contrary, the extension of the representative principle is accompanied by an abasement of political ideas and the vulgarisation of opinions in the mass of the electors. It shows also that this extension—in great States—was inspired by secret aims to the centralisation of power, or led directly to dictatorship. In France, universal suffrage was suppressed with the end of the Terror, and was re-established twice merely to affirm the autocracy of the two Napoleons. In Germany, the establishment of universal suffrage served merely to strengthen the high authority of a famous statesman who had acquired popularity by the success of his policy. What its ultimate consequences will be, Heaven only knows!

The manipulation of votes in the game of Democracy is of the commonest occurrence in most European states, and its falsehood, it would seem, has been exposed to all; yet few dare openly to rebel against it. The unhappy people must bear the burden, while the Press, herald of a supposititious public opinion, stifles the cry of the people with its shibboleth, "Great is Diana of the Ephesians." But to an impartial mind, all this is nothing better than a struggle of parties, and a shuffling with numbers and names. The voters, by themselves inconsiderable unities, acquire a value in the hands of dexterous agents. This value is realised by many means—mainly, by bribery in innumerable forms, from gifts of money and trifling articles, to the distribution of places in the services, the financial departments, and the administration. Little by little a class of electors has been formed which lives by the sale of votes to one or another of the political organisations. So far has this gone in France, for instance, that serious, intelligent, and industrious citizens in immense numbers abstain from voting, through the difficulty of contending with the cliques of political agents. With bribery go violence and threats, and reigns of terror are organised at elections, by the help of which the respective cliques advance their candidates; hence the stormy scenes at electoral demonstrations, in which arms have been used, and the field of battle strewn with the bodies of the killed and wounded.

Organisation and bribery—these are the two mighty instruments which are employed with such success for the manipulation of the mass of electors. Such methods are in no way new. Thucydides depicts in vivid colours their employment in the ancient republics of Greece. The history of the Roman Republic presents monstrous examples of corruption as the chief instrument of factions at elections. But in our times a new means has been found of working the masses for political aims, and joining them in adventitious alliances by provoking a fictitious community of views. This is the art of rapid and dexterous generalisation of ideas, the composition of phrase and formulas, disseminated with the confidence of burning conviction as the last word of science, as dogmas of politicology, as infallible appreciations of events, of men, and of institutions. At one time it was believed that the faculty of analysing facts, and deducing general principles was the privilege of a few enlightened minds and deep thinkers; now it is considered a universal attainment. . . .

THE GREAT FALSEHOOD
OF OUR TIME

I

. . . Among the falsest of political principles is the principle of the sovereignty of the people, the principle that all power issues from the people, and is based upon the national will—a principle which has unhappily become more firmly established since the time of the French Revolution. Thence proceeds the theory of Parliamentarism, which, up to the present day, has deluded much of the so-called "intelligence," and unhappily infatuated certain foolish Russians. It continues to maintain its hold on many minds with the obstinacy of a narrow fanaticism, although every day its falsehood is exposed more clearly to the world.

In what does the theory of Parliamentarism consist? It is supposed that the people in its assemblies makes its own laws, and elects responsible officers to execute its will. Such is the ideal conception. Its immediate realisation is impossible. The historical development of society necessitates that local communities increase in numbers and complexity; that separate races be assimilated, or, retaining their polities and languages, unite under a single flag, that territory extend indefinitely: under such conditions direct government by the people is impracticable. The people must, therefore, delegate its right of power to its representatives, and invest them with administrative autonomy. These representatives in turn cannot govern immediately, but are compelled to elect a still smaller number of trustworthy persons—ministers—to whom they entrust the preparation and execution of the laws, the apportionment and collection of taxes, the appointment of subordinate officials, and the disposition of the militant forces.

In the abstract this mechanism is quite symmetrical: for its proper operation many conditions are essential. The working of the political machine is based on impersonal forces constantly acting and completely balanced. It may act successfully only when the delegates of the people abdicate their personalities; when on the benches of Parliament sit mechanical fulfillers of the people's behests; when the ministers of State remain impersonal, absolute executors of the will of the majority; when the elected representatives of the people are capable of understanding precisely, and executing conscientiously, the programme of activity, mathematically expressed, which has been delivered to them. Given such conditions the machine would work exactly, and would accomplish its purpose. The law would actually embody the will of the people; administrative measures would actually emanate from Parliament; the pillars of the State would rest actually on the elective assemblies, and each citizen would directly and consciously participate in the management of public affairs.

Such is the theory. Let us look at the practice. Even in the classic countries of Parliamentarism it would satisfy not one of the conditions enumerated. The elections in no way express the will of the electors. The popular representatives are in no way restricted by the opinions of their constituents, but are guided by their own views and considerations, modified by the tactics of their opponents. In reality, ministers are autocratic, and they rule, rather than are ruled by, Parliament. They attain power, and lose power, not by virtue of the will of the people, but through immense personal influence, or the influence of a strong party which places them in power, or drives them from it. They dispose of the force and resources of the nation at will, they grant immunities and favours, they maintain a multitude of idlers at the expense of the people, and they fear no censure while they enjoy the support in Parliament of a majority which they maintain by the distribution of bounties from the rich tables which the State has put at their disposal. In reality, the ministers are as irresponsible as the representatives of the people. Mistakes, abuse of power, and arbitrary acts, are of daily occurrence, yet how often do we hear of the grave responsibility of a minister? It may be once in fifty years a minister is tried for his crimes, with a result contemptible when compared with the celebrity gained by the solemn procedure.

Were we to attempt a true definition of Parliament, we should say that Parliament is an institution serving for the satisfaction of the personal ambition, vanity, and self-interest of its members. The institution of Parliament is indeed one of the greatest illustrations of human delusion. Enduring in the course of centuries the tyranny of autocratic and oligarchical governments, and ignoring that the evils of autocracy are the evils of society itself, men of intellect and knowledge have laid the responsibility for their misfortunes on their rulers and on their systems of government, and imagined that by substituting for these systems government by the will of the people, or representative government, society would be delivered from all the evils and violence which it endured. What is the result? The result is that, *mutato nomine,* all has remained essentially as before, and men, retaining the weaknesses and failings of their nature, have transfused in the new institutions their former impulses and tendencies. As before, they are ruled by personal will, and in the interests of privileged persons, but this personal will is no longer embodied in the person of the sovereign, but in the person of the leader of a party; and privilege no longer belongs to an aristocracy of birth, but to a majority ruling in Parliament and controlling the State.

On the pediment of this edifice is inscribed: "All for the Public Good." This is no more than a lying formula: Parliamentarism is the triumph of egoism—its highest expression. All here is calculated to the service of the ego. In the Parliamentary fiction, the representative, as such, surrenders his personality, and serves as the embodiment of the will and opinions of his constituents; in reality, the constituents in the very act of election surrender all their rights in favour of their representative. In his addresses and speeches the candidate for election lays constant emphasis upon this fiction; he reiterates his phrases about the public welfare; he is nothing but a servant of the people; he will forget himself and his interests for its sake. But these are words, words, words alone—temporary steps of the staircase by which he climbs to the height he aspires to, and which he casts away when he needs them no longer. Then, so far from beginning to work for society, society becomes the instrument of his aims. To him his constituents are a herd, an aggregation of votes, and he, as their possessor, resembles those rich nomads whose flocks constitute their whole capital—the foundation of their power and eminence in society. Thus is developed to perfection the art of playing on the instincts and passions of the mass, in order to attain the personal ends of ambition and power. The people loses all importance for its representative, until the time arrives when it is to be played upon again; then false and flattering and lying phrases are lavished as before; some are suborned by bribery, others terrified by threats— the long chain of manœuvres spun which forms an invariable factor of Parliamentarism. Yet this electoral farce continues to deceive humanity, and to be regarded as an institution which crowns the edifice of State. Poor humanity! In truth may it be said: *mundus vult decipi, decipiatur.*

Thus the representative principle works in practice. The ambitious man comes before his fellow-citizens, and strives by every means to convince them that he more than any other is worthy of their confidence. What motives impel him to this quest? It is hard to believe that he is impelled by disinterested zeal for the public good.

In our time, nothing is so rare as men imbued with a feeling of solidarity with the people, ready for labour and self-sacrifice for the public good; this is the ideal nature, but such natures are little inclined to come into contact with the baseness of the world. He who, in the consciousness of duty, is capable of disinterested service of the community does not descend to the soliciting of votes, or the crying of his own praise at election meetings in loud and vulgar phrases. Such men manifest their strength in their own work, in a small circle of congenial friends, and scorn to seek popularity in the noisy market-place. If they approach the crowd, it is not to flatter it, or to pander to its basest instincts and tendencies, but to condemn its follies and expose its depravity. To men of duty and honour the procedure of elections is repellent; the only men who regard it without abhorrence are selfish, egoistic natures, which wish thereby to attain their personal ends. To acquire popularity such men have little scruple in assuming the mask of ardour for the public good. They cannot and must not be modest, for with modesty they would not be noticed or spoken of. By their positions, and by the parts which they have chosen, they are forced to be hypocrites and liars; they must cultivate, fraternise with, and be amiable to their opponents to gain their suffrages; they must lavish promises, knowing that they cannot fulfil them; and they must pander to the basest tendencies and prejudices of the masses to acquire majorities for themselves. . . .

II

The philosophy of the school of Rousseau has done much evil to humanity. This philosophy took possession of many minds; but at the same time it was all based on one false idea of human perfectibility, and on the assumption in every individual of capacity to comprehend and appreciate those principles of social organisation which it proclaimed.

The prevalent doctrine of the perfection of Democracy and of democratic government, stands on the same delusive foundation. This doctrine presupposes the capacity of the people to understand subtleties of political science which have a clear and substantial existence in the minds of its apostles only. Precision of knowledge is attainable only by the few minds which constitute the aristocracy of intellect; the mass, always and everywhere, is *vulgus,* and its conceptions of necessity are vulgar.

Democracy is the most complicated and the most burdensome system of government recorded in the history of humanity. For this reason it has never appeared save as a transitory manifestation, with few exceptions giving place before long to other systems. It is in no way surprising. The duty of the State is to act and to ordain: its dispositions are manifestations of a single will; without this government is inconceivable. But how can a multitude of men, or a popular assembly act with a single will? The upholder of Democracy takes little trouble over the decision of this question, but evades it by means of those favourite phrases and formulas: "The will of the people," "public opinion," "the supreme decision of the nation," "the voice of the people is the voice of God," and others of a like nature. All these phrases signify that a multitude of men on a multitude of questions may form a common conclusion, and, conformably with their conclusion, arrive at a common decision. This may be possible sometimes, but only on the simplest questions. Where questions present the slightest complexity their decision by a numerous assembly is possible only through the medium of men capable of judging them in all their details, and of persuading the people to accept their judgment. In the number of complex questions may be counted all political questions requiring great concentration of the intellectual forces of the most capable and experienced statesmen; on such questions it would be absurd to rely upon unanimity of thought and will in a numerous assembly; the decision of the people could only be ruinous to the State. The enthusiasts of Democracy contend that the people may manifest its will in affairs of State: this is a shallow theory. In reality, we find that popular assemblies are capable only of accepting —through enthusiasm—the opinion expressed by individuals or by a small minority—the opinion, for instance, of the recognised leader of their party, of some local worker of repute, of some organised association, or the impersonal opinion of an influential journal. Thus the discussions which precede decision become an absurd comedy played on a vast stage by a multitude of heads and voices, the greater the multitude the more unintelligible is the comedy, and the more the *dénouement* depends upon fortuitous and disorderly impulses.

To evade all these difficulties, the system of government by representation has been devised, a system first established, and first justified by success, in England. Thence, through the influence of fashion, it spread to other European countries, but proved successful only in the United States of America, and there by tradition and by right. Yet even in England, the land of their origin, representative institutions are in a critical epoch of their history. The very essence of the idea of representation has submitted already to modifications which have changed its primitive significance. In the beginning, the assemblies of electors, on a strictly limited franchise, sent to Parliament a certain number of persons whose duty it was to represent the opinions of the country, but who were not bound by any definite instructions from the mass of their constituents. It was assumed that these elected representatives were men who understood the real needs of their country, and who were capable of justly controlling the politics of the State. The problem was resolved simply and plainly: it was required to lessen, as far as possible, the difficulties of government by the people, by limiting in number the members of the assemblies summoned for the decision of questions of State. These men appeared in the capacity of free representatives of the people, and not as instruments of the opinions of factions; they were bound by no instructions. But in the course of time this system changed under the influence of that fatal delusion about the great value of public opinion, as enlightened by the periodical Press which gave to the people the capacity to participate directly in the decision of political questions. The idea of representation altogether lost its form, and reappeared as the idea of a *mandate*; or of specific commission. From this point of view each representative is accounted a representative of the dominant opinions of his constituency, or of the party under the banner of which his victory was gained. Thus he is no longer a representative of the country, or of the people, but a delegate bound by the instructions of his party. This change in the very essence of the idea of representation was the germ of the disease which has since devoured the whole system of representative government. With the disintegration of parties, elections have taken the character of personal struggles restricted by local interests and opinions, but independent of their primary purpose of subserving the advantage of the State.

21.

Imperialism:

"The Curse of the World"

There is no feature of history more sad, no
phase of human nature more dismal, than that
innate desire in man's heart to rule over his fellow
men. This ambition has been the curse of the
world.

—Sarah E. V. Emery, *Imperialism in America*

*During the first three quarters of the nineteenth century,
few of the states of Europe demonstrated much enthusiasm
for overseas expansion; in those instances where new holdings were established in Asia or Africa, this was not always
the result of conscious policy and was rarely accorded
much popular support. Then, about 1870 or 1880, a change
occurred. Colonial questions again came to the fore. The
powers of Europe not only consolidated their existing possessions but sought frantically to add to them. Europe
entered the "age of imperialism"—an era in which empire-
building became the accepted policy of all major powers
and was endorsed by public opinion with a passion that cut
across class and economic lines.*

*By 1900 the advanced countries had partitioned most of
the earth among themselves. In 1895 only one-tenth of
Africa remained unappropriated. It has been estimated that
in the last three decades of the nineteenth century the
Europeans expanded their colonial empire by over ten million square miles and by more than 120 million people.
Britain alone in this period annexed some thirty-nine separate areas. And she was mirrored in her scramble for*

empire by other nations. France added well over three million square miles of territory and twenty-six million people. Germany, fulfilling the dreams of ardent nationalists like Heinrich von Treitschke, a historian who was fond of enticing his students at the University of Berlin with the suggestion that "every virile people has established colonial power," added a million square miles and thirteen million people. Russia, Italy, and even Belgium followed suit.

In the 1890's America too embarked on a policy of imperialist expansion. It took possession of Guam, Puerto Rico, and the Philippines (1898), annexed the Hawaiian republic (1898), established itself in the Samoan Islands (1899), and, in 1902, assumed a protectorate over Cuba.

The imperial-mindedness shared by so many Americans and Europeans of the late nineteenth century fitted very neatly the preaching of Darwinian sociology, that human progress depended on struggle between races and nations and survival of the fittest. Obviously most eligible for the "fittest" were the white peoples of Europe and America, who told themselves that they owed it to science as well as to civilization to establish their supremacy over inferior populations in other countries. As Josiah Strong, a Congregationalist minister in the United States, expressed it, the "Anglo-Saxon race" had a sacred mission to carry the ideals of civil liberty and spiritual Christianity to "backward peoples." Rudyard Kipling, the widely acclaimed British poet, advanced a similar point of view in 1899, when he wrote:

> Take up the White Man's burden—
>   Send forth the best ye breed—
> Go, bind your sons to exile
>   To serve your captives' need;
> To wait, in heavy harness,
>   On fluttered folk and wild—
> Your new-caught sullen peoples
>   Half devil and half child.

Although sentiments like those expressed by Strong and Kipling had wide popularity, they were by no means unchallenged. Imperialism had its bitter critics as well as its zealous defenders. Wilfred S. Blunt, British diplomat, poet, and publicist, attacked the "massacring and pillaging and raping" that accompanied his country's overseas expansion; the great French novelist Anatole France warned that imperialism was "the new barbarism"; and hundreds of

American politicians and private citizens denounced colonial expansion in magazines, pamphlets, and newspapers, fought the acquisition of Hawaii, Puerto Rico, and the Philippines in Congress, and formed anti-imperialist leagues and associations.

The criticisms of American imperialism which follow were written in the years 1899–1902. The American Anti-Imperialist League, whose platform of October 18, 1899, makes up the first selection, came into being in 1898 as a protest against expansionists who advocated imperialism as the only path to national greatness. The second selection is a scathing denunciation of the "Blessings-of-Civilization Trust" by Mark Twain, the famous novelist and humorist. In the final selection Bolton Hall of New York City berates his government for embarking on "the policy of aggrandizement that characterizes European nations" and warns of the consequences.

I

*The Platform of the American Anti-Imperialist League, 1899**

We hold that the policy known as imperialism is hostile to liberty and tends toward militarism, an evil from which it has been our glory to be free. We regret that it has become necessary in the land of Washington and Lincoln to reaffirm that all men, of whatever race or color, are entitled to life, liberty and the pursuit of happiness. We maintain that governments derive their just powers from the consent of the governed. We insist that the subjugation of any people is "criminal aggression" and open disloyalty to the distinctive principles of our Government.

We earnestly condemn the policy of the present National Administration in the Philippines. It seeks to extinguish the spirit of 1776 in those islands. We deplore the sacrifice of our soldiers and sailors, whose bravery deserves admiration even in an unjust war. We denounce the slaughter

**Speeches, Correspondence and Political Papers of Carl Schurz.* Edited by Frederic Bancroft (New York: G. P. Putnam's Sons, 1913), Vol. VI, pp. 77–79. Copyright 1913 by Schurz Memorial Committee. Reprinted by permission.

of the Filipinos as a needless horror. We protest against the extension of American sovereignty by Spanish methods.

We demand the immediate cessation of the war against liberty, begun by Spain and continued by us. We urge that Congress be promptly convened to announce to the Filipinos our purpose to concede to them the independence for which they have so long fought and which of right is theirs.

The United States have always protested against the doctrine of international law which permits the subjugation of the weak by the strong. A self-governing state cannot accept sovereignty over an unwilling people. The United States cannot act upon the ancient heresy that might makes right.

Imperialists assume that with the destruction of self-government in the Philippines by American hands, all opposition here will cease. This is a grievous error. Much as we abhor the war of "criminal aggression" in the Philippines, greatly as we regret that the blood of the Filipinos is on American hands, we more deeply resent the betrayal of American institutions at home. The real firing line is not in the suburbs of Manila. The foe is of our own household. The attempt of 1861 was to divide the country. That of 1899 is to destroy its fundamental principles and noblest ideals.

Whether the ruthless slaughter of the Filipinos shall end next month or next year is but an incident in a contest that must go on until the Declaration of Independence and the Constitution of the United States are rescued from the hands of their betrayers. Those who dispute about standards of value while the foundation of the Republic is undermined will be listened to as little as those who would wrangle about the small economies of the household while the house is on fire. The training of a great people for a century, the aspiration for liberty of a vast immigration are forces that will hurl aside those who in the delirium of conquest seek to destroy the character of our institutions.

We deny that the obligation of all citizens to support their Government in times of grave National peril applies to the present situation. If an Administration may with impunity ignore the issues upon which it was chosen, deliberately create a condition of war anywhere on the face of the globe, debauch the civil service for spoils to promote the adventure, organize a truth-suppressing censorship and demand of all citizens a suspension of judgment and their unanimous support while it chooses to continue the fighting, representative government itself is imperiled.

We propose to contribute to the defeat of any person or party that stands for the forcible subjugation of any people. We shall oppose for reelection all who in the White House or in Congress betray American liberty in pursuit of un-American ends. We still hope that both of our great political parties will support and defend the Declaration of Independence in the closing campaign of the century .

We hold, with Abraham Lincoln, that "no man is good enough to govern another man without that other's consent. When the white man governs himself, that is self-government, but when he governs himself and also governs another man, that is more than self-government—that is despotism." "Our reliance is in the love of liberty which God has planted in us. Our defense is in the spirit which prizes liberty as the heritage of all men in all lands. Those who deny freedom to others deserve it not for themselves, and under a just God cannot long retain it."

We cordially invite the cooperation of all men and women who remain loyal to the Declaration of Independence and the Constitution of the United States.

II

*Mark Twain: To the Person Sitting in Darkness, 1901**

Shall we? That is, shall we go on conferring our Civilization upon the peoples that sit in darkness, or shall we give those poor things a rest? Shall we bang right ahead in our old-time, loud, pious way, and commit the new century to the game; or shall we sober up and sit down and think it over first? Would it not be prudent to get our Civilization-tools together, and see how much stock is left on hand in the way of Glass Beads and Theology, and Maxim Guns and Hymn Books, and Trade-Gin and Torches of Progress and Enlightenment (patent adjustable ones, good to fire villages with, upon occasion), and balance the books, and arrive at the profit and loss, so

*Mark Twain, "To the Person Sitting in Darkness," *The North American Review*, No. DXXXI (February, 1901), pp. 164–67.

that we may intelligently decide whether to continue the business or sell out the property and start a new Civilization Scheme on the proceeds?

Extending the Blessings of Civilization to our Brother who Sits in Darkness has been a good trade and has paid well, on the whole; and there is money in it yet, if carefully worked—but not enough, in my judgment, to make any considerable risk advisable. The People that Sit in Darkness are getting to be too scarce—too scarce and too shy. And such darkness as is now left is really of but an indifferent quality, and not dark enough for the game. The most of those People that Sit in Darkness have been furnished with more light than was good for them or profitable for us. We have been injudicious.

The Blessings-of-Civilization Trust, wisely and cautiously administered, is a Daisy. There is more money in it, more territory, more sovereignty, and other kinds of emolument, than there is in any other game that is played. But Christendom has been playing it badly of late years, and must certainly suffer by it, in my opinion. She has been so eager to get every stake that appeared on the green cloth, that the People who Sit in Darkness have noticed it—they have noticed it, and have begun to show alarm. They have become suspicious of the Blessings of Civilization. More— they have begun to examine them. This is not well. The Blessings of Civilization are all right, and a good commercial property; there could not be a better, in a dim light. In the right kind of a light, and at a proper distance, with the goods a little out of focus, they furnish this desirable exhibit to the Gentlemen who Sit in Darkness:

LOVE,	LAW AND ORDER,
JUSTICE,	LIBERTY,
GENTLENESS,	EQUALITY,
CHRISTIANITY,	HONORABLE DEALING,
PROTECTION TO THE	MERCY,
WEAK,	EDUCATION,
TEMPERANCE,	

—and so on.

There. Is it good? Sir, it is pie. It will bring into camp any idiot that sits in darkness anywhere. But not if we adulterate it. It is proper to be emphatic upon that point. This brand is strictly for Export—apparently. *Apparently*. Privately and confidentially, it is nothing of the kind. Privately and confidentially, it is merely an outside cover, gay and pretty and attractive, displaying the special patterns of our Civilization which we reserve for Home Consumption, while *inside* the bale is the Actual Thing that the Customer Sitting in Darkness buys with his blood and tears and land and liberty. That Actual Thing is, indeed, Civilization, but it is only for Export. Is there a difference between the two brands? In some of the details, yes.

We all know that the Business is being ruined. The reason is not far to seek. It is because our Mr. McKinley, and Mr. Chamberlain, and the Kaiser, and the Czar and the French have been exporting the Actual Thing *with the outside cover left off*. This is bad for the Game. It shows that these new players of it are not sufficiently acquainted with it.

It is a distress to look on and note the mismoves, they are so strange and so awkward. Mr. Chamberlain manufactures a war out of materials so inadequate and so fanciful that they make the boxes grieve and the gallery laugh, and he tries hard to persuade himself that it isn't purely a private raid for cash, but has a sort of dim, vague respectability about it somewhere, if he could only find the spot; and that, by and by, he can scour the flag clean again after he has finished dragging it through the mud, and make it shine and flash in the vault of heaven once more as it had shone and flashed there a thousand years in the world's respect until he laid his unfaithful hand upon it. It is bad play—bad. For it exposes the Actual Thing to Them that Sit in Darkness, and they say: "What! Christian against Christian? And only for money? Is *this* a case of magnanimity, forbearance, love, gentleness, mercy, protection of the weak—this strange and over-showy onslaught of an elephant upon a nest of field-mice, on the pretext that the mice had squeaked an insolence at him—conduct which 'no self-respecting government could allow to pass unavenged?' as Mr. Chamberlain said. Was that a good pretext in a small case, when it had not been a good pretext in a large one?—for only recently Russia had affronted the elephant three times and survived alive and unsmitten. Is this Civilization and Progress? Is it something better than we already possess? These harryings and burnings and desert-makings in the Transvaal—is this an improvement on our darkness? Is it, perhaps, possible that there are two kinds of Civilization—one for home consumption and one for the heathen market?"

Then They that Sit in Darkness are troubled, and shake their heads; and they read this extract from a letter of a British private, recounting his exploits in one of Methuen's victories, some days before the affair of Magersfontein, and they are troubled again:

> We tore up the hill and into the intrenchments, and the Boers saw we had them; so they dropped their guns and went down on their knees and put up their hands clasped, and begged for mercy. And we gave it them— *with the long spoon.*

The long spoon is the bayonet. See *Lloyd's Weekly,* London, of those days. The same number—and the same column—contained some quite unconscious satire in the form of shocked and bitter upbraidings of the Boers for their brutalities and inhumanities!

Next, to our heavy damage, the Kaiser went to playing the game without first mastering it. He lost a couple of missionaries in a riot in Shantung, and in his account he made an overcharge for them. China had to pay a hundred thousand dollars apiece for them, in money; twelve miles of territory, containing several millions of inhabitants and worth twenty million dollars; and to build a monument, and also a Christian church; whereas the people of China could have been depended upon to remember the missionaries without the help of these expensive memorials. This was all bad play. Bad, because it would not, and could not, and will not now or ever, deceive the Person Sitting in Darkness. He knows that it was an overcharge. He knows that a missionary is like any other man: he is worth merely what you can supply his place for, and no more. He is useful, but so is a doctor, so is a sheriff, so is an editor; but a just Emperor does not charge war-prices for such. A diligent, intelligent, but obscure missionary, and a diligent, intelligent country editor are worth much, and we know it; but they are not worth the earth. We esteem such an editor, and we are sorry to see him go; but, when he goes, we should consider twelve miles of territory, and a church, and a fortune, over-compensation for his loss. . . .

III

*Bolton Hall: Why I Am Opposed to Imperialism, 1902**

Only the remoteness of the Philippine Islands keeps our American people from realizing our cowardly policy toward the little brown men. It has been marked from the beginning by evasion, then by deception, followed naturally by violence—and all continued for more than three years. This is now a matter of common knowledge and need not be recited here, because details of iniquity are unimportant as compared with the principles of right.

Since the war with Spain, our Government has entered upon the policy of aggrandizement that characterizes European nations—reaching out for the property of weaker nations and pleading that this is done in the interests of civilization: the same plea that Britain made against the Boers. Such aggressions are never for the benefit of the oppressed, nor even for the advantage of the aggressing nation (though if they were, that would not justify them), but are for the benefit and enrichment of a few.

In the face of the declaration of the late President in the case of Cuba, that "forcible annexation could not so much as be thought of, because it would be criminal aggression," we have forcibly annexed the Philippines. For this action justification has been sought in a promised increase of trade. Aside from the folly of killing one's prospective customers, and the undisguised criminality of murder for gain, the result has shown that even in a material sense national crimes are national blunders. For by our conduct toward the Filipinos we have aroused a distrust among the nations of South America that will injure us commercially far more than we can possibly profit by possessing the Philippines. And it should be self-evident that peaceful relations with a grateful Filipino republic would have been far more advantageous than the ownership of desolated islands and the hatred of such inhabitants as

---

*Bolton Hall, "Why I Am Opposed to Imperialism," The Arena, XXVIII, No. 1 (July, 1902), pp. 4–7.

may remain when the process of assimilation shall have been completed.

Not only is foreign conquest immoral, but the consequences are fatal to the aggressor nation. While our victories engage our attention, and while our tariff-bled workers pay the interest on the bonds that paid for them, the trusts and their party rob and starve the people. "The fathers have eaten sour grapes, and the children's teeth are set on edge": the nation that disregards the law must pay the price. History has already begun to show us that our nation is no exception to the rule of the ages, and to the operation of that—

> Fixed arithmic of the universe,
> Which meteth good for good, and ill for ill.

Among the consequences of the violated law are official disregard for the rights of speech and press; censorship and suppression of news; the growth of the military spirit, with its glorification of brute force, threatening the gag and the noose for those who voice humanity's sighs, and branding as traitors those who protest against the betrayal of our allies.

Add to these the contempt engendered toward "inferior people," and the military cruelties practised on them. . . . And those whom we send to kill return to kill. Armies of conquest contract loathsome diseases, which are duly spread at home—"so close are sin and suffering joined."

Vainglorious actors in foreign conquests seldom tell of the hell of war, or of the woe of the vanquished. A victory is chronicled—so many killed, so many wounded, so many villages burned. Never is there mention of the lingering misery of the aged, of wives and children, nor of disease and starvation that await the helpless. Yet these are the natural fruits of the forcible annexation of a liberty-loving race.

Who of our people, if the decision rested solely with him, would set fire to his neighbors' houses and slaughter a thousand men to increase his business or demonstrate his strength? Yet the Filipino is our neighbor, and that which is done by our nation is the act of all who consent to it; and upon each the responsibility is as heavy for such crimes as if he were the sole criminal. Partnership does not diminish the guilt.

And the effect of wars of conquest is the stimulation of that patriotism which finds its expression in "My country, right or wrong!" That spirit ridicules morality, cows religious teaching, and is the forerunner of national decay. The Philosopher of Nazareth warned his disciples against the evils of the governing spirit. Though the princes of the Gentiles might exercise dominion, and they who are great might exercise authority, "it shall not be so with you." We are learning slowly the soundness of that advice, which indeed is the spirit of our homely phrase, "mind your own business."

But they who learn from history and philosophy are few. "Experience keeps a dear school, but fools will learn in none other." "The wise man foresees evil and hides himself, but the foolish pass on and are punished." As with the man, so with the nation.

Imperialism's other name is *Brutality;* and its end, if unchecked, is for the victor to deliver himself over to oppression and for the conquerors to find themselves enslaved.

22.

Capitalism and War

Capitalism, the insatiable monster that gnaws at
the vitals of man, woman and child, sparing not
even the tenderest, seizing Europe in its skeleton
clutches, has converted the old world into a hell
of horrors and now threatens to overwhelm and
deluge with blood the western shores.

—Eugene V. Debs, "The Red and the Dead," in
The American Socialist

*On the eve of World War I, socialism was almost uni-
versally regarded as dedicated to the preservation of peace.
In fact, it was widely believed in Europe at the beginning
of 1914 that the power of the socialist parties and their
cohesion in the Second International constituted an insur-
mountable obstacle to a major war. Yet, when war came
(August, 1914), the great majority of the socialists in each
of the belligerent nations rallied to the flag. "Bourgeois"
feelings of nationalism and patriotism triumphed over the
notion of working-class solidarity.*

*Because the American Socialist Party was not subjected
to the same historical pressure as its European counter-
parts, it was a pacifist island in a belligerent ocean. The
question that faced European socialists was whether or
not they would stand with their respective countries in this
international crisis. The traditional antiwar position of
socialists in the United States was subjected to no such
point-blank demand. While American socialists probably
would have followed the example of their European colleagues in resisting invasion, actual or threatened, no*

190

*such alternative was presented to them. When America
entered the war in 1917, no threat of foreign invasion was
involved. American participation in the conflict entailed the
sending of an expeditionary force to Europe. Hence the
traditional socialist pacifism asserted itself.*

*On April 7, 1917, the day after the declaration of war,
an emergency convention of the American Socialist Party
opened in St. Louis, Missouri, to announce its opposition
to the action. The convention adopted an antiwar proclamation that was essentially a restatement of the classic
Marxist analysis of war. Despite complaints on the part
of a number of dissident socialists that it should have
been labeled the "near-treason resolution," the St. Louis
proclamation received overwhelming support when submitted to a national referendum of the Socialist Party
membership.*

I

Proclamation on War and Militarism*
Adopted by the Emergency National
Convention of the Socialist Party
of the United States, St. Louis,
Missouri, April 7–14, 1917

The Socialist Party of the United States in the present
grave crisis, solemnly reaffirms its allegiance to the principle of internationalism and working-class solidarity the
world over, and proclaims its unalterable opposition to the
war just declared by the government of the United States.

Modern wars as a rule have been caused by the commercial and financial rivalry and intrigues of the capitalist
interests in the different countries. Whether they have been
frankly waged as wars of aggression or have been hypo-
critically represented as wars of "defense," they have always been made by the classes and fought by the masses.
Wars bring wealth and power to the ruling classes, and
suffering, death and demoralization to the workers.

*The American Labor Year Book 1917–18. Edited by Alexander
Trachtenberg (New York: The Rand School of Social Science,
1918), pp. 50–53.

They breed a sinister spirit of passion, unreason, race hatred and false patriotism. They obscure the struggles of the workers for life, liberty and social justice. They tend to sever the vital bonds of solidarity between them and their brothers in other countries, to destroy their organizations and to curtail their civic and political rights and liberties.

The Socialist Party of the United States is unalterably opposed to the system of exploitation and class rule which is upheld and strengthened by military power and sham national patriotism. We, therefore, call upon the workers of all countries to refuse support to their governments in their wars. The wars of the contending national groups of capitalists are not the concern of the workers. The only struggle which would justify the workers in taking up arms is the great struggle of the working class of the world to free itself from economic exploitation and political oppression, and we particularly warn the workers against the snare and delusion of so-called defensive warfare. As against the false doctrine of national patriotism we uphold the ideal of international working-class solidarity. In support of capitalism, we will not willingly give a single life or a single dollar; in support of the struggle of the workers for freedom we pledge our all.

The mad orgy of death and destruction which is now convulsing unfortunate Europe was caused by the conflict of capitalist interests in the European countries.

In each of these countries, the workers were oppressed and exploited. They produced enormous wealth but the bulk of it was withheld from them by the owners of the industries. The workers were thus deprived of the means to repurchase the wealth which they themselves had created.

The capitalist class of each country was forced to look for foreign markets to dispose of the accumulated "surplus" wealth. The huge profits made by the capitalists could no longer be profitably reinvested in their own countries, hence, they were driven to look for foreign fields of investment. The geographical boundaries of each modern capitalist country thus became too narrow for the industrial and commercial operations of its capitalist class.

The efforts of the capitalists of all leading nations were therefore centered upon the domination of the world markets. Imperialism became the dominant note in the politics of Europe. The acquisition of colonial possessions and the extension of spheres of commercial and political influence became the object of diplomatic intrigues and the cause of constant clashes between nations.

The acute competition between the capitalist powers of the earth, their jealousies and distrusts of one another and the fear of the rising power of the working class forced each of them to arm to the teeth. This led to the mad rivalry of armament, which, years before the outbreak of the present war, had turned the leading countries of Europe into armed camps with standing armies of many millions, drilled and equipped for war in times of "peace."

Capitalism, imperialism and militarism had thus laid the foundation of an inevitable general conflict in Europe. The ghastly war in Europe was not caused by an accidental event, nor by the policy or institutions of any single nation. It was the logical outcome of the competitive capitalist system.

The six million men of all countries and races who have been ruthlessly slain in the first thirty months of this war, the millions of others who have been crippled and maimed, the vast treasures of wealth that have been destroyed, the untold misery and sufferings of Europe, have not been sacrifices exacted in a struggle for principles or ideals, but wanton offerings upon the altar of private profit.

The forces of capitalism which have led to the war in Europe are even more hideously transparent in the war recently provoked by the ruling class of this country.

When Belgium was invaded, the government enjoined upon the people of this country the duty of remaining neutral, thus clearly demonstrating that the "dictates of humanity," and the fate of small nations and of democratic institutions were matters that did not concern it. But when our enormous war traffic was seriously threatened, our government calls upon us to rally to the "defense of democracy and civilization."

Our entrance into the European war was instigated by the predatory capitalists in the United States who boast of the enormous profit of seven billion dollars from the manufacture and sale of munitions and war supplies and from the exportation of American food stuffs and other necessaries. They are also deeply interested in the continuance of war and the success of the allied arms through their huge loans to the governments of the allied powers and through other commercial ties. It is the same interests which strive for imperialistic domination of the Western Hemisphere.

The war of the United States against Germany cannot

be justified even on the plea that it is a war in defense of American rights or American "honor." Ruthless as the unrestricted submarine war policy of the German government was and is, it is not an invasion of the rights of the American people, as such, but only an interference with the opportunity of certain groups of American capitalists to coin cold profits out of the blood and sufferings of our fellow men in the warring countries of Europe.

It is not a war against the militarist regime of the Central Powers. Militarism can never be abolished by militarism.

It is not a war to advance the cause of democracy in Europe. Democracy can never be imposed upon any country by a foreign power by force of arms.

It is cant and hypocrisy to say that the war is not directed against the German people, but against the Imperial Government of Germany. If we send an armed force to the battlefields of Europe, its cannon will mow down the masses of the German people and not the Imperial German Government.

Our entrance into the European conflict at this time will serve only to multiply the horrors of the war, to increase the toll of death and destruction and to prolong the fiendish slaughter. It will bring death, suffering and destitution to the people of the United States and particularly to the working class. It will give the powers of reaction in this country the pretext for an attempt to throttle our rights and to crush our democratic institutions, and to fasten upon this country a permanent militarism.

The working class of the United States has no quarrel with the working class of Germany or of any other country. The people of the United States have no quarrel with the people of Germany or any other country. The American people did not want and do not want this war. They have not been consulted about the war and have had no part in declaring war. They have been plunged into this war by the trickery and treachery of the ruling class of the country through its representatives in the National Administration and National Congress, its demagogic agitators, its subsidized press, and other servile instruments of public expression.

We brand the declaration of war by our government as a crime against the people of the United States and against the nations of the world.

In all modern history there has been no war more unjustifiable than the war in which we are about to engage.

No greater dishonor has ever been forced upon a people

than that which the capitalist class is forcing upon this nation against its will.

In harmony with these principles, the Socialist Party emphatically rejects the proposal that in time of war the workers should suspend their struggle for better conditions. On the contrary, the acute situation created by war calls for an even more vigorous prosecution of the class struggle, and we recommend to the workers and pledge ourselves to the following course of action:

1. Continuous, active, and public opposition to the war, through demonstrations, mass petitions, and all other means within our power.

2. Unyielding opposition to all proposed legislation for military or industrial conscription. Should such conscription be forced upon the people, we pledge ourselves to continuous efforts for the repeal of such laws and to the support of all mass movements in opposition to conscription. We pledge ourselves to oppose with all our strength any attempt to raise money for payment of war expense by taxing the necessaries of life or issuing bonds which will put the burden upon future generations. We demand that the capitalist class, which is responsible for the war, pay its cost. Let those who kindled the fire, furnish the fuel.

3. Vigorous resistance to all reactionary measures, such as censorship of press and mails, restriction of the rights of free speech, assemblage, and organization, or compulsory arbitration and limitation of the right to strike.

4. Consistent propaganda against military training and militaristic teaching in the public schools.

5. Extension of the campaign of education among the workers to organize them into strong, class-conscious, and closely unified political and industrial organizations, to enable them by concerted and harmonious mass action to shorten this war and to establish lasting peace.

6. Widespread educational propaganda to enlighten the masses as to the true relation between capitalism and war, and to rouse and organize them for action, not only against present war evils, but for the prevention of future wars and for the destruction of the causes of war.

7. To protect the masses of the American people from the pressing danger of starvation which the war in Europe has brought upon them, and which the entry of the United States has already accentuated, we demand—

(a) The restriction of food exports so long as the present shortage continues, the fixing of maximum prices and whatever measures may be necessary to prevent the food speculators from holding back the supplies now in their hands;

(b) The socialization and democratic management of the great industries concerned with the production, transportation, storage, and the marketing of food and other necessaries of life;

(c) The socialization and democratic management of all land and other natural resources now held out of use for monopolistic or speculative profit.

These measures are presented as means of protecting the workers against the evil results of the present war. The danger of recurrence of war will exist as long as the capitalist system of industry remains in existence. The end of wars will come with the establishment of socialized industry and industrial democracy the world over. The Socialist Party calls upon all the workers to join it in its struggle to reach this goal, and thus bring into the world a new society in which peace, fraternity, and human brotherhood will be the dominant ideals.

II

Eugene V. Debs: Speech at
Nimisilla Park, Canton, Ohio,
June 16, 1918

There was no more bitter opponent of World War I than Eugene V. Debs (1855–1926), the great moral force of American socialism. A born crusader with a burning hatred of all forms of social injustice, who was five times the socialist candidate for President of the United States, there is no question that Debs was the most controversial —yet popular and effective—socialist figure ever to appear in America. Clarence Darrow, the famous lawyer, considered him the kindliest, gentlest, most generous man he had ever known; the British-American novelist, critic, and biographer Frank Harris wrote of him as "the man who had more of the spirit of Jesus in him than any man I have ever met"; and on the occasion of his death The Nation asserted that he belonged "to the republic of the

Writings and Speeches of Eugene V. Debs (New York: Hermitage Press, Inc., 1948), pp. 417–18, 421–22, 425–26, 429–33.

immortals whose memory is a living inspiration to mankind." In sharp contrast, Justice Oliver Wendell Holmes dismissed him as a "noted agitator," the Chicago Herald described him as a "reckless, ranting . . . law breaker," and the New York Times referred to him on one occasion as "an enemy of the human race."

From the beginning of his career as a socialist, Debs was an outspoken opponent of war, holding that modern wars have invariably been due to economic competition and commercial rivalry among nations in their struggle for world power. Consistent with this position, when World War I broke out he branded it as a conflict between two groups of capitalists in which the proletariat of each side had nothing to win and much to lose. Although he did not attend the Socialist Party's emergency national convention in St. Louis in 1917, he staunchly supported its antiwar proclamation and—countering the charge that the proclamation was "treasonable"—announced that there are times "when to be 'treasonable' is to be true to revolutionary principles and the cause of humanity."

After April, 1917, American critics of the war had a difficult time. The Espionage Act of June, 1917, and the Sedition Act of May, 1918, practically guaranteed that any opposition to the status quo could be interpreted as traitorous. Otherwise sane and responsible citizens, prominent clergymen among them, demanded that opponents of the war be silenced—some (including Dr. Henry Van Dyke, American Minister to Holland) even suggested that dissidents should be hanged. So deep and unreasoning was the hatred and fear of the enemy by the spring of 1918 that the Montana State Council, in an action that was not at all as unusual as it might appear, ordered the public schools to cease using a textbook on ancient history that gave what was considered to be too favorable a treatment of the Teutonic tribes prior to the year 812 A.D.

The persecution of war protesters, many of them old and devoted friends, deeply disturbed Debs, and in the summer of 1918—apparently feeling that he had no right to be free when others were in prison for saying what he believed—he decided to abandon any appearance of restraint and assail the war with even greater vigor. He chose to make his stand at Nimisilla Park in Canton, Ohio, where he spoke on June 16, 1918, before the final session of the Ohio state socialist convention. He did not choose Ohio accidentally. The Buckeye state had long been a radical

*stronghold and already a number of Ohio socialists had
been arrested.*

*Debs's speech was a catalogue of socialist persecutions
and a reaffirmation of his radical principles. Though
couched in militant language, it contained little that was
new, nothing that he had not said before, and much that
was not incendiary. Indeed, when read today the speech
may not appear to be a strong criticism of America's role
in World War I. But at the time the atmosphere was full
of tension and the audience recognized that Debs's re-
marks were directed at the current war.*

*If Debs was daring the authorities to arrest and place
him on trial, as many believe he was, his speech had the
intended effect. He was indicted on June 29, 1918, for
violating the Sedition Act, which made it a crime to express
antiwar sentiments to an audience which included men of
draft age, and tried in Cleveland, Ohio, in September,
1918. The verdict of guilty and the ten-year prison sentence
was no great surprise to Debs, but he was both hurt and
angered by the charge of the Cleveland Press that he had
done "more to aid the Hun Kaiser than all the pro-German
Germans in America." His case was appealed to the
Supreme Court, which handed down its decision on March
10, 1919, upholding the verdict and the sentence. He
entered prison on April 13, 1919, seven months after
World War I ended, and, though he never recanted a word
which he had uttered in condemnation of the American
participation in the war, was released through the intercession of President Harding on Christmas Day, 1921.*

. . . To speak for labor; to plead the cause of the men
and women and children who toil; to serve the working
class, has always been to me a high privilege; a duty of
love.

I have just returned from a visit over yonder (pointing
to the workhouse), where three of our most loyal comrades
are paying the penalty for their devotion to the cause of

the working class. They have come to realize, as many of us have, that it is extremely dangerous to exercise the constitutional right of free speech in a country fighting to make democracy safe in the world.

I realize that, in speaking to you this afternoon, there are certain limitations placed upon the right of free speech. I must be exceedingly careful, prudent, as to what I say, and even more careful and prudent as to how I say it. I may not be able to say all I think; but I am not going to say anything that I do not think. I would rather a thousand times be a free soul in jail than to be a sycophant and coward in the streets. They may put those boys in jail—and some of the rest of us in jail—but they cannot put the Socialist movement in jail. Those prison bars separate their bodies from ours, but their souls are here this afternoon. They are simply paying the penalty, that all men have paid in all the ages of history, for standing erect, and for seeking to pave the way to better conditions for mankind.

If it had not been for the men and women, who, in the past, have had the moral courage to go to jail, we would still be in the jungles. . . .

. . . Are we opposed to Prussian militarism? Why, we have been fighting it since the day the Socialist movement was born; and we are going to continue to fight it, day and night, until it is wiped from the face of the earth. Between us there is no truce—no compromise. . . .

. . . I hate, I loathe, I despise Junkers and junkerdom. I have no earthly use for the Junkers of Germany, and not one particle more use for the Junkers in the United States.

They tell us that we live in a great free republic; that our institutions are democratic; that we are a free and self-governing people. This is too much, even for a joke. But it is not a subject for levity; it is an exceedingly serious matter.

To whom do the Wall Street Junkers in our country marry their daughters? After they have wrung their countless millions from your sweat, your agony and your life's blood, in a time of war as in a time of peace, they invest these untold millions in the purchase of titles of broken-down aristocrats, such as princes, dukes, counts and other parasites and no-accounts. Would they be satisfied to wed their daughters to honest workingmen? To real democrats? Oh, no! They scour the markets of Europe for vampires

who are titled and nothing else. And they swap their
millions for the titles, so that matrimony with them becomes literally a matter of money.

These are the gentry who are today wrapped up in the
American flag, who shout their claim from the housetops
that they are the only patriots, and who have their magnify-
ing glasses in hand, scanning the country for evidence of
disloyalty, eager to apply the brand of treason to the men
who dare to even whisper their opposition to Junker rule
in the United States. No wonder Sam Johnson declared that
"patriotism is the last refuge of the scoundrel." He must
have had this Wall Street gentry in mind, or at least their
prototypes, for in every age it has been the tyrant, the
oppressor and the exploiter who has wrapped himself in
the cloak of patriotism, or religion, or both to deceive and
overawe the people. . . .

. . . Wars throughout history have been waged for
conquest and plunder. In the Middle Ages when the feudal
lords who inhabited the castles whose towers may still be
seen along the Rhine concluded to enlarge their domains, to
increase their power, their prestige and their wealth they
declared war upon one another. But they themselves did
not go to war any more than the modern feudal lords, the
barons of Wall Street go to war. The feudal barons of the
Middle Ages, the economic predecessors of the capitalists
of our day, declared all wars. And their miserable serfs
fought all the battles. The poor, ignorant serfs had been
taught to revere their masters; to believe that when their
masters declared war upon one another, it was their
patriotic duty to fall upon one another and to cut one
another's throats for the profit and glory of the lords and
barons who held them in contempt. And that is war in a
nutshell. The master class has always declared the wars;
the subject class has always fought the battles. The master
class has had all to gain and nothing to lose, while the
subject class has had nothing to gain and all to lose—
especially their lives. . . .

And here let me emphasize the fact—and it cannot be
repeated too often—that the working class who fight all
the battles, the working class who make the supreme
sacrifices, the working class who freely shed their blood
and furnish the corpses, have never yet had a voice in
either declaring war or making peace. It is the ruling class
that invariably does both. They alone declare war and they
alone make peace.

Yours not to reason why:
Yours but to do and die.

That is their motto and we object on the part of the
awakening workers of this nation. . . .

What a compliment it is to the Socialist movement to
be persecuted for the sake of the truth! The truth alone
will make the people free. And for this reason the truth
must not be permitted to reach the people. The truth has
always been dangerous to the rule of the rogue, the
exploiter, the robber. So the truth must be ruthlessly suppressed. That is why they are trying to destroy the Socialist
movement; and every time they strike a blow they add a
thousand new voices to the hosts proclaiming that Socialism
is the hope of humanity and has come to emancipate the
people from their final form of servitude. . . .

. . . It is the minorities who have made the history of
this world. It is the few who have had the courage to take
their places at the front; who have been true enough to
themselves to speak the truth that was in them; who have
dared oppose the established order of things; who have
espoused the cause of the suffering, struggling poor; who
have upheld without regard to personal consequences the
cause of freedom and righteousness. It is they, the heroic,
self-sacrificing few who have made the history of the race
and who have paved the way from barbarism to civilization.
The many prefer to remain upon the popular side. They
lack the courage and vision to join a despised minority that
stands for a principle; they have not the moral fibre that
withstands, endures and finally conquers. They are to be
pitied and not treated with contempt for they cannot help
their cowardice. But, thank God, in every age and in
every nation there have been the brave and self-reliant
few, and they have been sufficient to their historic task;
and we, who are here today, are under infinite obligations
to them because they suffered, they sacrificed, they went
to jail, they had their bones broken upon the wheel, they
were burned at the stake and their ashes scattered to the
winds by the hands of hate and revenge in their struggle
to leave the world better for us than they found it for
themselves. We are under eternal obligations to them because of what they did and what they suffered for us and
the only way we can discharge that obligation is by doing
the best we can for those who are to come after us. . . .

. . . The capitalist system affects to have great regard
and reward for intellect, and the capitalists give them-

selves full credit for having superior brains. When we have ventured to say that the time would come when the working class would rule they have bluntly answered "Never! it requires brains to rule." The workers of course have none. And they certainly try hard to prove it by proudly supporting the political parties of their masters under whose administration they are kept in poverty and servitude. . . .

It is true that they have the brains that indicate the cunning of the fox, the wolf, but as for brains denoting real intelligence and the measure of intellectual capacity they are the most woefully ignorant people on earth. Give me a hundred capitalists and let me ask them a dozen simple questions about the history of their own country and I will prove to you that they are as ignorant and unlettered as any you may find in the so-called lower class. They know little of history; they are strangers to science; they are ignorant of sociology and blind to art but they know how to exploit, how to gouge, how to rob, and do it with legal sanction. They always proceed legally for the reason that the class which has the power to rob upon a large scale has also the power to control the government and legalize their robbery. I regret that lack of time prevents me from discussing this phase of the question more at length.

They are continually talking about your patriotic duty. It is not *their* but *your* patriotic duty that they are concerned about. There is a decided difference. Their patriotic duty never takes them to the firing line or chucks them into the trenches.

And now among other things they are urging you to "cultivate" war gardens, while at the same time a government war report just issued shows that practically 52 percent of the arable, tillable soil is held out of use by the landlords, speculators and profiteers. They themselves do not cultivate the soil. They could not if they would. Nor do they allow others to cultivate it. They keep it idle to enrich themselves, to pocket the millions of dollars of unearned increment. Who is it that makes this land valuable while it is fenced in and kept out of use? It is the people. Who pockets this tremendous accumulation of value? The landlords. And these landlords who toil not and spin not are supreme among American "patriots."

In passing I suggest that we stop a moment to think about the term "landlord." "LANDLORD!" Lord of the Land! The Lord of the land is indeed a super-patriot. This lord who practically owns the earth tells you that we are fighting this war to make the world safe for democracy—he, who shuts out all humanity from his private domain; he who profiteers at the expense of the people who have been slain and mutilated by multiplied thousands, under pretense of being the great American patriot. It is he, this identical patriot who is in fact the arch-enemy of the people; it is he that you need to wipe from power. It is he who is a far greater menace to your liberty and your well-being than the Prussian Junkers on the other side of the Atlantic Ocean....

... There are few men who have the courage to say a word in favor of the I. W. W. [Industrial Workers of the World].[1] I have. Let me say here that I have great respect for the I. W. W. Far greater than I have for their infamous detractors.

It is only necessary to label a man "I. W. W." to have him lynched. War makes possible all such crimes and outrages. And war comes in spite of the people. When Wall Street says war the press says war and the pulpit promptly follows with its *Amen*. In every age the pulpit has been on the side of the rulers and not on the side of the people. That is one reason why the preachers so fiercely denounce the I. W. W....

... When we unite and act together on the industrial field and when we vote together on election day we shall develop the supreme power of the one class that can and will bring permanent peace to the world. We shall then have the intelligence, the courage and the power for our great task. In due time industry will be organized on a co-operative basis. We shall conquer the public power. We shall then transfer the title deeds of the railroads, the telegraph lines, the mines, mills and great industries to the people in their collective capacity; we shall take possession of all these social utilities in the name of the people. We shall then have industrial democracy. We shall be a free nation whose government is of and by and for the people....

[1] A radical labor organization which preached antimilitarism and antipatriotism as basic principles.

23.

Picketing the White House:
Women Demand the Vote*

Shout the revolution
  Of women, of women,
Shout the revolution,
For liberty.
Rise, glorious women of the earth,
  The voiceless and the free
United strength assures the birth
  Of true democracy.

—From the song "Shout the Revolution of Women" (1917)

*Max Lerner's assertion that women have been the most
continuous revolutionaries in America[1] appears well
founded. From colonial times until today American women
have been engaged in a series of hard-fought "revolutions"
for equality, perhaps the most dramatic of which has been
the "suffrage revolution"—the successful struggle for
equality before the ballot box.*

*Although the woman's suffrage movement began in
America about the middle of the nineteenth century, by the
end of 1914 only eleven states and the territory of Alaska
had extended equal political rights to women. Opponents
of woman suffrage, countering the ladies' assertion that
unless they had the vote the Declaration of Independence
was a mockery, emphasized the degrading nature of*

*Doris Stevens, *Jailed for Freedom* (New York: Liveright Publishing Co., 1920), pp. 122–24, 125–29, 212–13. Reprinted by
permission of Jonathan Mitchell, executor of Miss Stevens' estate.

[1]Max Lerner, *America as a Civilization: Life and Thought in the
United States* (New York: Simon and Schuster, 1957), p. 603.

politics and insisted that "woman's place is in the home."

Despairing of ever getting men to listen to reason, some of the more persistent "suffragettes," as in England at the same time, turned to militancy. They picketed the White House and sought to promote their cause by other types of disturbances. The activities of these self-styled "sentinels of liberty" during the "August Riots" of 1917 are recorded below in an account by one of the participants.

Within a few years of the "August Riots" the long battle for woman's suffrage ended in victory. In the fall of 1918 a resolution to amend the Constitution by providing that "the right of citizens of the United States to vote shall not be denied or abridged by the United States on account of sex" was passed by the House of Representatives. After twice defeating the amendment, the Senate approved it in a special session called by President Wilson in 1919. The amendment was ratified by the necessary thirty-six states in 1920.

Imprisoning women had met with considerable public disapproval, and attendant political embarrassment to the Administration. That the presidential pardon would end this embarrassment was doubtless the hope of the Administration. The pickets, however, returned to their posts in steadily increasing numbers. Their presence at the gates was desired by the Administration no more now than it had been before the arrests and imprisonments. But they had found no way to rid themselves of the pickets. And as another month of picketing drew to an end the Administration ventured to try other ways to stop it and with it the consequent embarrassment. Their methods became physically more brutal and politically more stupid. Their conduct became lawless in the extreme.

Meanwhile the President had drafted the young men of America in their millions to die on foreign soil for foreign democracy. He had issued a special appeal to women to give their work, their treasure and their sons to this enterprise. At the same time his now gigantic figure stood obstinately across the path to our main objective. It was our daily task to keep vividly in his mind that objective. It was our responsibility to compel decisive action from him.

Using the return of Envoy Root[1] from his mission to Russia as another dramatic opportunity to speak to the President we took to the picket line these mottoes:

TO ENVOY ROOT

You say that America must throw its manhood to the support of liberty.

Whose liberty?

This nation is not free. Twenty million women are denied by the President of the United States the right to representation in their own government.

Tell the President that he cannot fight against liberty at home while he tells us to fight for liberty abroad.

Tell him to make America safe for democracy before he asks the mothers of America to throw their sons to the support of democracy in Europe.

Ask him how he can refuse liberty to American citizens when he is forcing millions of American boys out of their country to die for liberty.

At no time during the entire picketing was the traffic on Pennsylvania Avenue so completely obstructed as it was for the two hours during which this banner made its appearance on the line. Police captains who three weeks before were testifying that the police could not manage the crowds, placidly looked on while these new crowds increased.

We did not regard Mr. Wilson as *our* President. We felt that he had neither political nor moral claim to our allegiance. War had been made without our consent. The war would be finished and very likely a bad peace would be written without our consent. Our fight was becoming increasingly difficult—I might almost say desperate. Here we were, a band of women fighting with banners, in the

---

[1] Elihu Root, the American statesman and lawyer, was appointed by President Wilson in 1917 to a special diplomatic mission to Russia.

midst of a world armed to the teeth. And so it was not very difficult to understand how high spirited women grew more resentful, unwilling to be a party to the President's hypocrisy, the hypocrisy so eager to sacrifice life without stint to the vague hope of liberty abroad, while refusing to assist in the peaceful legislative steps which would lead to self-government in our own country. As a matter of fact the President's constant oratory on freedom and democracy moved them to scorn. They were stung into a protest so militant as to shock not only the President but the public. We inscribed on our banner what countless American women had long thought in their hearts.

The truth was not pleasant but it had to be told. We submitted to the world, through the picket line, this question:

KAISER WILSON

HAVE YOU FORGOTTEN HOW YOU SYMPATHIZED WITH THE POOR GERMANS BECAUSE THEY WERE NOT SELF-GOVERNED?

20,000,000 AMERICAN WOMEN ARE NOT SELF-GOVERNED.

TAKE THE BEAM OUT OF YOUR OWN EYE.

. . . And so those excited boys of the Army and Navy attacked the women and the banner. The banner was destroyed. Another was brought up to take its place. This one met the same fate. Meanwhile a crowd was assembling in front of the White House either to watch or to assist in the attacks. At the very moment when one banner was being snatched away and destroyed, President and Mrs. Wilson passed through the gates on their way to a military review at Fort Myer. *The President saw American women being attacked, while the police refused them protection.*

Not a move was made by the police to control the growing crowd. Such inaction is always a signal for more violence on the part of rowdies. As the throng moved to and fro between the White House and our Headquarters immediately opposite, so many banners were destroyed that finally Miss Lucy Burns, Miss Virginia Arnold and Miss Elizabeth Stuyvesant took those remaining to the second and third floor balconies of our building and hung them out. At this point there was not a picket left on the street. The crowd was clearly obstructing the traffic, but no attempt was made to move them back or to protect the women, some of whom were attacked by

sailors on their own doorsteps. The two police officers
present watched without interference while three sailors
brought a ladder from the Belasco Theater in the same
block, leaned it against the side of the Cameron House,
the Headquarters, climbed up to the second floor balcony,
mounted the iron railing and tore down all banners and
the American flag. One sailor administered a severe blow in
the face with his clenched fist upon Miss Georgina Sturgis
of Washington.

"Why did you do that?" she demanded.

The man halted for a brief instant in obvious amazement
and said, "I don't know." And with a violent wrench he
tore the banner from her hands and ran down the ladder.

The narrow balcony was the scene of intense excitement.

But for Miss Burns' superb strength she would have been
dragged over the railing of the balcony to be plunged to
the ground. The mob watched with fascination while she
swayed to and fro in her wrestle with two young sailors.
And still no attempt by the police to quell the riot!

The climax came when in the late afternoon a bullet
was fired through one of the heavy glass windows of the
second floor, embedding itself in the ceiling. The bullet
grazed past the head of Mrs. Ella Morton Dean of Montana. Captain Flather of the 1st Precinct, with two de-
tectives, later examined the holes and declared they had
been made by a 38 caliber revolver, but no attempt was
ever made to find the man who had drawn the revolver. . . .

. . . This entire spectacle was enacted on August 14,
within a stone's throw of the White House.

Miss Paul summed up the situation when she said:

"The situation now existing in Washington exists because President Wilson permits it. Orders were first handed
down to the police to arrest suffragists. The clamor over
their imprisonments made this position untenable. The
police were then ordered to protect suffragists. They were
then ordered to attack suffragists. They have now been
ordered to encourage irresponsible crowds to attack suffragists. No police head would dare so to besmirch his record without orders from his responsible chief. The responsible chief in the National Capital is the President
of the United States." . . .

. . . On August 15th the pickets again attempted to
take their posts on the line.

On this day one lettered banner and fifty purple, white
and gold flags were destroyed by a mob led by sailors in

uniform. Alice Paul was knocked down three times by a sailor in uniform and dragged the width of the White House sidewalk in his frenzied attempt to tear off her suffrage sash.

Miss Katharine Morey of Boston was also knocked to the pavement by a sailor, who took her flag and then darted off into the crowd. Miss Elizabeth Stuyvesant was struck by a soldier in uniform and her blouse torn from her body. Miss Maud Jamison of Virginia was knocked down and dragged along the sidewalk. Miss Beulah Amidon of North Dakota was knocked down by a sailor.

In the midst of these riotous scenes, a well-known Washington correspondent was emerging from the White House, after an interview with the President. Dr. Cary Grayson, the President's physician, accompanying him to the door, advised:

"You had better go out the side entrance. Those damned women are in the front." . . .

. . . Finding that riots and mob attacks had not terrorized the pickets, the Administration decided again to arrest the women in the hope of ending the agitation. Having lost public sympathy through workhouse sentences, having won it back by pardoning the women, the Administration felt it could afford to risk losing it again, or rather felt that it had supplied itself with an appropriate amount of stage-setting. . . .

. . . Nothing in the world so baffles the pompous dignity of a court as non-resistant defendants. The judge cleared his throat and the attendants made meaningless gestures.

"Will the prisoners stand up and be sworn?"

They will not.

"Will they question witnesses?"

They will not.

"Will they speak in their own behalf?"

The slender, quiet-voiced Quaker girl arose from her seat. The crowded courtroom pressed forward breathlessly. She said calmly and with unconcern: "We do not wish to make any plea before this court. We do not consider ourselves subject to this court, since as an unenfranchised class we have nothing to do with the making of the laws which have put us in this position."

What a disconcerting attitude to take! Miss Paul sat down as quietly and unexpectedly as she had arisen. The judge moved uneasily in his chair. The gentle way in which it was said was disarming. Would the judge hold them in contempt? He had not time to think. His part of the comedy he had expected to run smoothly, and here was this defiant little woman calmly stating that we were not subject to the court, and that we would therefore have nothing to do with the proceedings. The murmurs had grown to a babel of conversation. A sharp rap of the gavel restored order and permitted Judge Mullowny to say: "Unfortunately, I am here to support the laws that are made by Congress, and, of course, I am bound by those laws; and you are bound by them as long as you live in this country, notwithstanding the fact that you do not recognize the law."

Everybody strained his ears for the sentence. The Administration had threatened to "get" the leader. Would they dare?

Another pause!

"I shall suspend sentence for the time being," came solemnly from the judge.

Was it that they did not dare confine Miss Paul? Were they beginning actually to perceive the real strength of the movement and the protest that would be aroused if she were imprisoned? Again we thought perhaps this marked the end of the jailing of women.

But though the pickets were released on suspended sentences, there was no indication of any purpose on the part of the Administration of acting on the amendment. Two groups, some of those on suspended sentence, others first offenders, again marched to the White House gates. . . .

24.

Intellectuals in Revolt: The Quest for Freedom of Expression in Soviet Russia

> Every artist, and every one who regards himself as such, claims as his proper right the liberty to work freely according to his ideal, whether it is good or not. There you have the ferment, the experiment, the chaos. Nevertheless we are Communists, and must not quietly fold our hands and let chaos bubble as it will. We must also try to guide this development consciously, clearly, and to shape and determine its results.
>
> —Vladimir Lenin as quoted in Donald W. Treadgold, *Twentieth Century Russia*

Although Lenin declared soon after coming to power that the regime, not the artist, should and would determine the outcome in the arts, he did not try to enforce his preferences. He attacked what he regarded as "unhealthy" schools of the arts, but refrained from prohibiting other artists from working. In similar fashion, the cultivated old Bolshevik A. V. Lunacharsky, who until 1929 was responsible for general Party supervision of literary and artistic affairs, exercised great tact in the handling of cultural problems. In large part as a consequence of this relatively mild stewardship, the 1920's were clearly the most productive years of cultural creativeness in Soviet history. Literature, in particular, enjoyed its best years.

The emergence of Joseph Stalin as absolute dictator at the end of the 1920's, and his subsequent determination to

211

plunge the country into a policy of rapid industrialization and collectivization, however, spelled the end of cultural freedom and the beginning of an enforced state of "entropy" which went on for the next two decades. At the beginning of the 1930's there developed under Stalin's direction a new style known as "Socialist realism." In theory, the new trend, in force until Stalin's death (and to a lesser degree even afterwards), sought to develop "artistic works worthy of the great age of Socialism." In practice, it demanded of all writers and artists absolute conformity, producing, in the words of one observer, a "cultural wilderness." Literature was to be "of one flesh and blood with Socialist construction," and writers were to be "engineers of the human soul" who depicted "reality in its revolutionary development."

Evgeni Zamyatin (1884–1937), perhaps the most interesting and original Russian writer of the twentieth century, was one of a handful of Soviet intellectuals who refused to make compromises or rationalizations in the face of oppression. Had his example (as well as that of Boris Pasternak) been emulated by other writers and artists, it is possible that Stalin would not have succeeded in establishing his ascendancy over the USSR.

Long before the Communist victory in 1917, Zamyatin enjoyed the credentials of a bona fide *political revolutionary. An early member of the Bolshevik faction of the Social Democratic Party, he had served several months in solitary confinement in a St. Petersburg prison for his participation in the Revolution of 1905. The Bolshevik Revolution, however, which succeeded at the expense of democratic ideals, caused him to recoil from his earlier affiliations, and from then until his death twenty years later he remained irreconcilably hostile to Bolshevism. His best-known work, the satirical novel* We *(published in Prague in 1924), was a humanitarian attack on Soviet Utopianism, which Zamyatin already foresaw would lead to a dehumanized monster state founded on conformism and the suppression of freedom.*

In "On Literature, Revolution, and Entropy," published in Moscow in 1924 and again in 1926, Zamyatin boldly asserted that "dogmatism is the entropy of thought" and argued the need for heresy in literature. When, in 1929, he was falsely accused together with Boris Pilnyak (then chairman of the All-Russian Union of Writers) of having deliberately arranged for the publication abroad of works which had not been approved by the Soviet censorship,

*he refused to grovel and, probably through the intercession
of Maxim Gorky, was permitted to emigrate to Paris. He
died in that foreign capital in 1937.*

I

Evgeni Zamyatin: On Literature,
*Revolution, and Entropy**

. . . Revolution is everywhere and in all things; it is
infinite, there is no final revolution, no end to the sequence
of integers. Social revolution is only one in the infinite
sequence of integers. The law of revolution is not a social
law, it is immeasurably greater, it is a cosmic, universal
law—such as the law of the conservation of energy and
the law of the loss of energy (entropy). Some day an
exact formula will be established for the law of revolution.
And in this formula nations, classes, stars—and books will
be expressed as numerical values.

Red, fiery, death-dealing is the law of revolution; but
that death is the birth of a new life, of a new star. And
cold, blue as ice, as the icy interplanetary infinities, is the
law of entropy. The flame turns from fiery red to an even,
warm pink, no longer death-dealing but comfort-producing;
the sun ages and becomes a planet suitable for highways,
shops, beds, prostitutes, prisons: that is a law. And in
order to make the planet young again, we must set it afire,
we must thrust it off the smooth highway of evolution:
that is a law.

The flame, true enough, will grow cold tomorrow or the
day after tomorrow (in the Book of Genesis days are years
and even aeons). But already today there should be
somebody who can foresee that; there should be somebody
today to speak heretically of tomorrow. Heretics are the
only (bitter-tasting) remedy for the entropy of human
thought.

When (in science, religion, social life, art) a flaming,

*Copyright © 1961 by *Partisan Review*. Reprinted from
Dissonant Voices in Soviet Literature, edited by Patricia Blake and
Max Hayward, by permission of Pantheon Books, Inc., a Division
of Random House, Inc. Acknowledgment is also made to George
Allen & Unwin Ltd.

seething sphere grows cold, the fiery molten rock becomes covered with dogma—with a hard, ossified, immovable crust. In science, religion, social life, and art, dogmatization is the entropy of thought; what has been dogmatized no longer inflames, it is merely warm—and soon it is to be cool. The sermon on the Mount, delivered beneath the scorching sun to upstretched arms and rending sobs, gives way to slumberous prayer in some well-appointed abbey. Galileo's tragic *"E pur si muove"* gives way to calm calculations in some well-heated office in an observatory. On the Galileos the epigones build—slowly, coral upon coral, forming a reef: this is the path of evolution. Till one day a new heresy explodes and blows up the dogma's crust, together with all the ever so stable, rocklike structures that had been erected on it.

Explosions are not comfortable things. That is why the exploders, the heretics, are quite rightly annihilated by fire, by axes, and by words. Heretics are harmful to everybody today, to every evolution, to the difficult, slow, useful, so very useful, constructive process of coral reef building; imprudently and foolishly they leap into today from tomorrow. They are romantics. It was right and proper that in 1797 Babeuf had his head cut off: he had leaped into 1797, skipping one hundred and fifty years. It is equally right and proper that heretical literature, literature that is damaging to dogma, should also have its head cut off: such literature is harmful.

But harmful literature is more useful than useful literature: because it is anti-entropic, it militates against calcification, sclerosis, encrustedness, moss, peace. It is utopian and ridiculous. Like Babeuf in 1797 it is right one hundred and fifty years later.

We know Darwin, we know that after Darwin came mutations, Weismannism, neo-Lamarckism. But these are only penthouses and balconies while Darwin is the building itself. And the building contains not only tadpoles and toadstools, it also contains man. Fangs grow sharp only if there is someone to gnaw on; the domestic hen's wings serve only to flap with. Ideas and hens obey the same law: ideas which feed on minced meat lose their teeth just as civilized men do. Heretics are necessary to health. If there are no heretics, they have to be invented.

Live literature does not set its watch by yesterday's time, nor by today's, but by tomorrow's. Live literature is like a

sailor who is sent aloft; from the masthead he can descry
sinking vessels, icebergs, and maelstroms which are not yet
visible from the deck. You can drag him down from the
mast and put him to work in the boiler room or on the
capstan, but that won't change a thing: the mast is still
there and from the masthead another sailor will be able
to see what the first sailor has seen.

In stormy weather you need a man aloft. And right now
the weather is stormy. SOS signals are coming in from all
directions. Only yesterday the writer was able to stroll calmly on deck, taking snapshots of "real life"; but who wants
to look at pictures of landscapes and scenes from daily
life when the world has taken on a forty-five degree list,
when the green waves are threatening to swallow us and the
ship is breaking up? Right now we can look and think
only as men do in the face of death: we shall die—and
what then? How have we lived? If we are to live all over
again in some new way, then by what shall we live, and
for what? Right now we need in literature the vast philosophical horizon, the vast sweep from the masthead, from
the sky above, we need the most ultimate, the most fear-
some, the most fearless "Whys?" and "What nexts?" . . .

. . . Organic chemistry has blurred the dividing line between living and dead matter. It is a mistake to divide
people into the living and the dead: there are live-dead
people and live-live people. The live-dead people also
write, walk, talk, act. But they do not make mistakes; only
machines produce without mistakes, but they produce only
dead things. The live-live people are all mistakes, search-
ings, questions, torments.

So too what we write also walks and talks, but it can
be live-dead or live-live. The genuinely live, stopping at
nothing, brooking no obstacle or hindrance, searches for
the answers to foolish, "childish" questions. The answers
may be wrong, the philosophy erroneous—but errors are of
greater value than truths: truth is machinelike, error is
alive, truth reassures, error unsettles. And even if the
answers are quite impossible, so much the better: to ask
answered questions is the privilege of minds constructed
on the same principle as the cow's stomach, which is ideally
suited, as well we know, to chewing the cud.

If there were in nature something fixed, if there were
truths, all this would, of course, be wrong. But happily
all truths are erroneous. This is precisely the significance

of the dialectic process: today's truths become tomorrow's errors; there is no final integer.

This (one and only) truth is only for the strong: weak-nerved minds unfailingly require a finite universe, a final integer; they require, as Nietzsche said, "the crutches of assurance." The weak-nerved do not have the strength to include themselves in the dialectic syllogism. True, this is difficult. But it is the very thing that Einstein did succeed in doing: he managed to remember that he, Einstein, with watch in hand observing motion, was also moving; he succeeded in looking at the earth's movements *from outside*.

That is precisely how great literature—literature that knows no final integer—looks at the earth's movements.

The formal characteristic of live literature is the same as its inner characteristic: the negation of truth, that is, the negation of what everyone knows and what I knew up to this moment. Live literature leaves the canonical rails, leaves the broad highway.

. . . Today's literature has the same relation to the plane surface of real life as an aircraft has to the earth: it is nothing more than a runway from which to take off and soar aloft from real life to reality, to philosophy, to the realm of the fantastic. Leave the carts of yesterday to creak along the great highways. The living have strength enough to cut off their yesterdays. . . .

. . . A new form is not intelligible to all; for many it is difficult. Maybe. The habitual, the banal is of course simpler, pleasanter, more comfortable. Euclid's world is very simple and Einstein's world is very difficult; nevertheless it is now impossible to return to Euclid's. No revolution, no heresy is comfortable and easy. Because it is a leap, it is a rupture of the smooth evolutionary curve, and a rupture is a wound, a pain. But it is a necessary wound: most people suffer from hereditary sleeping sickness, and those who are sick with this ailment (entropy) must not be allowed to sleep, or they will go to their last sleep, the sleep of death.

This same sickness is common to artists and writers: they go contentedly to sleep in their favorite artistic form which they have devised, then twice revised. They do not have the strength to wound themselves, to cease to love what has become dear to them. They do not have the strength to come out from their lived-in, laurel-scented rooms, to come out into the open air and start anew.

To wound oneself, it is true, is difficult, even dangerous. But to live today as yesterday and yesterday as today is even more difficult for the living.

II

Solzhenitsyn's Letter
to the Fourth Congress of Soviet Writers*

Stalin's death in 1953, the ensuing struggle for succession, and de-Stalinization produced in the Soviet Union an interesting intellectual ferment popularly labeled "the thaw" (after a novel of the same name by Ilya Ehrenburg, which suggested that there had been a paralyzing freeze in Soviet life, but that with Stalin dead, better things might be hoped for). Despite an undeniable growth of freedom, however, a considerable number of writers who took the opportunity in the late 1950's and throughout the 1960's to criticize various aspects of Soviet society found themselves officially attacked and often personally disadvantaged—in extreme cases carried off to lunatic asylums or sentenced to hard labor. In February, 1966, for example, the dissident authors Andrei Sinyavsky ("Abram Tertz") and Yuli Daniel ("Nikolai Arzhak"), whose work had been published pseudonymously in the West, were tried, convicted of having slandered Lenin, the Red Army, and "everything dear to the Soviet man," and sentenced to seven and five years hard labor, respectively.

Alexander Solzhenitsyn (1918–   ), another literary opponent of the Soviet Establishment, is widely acknowledged as the most powerful writer and most versatile stylist in Russia today. Imprisoned in 1945 for criticizing Stalin in a letter to a friend, in 1962 he rocketed to international fame with the publication in Russia and abroad of One Day in the Life of Ivan Denisovich, *a narrative of life in a Stalinist concentration camp. Since then, two of his novels—*The First Circle *and* Cancer Ward *(both of them strong polemics against the official norms in Soviet*

*"An Open Letter to the Fourth Congress of Soviet Writers from Alexander Solzhenitsyn," *Survey: A Journal of Soviet and East European Studies,* No. 64 (July, 1967), pp. 177–81. Reprinted by permission.

literature)—*have been smuggled out of the Soviet Union
and published amid wide acclaim in the West. Neither
of these works has been judged fit to be printed in the
author's native land.*

*Since 1967, Solzhenitsyn has been leading the struggle
to do away with literary censorship in the Soviet Union.
In May of that year he took the fight to the national congress of the Writer's Union. His letter to that assembly re-
flects the struggle of Solzhenitsyn for his rights as an author and a citizen, and his concern about the future of
Soviet literature.*

*At this writing, Solzhenitsyn, though a free man, is a
literary "unperson." In November, 1969, he was cast out
of the Writers' Union for "antisocial" behavior and the
decision was made to strike his name from the next edition
of the official Soviet* Who's Who. *In October, 1970,
Solzhenitsyn won and accepted the Nobel prize in literature, but did not go to Stockholm to receive the award
personally for fear he would be banished from his home-
land.*

Since I am unable to speak from the platform, I would
ask the congress to consider the following questions:

(1) The oppression, insupportable in the long run, to
which our literature has for decades and decades been
subjected, on the part of the censorship, and which the
Writers' Union can no longer tolerate.

The censorship, for which there is no provision in the
Constitution and which is therefore illegal, the censorship
which never passes under its own name, has imposed its
yoke on literature under the obscure name of "Glavlit." It
gives to literary illiterates the possibility of taking arbitrary
measures against writers. The censorship, this survival of
the Middle Ages, has managed, like a kind of Methuselah,
to live almost into the twenty-first century. In its refuge,
it tries to assume the attributes of timelessness and to sort
out the good books from the bad.

There is no suggestion, and no recognition of the right of our writers to state publicly their opinions about the moral life of men and of society, to elucidate in their own way the social problems or the historical experiences which have so profoundly affected our country. Works which could have expressed the thoughts matured among the people, which might in time have exercised a valuable influence in the spiritual domain or on the evolution of the social conscience, are prohibited or distorted by the censorship as a result of calculations which, from the point of view of the people, are pettifogging, egotistic, and short-sighted.

Excellent manuscripts by young authors, still completely unknown, are today rejected by editors on the sole ground that they "will not pass" the censor. Many members of the Union, and even delegates to this congress, know how they themselves have had to bow to the pressures of the censorship, to capitulate on matters concerning the structure and orientation of their works. They have rewritten chapters, pages, paragraphs, phrases; they have sweetened them only because they wanted to have them published; and in so doing they have damaged them irreparably. If we bear in mind the special character of literary works, it is obvious that these mutilations are pernicious for works of talent, but quite imperceptible in others. What is best in our literature is mutilated when it appears.

At the same time the labels used by the censorship ("ideologically pernicious," "incorrect") are very ephemeral. They are changed and discarded before our eyes. Even Dostoevsky, the pride of world literature, could not at one time be published in our country (even today he is not published in full). He was excluded from educational curricula, he was made inaccessible to the reader, he was slandered. For how many years was Esenin considered a "counter-revolutionary" (and were not people imprisoned for possessing his books)? Was not Mayakovsky branded an "anarchist," a "political hooligan"? For decades the immortal poems of Akhmatova were considered to be "anti-Soviet." The first modest publication of the dazzling poetry of Tsvetaeva, which appeared about ten years ago, was declared a "crude political error." It was only after a delay of twenty or thirty years that we have been given the works of Bunin, Bulgakov, Platonov, Mandelshtam, Voloshin, Gumilev, Klyuev. "Recognition" of Zamyatin and Remizov could not be avoided. This is the decisive moment: after the death of an inconvenient writer, he is sooner or

later given back to us "with the explanation of his errors."
For a long time Pasternak's name could not be spoken
aloud. Now he is dead: now his books are published and
his poems are even quoted on ceremonial occasions.

Truly they bear witness to the truth of Pushkin's words:
"they are capable of loving only the dead."

But the late publication or the "acceptance" of a name
does not compensate at all for the social and artistic losses
suffered by our people because of these monstrous delays,
this stifling of the artistic conscience (in particular, there
were the writers of the twenties, Pilnyak, Platonov, Mandelshtam, who at a very early stage denounced the birth
of the personality cult and the characteristic traits of
Stalin, but they were annihilated, they were stifled, instead
of being listened to). Literature cannot develop between
the categories "permitted" and "not permitted," you can
write about this, you can't write about that. Literature
which does not breathe the same air as contemporary
society, which cannot communicate to it its pains and fears,
which cannot give warning in time against moral and social
dangers, does not deserve the name of literature. It deserves only the name of literary make-up. Such a literature
loses the confidence of its people. Its books do not deserve
to be read. They are nothing but printed paper.

Our literature has lost the leading position which it occupied in the world at the end of the last century and the
beginning of this; it has also lost the passion for experimen-
tation which distinguished it during the twenties. The
literature of our country appears today to all the world
as infinitely poorer, more flat and worthless than it is in
reality, than it would look if it were not being restricted,
if it were not being prevented from developing. The loser
is our country, as it is being judged by world opinion, and
world literature is also the loser. If it had before it all the
fruits of our literature, without restrictions, if it could
gain a deeper insight as a result of our spiritual experience,
the artistic evolution of the entire world would be different; it could find a new vigour and reach a new artistic
level.

I propose that the congress should demand and obtain
the abolition of all censorship—open or concealed—of
artistic works, that it should free the publishing houses of
their obligation to obtain permission from the authorities
before publishing any work.

(2) The obligations of the Union to its members. These
obligations are not clearly formulated in its statutes ("pro-

tection of rights of authorship" and "measures to protect the other rights of authors"). It is painful to have to state that for a third of a century the Union has not protected either these "other rights" or even the authorship rights of writers.

In their lifetime many writers have been exposed, in the press and from the platform, to insults and slander without having any opportunity of replying. More, they have been exposed to violence and physical persecution (Bulgakov, Akhmatova, Tsvetaeva, Pasternak, Zoshchenko, Platonov, Alexander Grin, Vasily Grossman). Not only did the Union of Writers not offer them the columns of its journals for them to reply and defend themselves; not only did it not intervene on their behalf; the board of the Union always placed itself at the head of the persecutors. Those who are an ornament of our twentieth-century poetry have been excluded from the Union, assuming they were ever admitted. More still: the board of the Union in cowardly fashion abandoned to their misfortune those whom persecution finally condemned to exile, to the concentration camp, to death (Paul Vasiliev, Mandelshtam, Artem Vesely, Pilnyak, Babel, Tabidze, Zabolotsky and others). We have had to break off the list with "and others." After the twentieth party congress we learned that there were more than six hundred writers who were guilty of no crime and whom the Union obediently left to their fate in the prisons and the camps. But the list is still longer. Our eyes have not seen, and never will see, the end of the list, for it will never be fully unrolled. It contains the names of young writers and poets of whom we learnt only by chance, thanks to personal meetings, men whose talent withered in the camps before coming to flower, men whose writings have not been rescued from the offices of the security services since the days of Yagoda, Ezhov, Beria, Abakumov.

There is no reason in history for the board of the Union now elected to share with its predecessors responsibility for the past.

I propose that paragraph 22M of the statutes of the Union should formulate clearly all the guarantees of protection that the Union affords to those of its members who are exposed to slander and to unjustified persecution, in such a way as to make a repetition of the illegalities of the past impossible.

If the congress does not remain indifferent to what I have said, I ask it to pay attention to the prohibitions and persecutions to which I have myself been subjected:

(i) My novel *The First Circle* was taken from me nearly two years ago by the State Security Service, which has prevented me from submitting it to publishers. On the other hand, against my will and even without my being informed, this novel has been "published" in a "closed" edition, to be read by a selected but unnamed few. My novel has been made accessible to literary officials, but it has been concealed from the majority of writers. I am unable to get it openly discussed in the writers' sections of the Union, and I cannot prevent its being misused or plagiarised.

(ii) At the same time as the novel, my literary archives, collected over fifteen or twenty years, papers which were not intended for publication, were confiscated. Now tendentious extracts from these archives are being distributed in "closed editions" among the same selected circle. Some verses called "The Banquet of the Victors," which I wrote and learned by heart in the camp, and in which I appear under four different numbers (when we were abandoned to death, forgotten by society, and outside the camp nobody rose to our defence), these verses which I have long left far behind me, are now being described as my most recent piece of writing.

(iii) For the last three years an irresponsible campaign of slander has been waged against me, who spent the entire war as commander of a battery and received military decorations. It is now being said that I passed the war years as a common prisoner, or that I surrendered to the enemy (I was never a prisoner of war), that I "betrayed my country," "served the Germans." That is how they explain the eleven years which I spent in the camps and in exile, where I was sent for having criticised Stalin. This slander has been spread at meetings and at closed sessions by persons holding official positions. I have tried, but in vain, to stop the slander by appealing to the Russian Writers' Union and to the press. I did not even get an answer from the Union, and no paper published my reply to the slanderers. On the contrary! Last year, the slander spread against me was reinforced, became sharper; they are using a distorted version of materials taken from my confiscated archives, and I am deprived of any possibility of replying.

(iv) My story, *The Cancer Ward* (25 folios), which was recommended for publication (first part) by the prose-writers' section of the Moscow writers' organisation, cannot be published either in separate parts (five periodicals have rejected it), nor as a whole (rejected by *Novy Mir, Zvezda,* and *Prostor*).

(v) The Sovremennik Theatre, which accepted my play called "The Stag and the Camp Prostitute" in 1962, has still not been given permission to present it.

(vi) The scenario of the film "The Tanks Know the Truth," the play "The light within you," some short stories ("The true touch," and some other short pieces) have found neither a publisher nor producer.

(vii) Those of my stories which have been published in *Novy Mir* have never appeared in book form. Everybody has refused (Soviet Writers Publishing House, State Literary Publishing House, the Ogonek Library). They remain, therefore, inaccessible to the public at large.

(viii) At the same time I have been forbidden to make any other contacts with my readers, including public readings of my works (in November 1966 nine sessions out of eleven arranged were at the last moment cancelled), and radio broadcasts. Even the simple act of giving a manuscript for "reading and copying" is now something criminal in our country (the old Russian scribes could do it without hindrance five centuries ago).

In this way my work has been strangled, it has been slain and damned.

Will the fourth congress of the Writers' Union take it upon itself to defend me against such a scurrilous attack on my rights as an author and my "other" rights? Yes or no? It seems to me that the choice to be made is not without importance for the literary future of many congress delegates.

I have a clear conscience, because I have fulfilled my duties as a writer in all circumstances and because I will fulfil them even more successfully, more indisputably, when I am dead than I can while I am still alive. Nobody can bar the road to the truth. I am ready to accept death for the sake of the movement. But how many lessons do we need to teach us that the writer's pen should not be stopped while he still lives? Never once in our history have we been able to say this is so.

III

Anatoly Kuznetsov:
*I Could No Longer Breathe**

*In August, 1969, the Soviet writer Anatoly Kuznetsov—
declaring that he had "arrived at the complete rejection of
Marxism-Leninism" and that he had "come to realize the
utter falsity, stupidity and reactionary nature of 'Socialist
realism' "—defected to the West. The author of the best-
selling documentary novel* Babi Yar *(1966) and one of
the Soviet Union's most celebrated young writers,
Kuznetsov had been a member of the Communist Party
since 1955. In 1967 he had refused Solzhenitsyn's request
that he sign the latter's controversial letter to the Writers'
Union, later explaining that he had lacked the courage
and "probably fully deserved Solzhenitsyn's contempt."*

*The following selection is Kuznetsov's explanation of
why he defected. It is a clear expression of the belief that
the ends of literature should be determined by the intellect
or conscience of the artist and freely chosen by him.*

You will say it's hard to understand. Why should a writer
whose books have sold millions of copies, and who is extremely popular and well-off in his own country, suddenly
decide not to return to that country, which, moreover, he
loves?

The loss of hope: I simply cannot live there any longer.
This feeling is something stronger than me. I just can't

*Anatoly Kuznetsov, "I Could No Longer Breathe," *Time*,
August 8, 1969, pp. 30–31. Reprinted by permission of *The Daily
Telegraph* and *Morning Post*, London, England.

go on living there. If I were now to find myself again in the Soviet Union, I should go out of my mind. If I were not a writer, I might have been able to bear it. But, since I am a writer, I can't. Writing is the only occupation in the world that seriously appeals to me. When I write, I have the illusion that there is some sort of sense in my life. Not to write is for me roughly the same as for a fish not to swim. I have been writing as long as I can remember. My first work was published twenty-five years ago.

In those twenty-five years, not a single one of my works has been printed in the Soviet Union as I wrote it. For political reasons, the Soviet censorship and the editors shorten, distort and violate my works to the point of making them completely unrecognizable. Or they do not permit them to be published at all. So long as I was young, I went on hoping for something. But the appearance of each new work of mine was not a cause for rejoicing but for sorrow. Because my writing appears in such an ugly, false and misshapen form, and I am ashamed to look people in the face. To write a good book in the Soviet Union, that is still the simplest thing to do. The real trouble begins only later, when you try to get it published. For the past ten years, I have been living in a state of constant, unavoidable and irresolvable contradiction. Finally, I have simply given up.

I wrote my last novel, *The Fire,* with no feeling left in my heart, without faith and without hope. I knew in advance for certain that, even if they published it, they would ruthlessly cut everything human out of it, and that at best it would appear as just one more "ideological" potboiler. (And that is, incidentally, exactly what happens.)

I came to the point where I could no longer write, no longer sleep, no longer breathe.

A writer is above all an artist who is trying to penetrate into the unknown. He must be honest and objective, and be able to do his creative work in freedom. These are all obvious truths. These are the very things that writers are forbidden in the Soviet Union.

Artistic freedom in the Soviet Union has been reduced to the "freedom" to praise the Soviet system and the Communist Party and to urge people to fight for Communism. The theoretical basis for this is an article that Lenin wrote sixty years ago on "The Party Organization and Party Literature," which laid it down that every writer is a propagandist for the party. His job is to receive slogans and orders from the party and make propaganda out of them.

This means that writers in Russia are faced with the following choices:

(a) Simply to go along with this idiocy—to let their brains and their consciences have no effect on their actions. If Stalin is on top, then praise Stalin. If they order people to plant maize, then write about maize. If they decide to expose Stalin's crimes, then expose Stalin. And when they stop criticizing him, you stop too. There are so very many Soviet "writers" who are just like that.

But real life will not forgive a man who violates his conscience. Those writers have all become such cynics and spiritual cripples and their hidden regret for their wasted talent eats away at them to such an extent that their wretched existence cannot be called life but rather a caricature of life. It would probably be difficult to think up a worse punishment for oneself than to have to spend one's whole life trembling, cringing, trying fearfully to get the sense of the latest order and fearing to make the slightest mistake. Oh, God!

(b) To write properly, as their ability and consciences dictate.

It is then 100-to-1 that what they write will not be published. It will simply be buried. It may even be the cause of the author's physical destruction. It is a sad thought that Russia has long and deep "traditions" in this connection. The best Russian writers were always persecuted, dragged before the courts, murdered or reduced to suicide.

(c) To try and write honestly "as far as possible." To choose subjects that are not dangerous. To write in allegories. To seek out cracks in the censorship. To circulate your works from hand to hand in manuscript form. To do at least something: a sort of compromise solution. I was one of those who chose this third way. But it didn't work for me. The censors always managed to bring me to my knees. My anxiety to save at least something from what I had written, so that something would reach the reader, meant only that in the end all my published writings were neither genuine literature nor utterly contemptible but something in between.

However much I protested or tried to prove some point, it was like beating my head against a wall. Literature in the Soviet Union is controlled by people who are ignorant, cynical, and themselves very remote from literature. But they are people with excellent knowledge of the latest instructions from the men at the top of the prevailing Party dogmas. I could not force my way through their ranks. [Evgeny] Evtushenko managed to achieve a little in this way. [Alexander] Solzhenitsyn managed a little more, but even that is all over now. The cracks were noticed and cemented up. Russian writers go on writing and keep hoping for something. It is a nightmare.

My mania: So for a quarter of a century I went on dreaming about a happy state of affairs, which is unthinkable for a Soviet writer—to be able to write and publish his writings without restriction and without fear. Not to choke off his own song. To have no thought for party instructions, government-appointed editors and political censors. Not to start trembling at every knock on the door. Not to be hiding his manuscripts away in a hole in the ground almost before the ink on them is dry.

Oh, the number of holes I have dug in the ground to conceal my jam jars full of "dangerous" and "doubtful" manuscripts. I couldn't keep them in my desk because whenever I wasn't there my flat could be broken into and searched and my manuscripts confiscated, as happened with Solzhenitsyn and many others. My writing desk, in fact, had no drawers at all. The Russian earth itself served as my desk and my safe. It became a real mania for me to be able to see my writing published in the form in which I had written it. I wanted to see it just once, and then they could do what they liked with me. Yes, in that sense I was a sick man, I was a maniac.

As a boy I saw books being burned in Russia in 1937, under Stalin. I saw books being burned in 1942 in occupied Kiev, under Hitler, and now it has pleased God to let me know in my lifetime that my own books are being burned. Because now that I have left the Soviet Union, my books will, of course, be destroyed there too. In fact, I pray that my published works should be destroyed down to the very last one. Since they are not what I actually wrote and wanted to say to my readers, that means, after all, that they are not my books! I disassociate myself from them.

And so: I hereby, publicly and definitively, disassociate myself from everything that has been published under the name of "Kuznetsov" in the USSR or has appeared in translation from Soviet editions in other countries of the world. I solemnly declare that Kuznetsov is a dishonest, conformist, cowardly author. I renounce this name. I want to be, at last, an honest man and an honest writer. All my writings published from this day onward will bear the signature "A. Anatol." I request you to regard only such works as being mine.

What do I hope for? In recent years I have, from time to time, locked securely in my room, permitted myself a treat: I wrote as I pleased. It was a painful and unusual experience. It was as if, in a world where everybody went on all fours, somebody, shut in a cellar, had stood up and walked upright.

Then for some months, I dug my manuscripts up from their hiding places in the ground, photographed them and buried them again. I have succeeded in bringing those films across the frontier with me—thousands of pages on film, everything I have ever written in my life. They include my known works, such as *Babi Yar*, but in its true form. They also include things that could not be published in Russia. And some that I doubt whether I shall be able to publish in the West.

But now I have hope, at least. In any case, these are not the words of Kuznetsov but of a quite different author. Not a Soviet author and not a Western author, not a Red one and not a White one, but just an author living in this twentieth century on this earth. And what is more, a writer who has made a desperate effort to be in this century, an honest writer who wants to associate himself with those who strive for humanity in the present wild, wild, wild life of this mad, mad world.

25.

Malcolm Boyd:

Rejecting a Middle-Class

Christianity*

Today's heretics are tomorrow's saints.—Harvey
Cox, *Playboy*, January, 1967

GOD IS DEAD. At least *a* god is dead. The white
god, the nationalistic American god, he's dead,
dead, dead. Goddamn it! *Dead!*—Malcolm Boyd,
Playboy, April, 1967

*Since the beginning of the 1960's, Christianity has been
in the first stages of a new reformation. Both in America
and abroad, churches have plunged into a tempest of
liturgical experiment, theological innovation, and social
activism. Rejecting the view that the church must concern
itself with inner rectitude and man's relation to God, an
increasing number of "pro-world" Christians are calling
upon the church to address itself to rampant social abuses.*

*In the forefront of such new-breed Christians is Malcolm
Boyd (1923–   ), an Episcopal priest, Freedom Rider,
playwright, and film critic who left a successful career in
advertising and television to become one of the best-
known religious figures of this generation. For Boyd, God is
neither "an upper-middle-class snob in a private 'holy of
holies'" nor "an impersonal I.B.M. machine computing
petty sins in some celestial office building above the*

*From *Free to Live, Free to Die* by Malcolm Boyd, pp. 18–20, 30,
33–34, 54–57, 73, 82–83. Copyright © 1967 by Malcolm Boyd.
Reprinted by permission of Holt, Rinehart and Winston, Inc.

clouds."¹ *God is attainable. He may be encountered in the
complexity of everyday life in the world—in gay bars and
slums as well as in churches.*

*Though denounced by conservative Episcopalians, the
appeal of Boyd's contemporary approach to religion became apparent when a collection of his "pop prayers,"*
Are You Running With Me, Jesus? *(1965), made the best-
seller lists. The selections which follow are from his* Free
to Live, Free to Die, *a book couched in the style of
"secular meditations." They should be read in the context
of their outspoken author's conviction that "the Church
should get off its ass."²*

"God spelled backward," the young man reminded me,
"spells dog." He was twenty-one, Negro, wearing a T-shirt
and levis, and had not finished high school. He spoke to
me in the Watts ghetto area of Los Angeles, where rioting
had occurred just a few hours earlier.

"You wet a white man's hair and a dog's, and it smells
the same way. A black man's wet hair doesn't smell that
way. I've seen whites treat a dog better than me. A white
man would sleep with a dog. I wouldn't. I wouldn't even
allow my dog in my house. So I identify a white man with
a dog. Then whites speak to me of their *culture*.

"I really don't hate the white man. I just want the Man
to leave me alone. Just back up and keep his distance. I
used to sit in school every day. A man there tells me
Christopher Columbus discovered the new world. Another
man says an Italian cat whose name began with V did it.
I don't know why the white man keeps confusing me.
Blacks have been here for a long time. I want to hear
something about *me*. But I can't find out.

"You come to a man and try to tell him, over and over,
but he never listens. Why, the Man has always been kill-

¹Malcolm Boyd, *Are You Running With Me, Jesus?* (New York:
Holt, Rinehart and Winston, 1965), p. 5.
²As quoted in *Playboy*, Vol. XIV, No. 4 (April, 1967), p. 154.

ing. He first drove the Indians out. Now *my* arm's almost been bit off. I've got to bite back. The riot? There'll be more of the same until the Man opens up his eyes and says, 'We're going to give it to you because we're tired.'

"A few whites I'll let to get know me. I know some whites who are okay. Others I can't have anything to do with. There's one white guy I knew at school—he *could* be a soul brother if he was black. I don't know any middle-class Negroes. Pride makes you rich. Material things don't matter. If a Negro is dressed well, the white man thinks, 'That's one of those niggers who did all right.' So I never dress well.

"We just found out the white man has been killing the colored man with those birth control pills. He gave us birth control pills, but he gave *his* women hormones so they could have quintuplets. The white man is trying to get rid of Indians *and* black men. If the white man doesn't like me because of the color of my skin, why this Man-Tan? If the police chief considers us monkeys, why do his men proposition Negro women? The Beatles' haircut is long like ours used to be, so now we cut ours short. They try to get on the band wagon and be like us. They try to sing like us. Everything we do, we do good. The black man is just great. Cassius Clay proved that.

"A community organization might be all right here. Not preachers or Toms or soul-saving sisters. The answer is the young black man. The old man can't help right now. No, we're not organized. You don't find a rat until you throw a piece of cheese out there. Then everybody's on the scene. My idol was Malcolm X. When he died I knew a brother was gone. But I didn't cry for him. If my mother fell down and died, I couldn't feel anything. I've got no tears for nobody.

"The police beat me on the head after they handcuffed my hands. I know hate isn't going to do any good. But I'm not going to love a white. Nobody can define love to me. I might want to make love to a white, but I can't love a white. And I'm tired of hearing that old thing about the good old Jesus Christ, how he walks on water, with his blue eyes and blond hair. The cross is a sign of death, that's all there is to it. Jesus Christ hung from it. The church people, with their Book, do you think they're going to tell me what's right and wrong? I want them to leave me alone. Preachers don't make sense. The Bible says, "Do unto others as you would have them do unto you.' So?" ...

. . . The young man is going to war. He doesn't want to lose either precious time *or* his life, yet he's anxious now to get into the damned uniform and fight. He feels it's his duty.

He asks himself, "What does war mean?" Or, "*Why* is war?" It seems to him that it is madness, murder, pain, and the denial of love.

A clergyman is saying a prayer over him and three other young men who are going overseas with him.

"O holy God, bless these our young men who are about to go forth into battle. Strengthen them for victory over the enemy as they prepare to render service to Thee and Thy Kingdom. O God, preserve our nation and our way of life, execute this war according to Thy holy purpose, and give us victory, through Jesus Christ our Savior. Amen."

He listens to the words but is unable to pray them. . . .

COLLECT TO THE GOD WHO IS DEAD

It was great knowing you all those years, even when I realized you were no longer around. Then it became somehow more comforting than ever before, in a strange, crazy way.

I'm not sure what "worship" means. But I worshiped you once. I was quite sincere about it. I was afraid of you at times. I actually thought you might strike me dead on occasion, or throw a fiery thunderbolt at my feet if I committed one indiscretion or another. Then, when I found I was still alive and that you hadn't killed me off or maimed me for life, I realized how indulgently kind you were. I couldn't exactly pull the wool over your eyes, but I could play games with you. I could go to church for one hour a week and have you on my side. If I really got frightened and was altogether sincere, you would heal my sore throat so I could go to work. If I prayed hard enough —more time on my knees—you would even turn me into the sort of person I thought I wished to become.

Well, it's over, isn't it? You're not here and I still am. But, needless to say, I miss you. It was great having a god on my side. . . .

ONCE UPON A TIME A CHURCH
OPENED A COFFEE HOUSE

Once upon a time a church made up its mind to open a coffee house, to be located in a bohemian section of the city, many miles away from the church building itself. The congregation felt it was time to be daring and avantgarde. In fact, the evening newspaper congratulated them for it on the church page.

Church board members were generally rather enthusiastic. They believed church-operated coffee houses would keep young people out of non-church-operated coffee houses, and, at the same time, the church would show its involvement with the real world. At least, that was the majority argument at the decisive board meeting.

A discreet censorship, it was felt, could be placed on all dramatic and musical material to be used in the place. Toned-down profanity of the Theater of the Absurd might be used without scandal, but it was understood from the outset that folk songs would have to be substituted for hymns.

"There will be conversions," one church board member had said at a morning meeting over coffee and doughnuts. "Jesus himself mixed with winebibbers and publicans."

The name of the coffee house had to be both biblical and interesting to secularists. It was decided, after considerable discussion, to call it "The Scapegoat." A gold sign, with a goat drawn on it in deep red, was placed outside. Some advertisements were placed in student, beatnik, and civil rights publications, but they avoided any explicit reference to Christianity, and utilized a galloping italic type copied from a French film ad in a recent Sunday *Times*.

The site of the coffee house was a converted bar, though the house itself had served a number of different purposes. It was in a neighborhood where many students wore beards, interracial couples could be seen on the street, and what one church official described as "queer people of all stripes" hung out.

Although expensive, a real espresso coffee machine was mandatory. People could be served espresso coffee, cappuccino, cider, tea, a slightly more expensive punch made with a fruit-juice base, sweet rolls, and sandwiches. But all this was just a subterfuge: what the place was really serving was *dialogue*.

There would be folk singing, with an emphasis on the very fashionable freedom songs. In fact, a couple of talented folk singers would be lured away from a non-church-operated coffee house to provide the desired musical setting. Lighting would be romantic but in the brusque, acceptable fashion: candlelight would pick up the strong beam of the wood on the ceiling and the old bar.

Publicity posed problems, but it was recognized that "The Scapegoat" must do something rather special to attract people. Finally, a terse, succinct press release was okayed by the board and sent to all local publications:

We want dialogue with YOU. We are *trying* to be Christians. Do you know who YOU are? We are all bound together by the crucial problem of identity.

We invite you to share the existential journey (within the pilgrimage of being) with us at "The Scapegoat." There will be coffee, ideas, and ourselves. We are motivated by no idea of religious paternalism, but seek only a genuine I-thou encounter. Be with us next Thursday night to help us create the spirit of agape as we open our new Christian coffee house.

Well, the opening night finally arrived. Even some church board members came, having decided to mingle unobtrusively with whatever crowd might be coming.

A graduate student wearing a beard (he was white) was photographed with a white ex-Freedom Rider and a Negro woman social worker for the front page of the big-circulation Sunday edition of the most important paper. This took care of all p.r. problems; the place was "in" for the outs who were "in."

In fact, the success of "The Scapegoat" surprised even its strongest early advocates. Six months later it was moved to much larger quarters in the basement of the church building; the church board was delighted that it had learned to *listen* to the world, and stated that a coffee house is a "must" for today's evangelism.

Some of the younger business executives in the congregation started wearing beards, hymns were substituted for folk songs, New Testament readings began to be favored over one-act plays, and twenty-three conversions were specifically credited to "The Scapegoat."

One Sunday evening, after prayers, the coffee house in

the church basement was renamed. One of the clergy described it as being "like a dramatic baptism of our very culture." From then on "The Scapegoat" was officially called "Lazarus' Tomb." . . .

LITANY TO THE BITCH GODDESS

O Thou who art truly god,
Bestow upon us success.
O Thou who dost oversee the affairs of men and nations, and dost manipulate all things for good, and dost hold the reins of the hearts of all, male and female, black and white, rich and poor,
Bestow upon us success.
O Thou who art most truly beneficent, and the reward of all who are faithful to Thee, grant unto us such devotion and obedience that we may follow in Thy footsteps all the days and nights of our lives,
Bestow upon us success.
O Thou who art all-merciful, accept the sacrifice of our loved ones, especially those who are dearest and nearest to us, when two or three of us are gathered together, and show that you are mindful of the ancient covenant between us by granting us our deepest desires.
Bestow upon us success.
In the name of Applause, Happy Smiles, and the Dollar. Amen. . . .

. . . Saint or slut—it depends on who you're talking to. She is almost oblivious to both judgments made about her.

Middle class in background, educated in the right schools, she is now living among the poor, sharing their life without reservation. Nothing she could have done would have so outraged her former friends and associates.

Because it isn't "charity" but something real. The paternalism is out of it, the risks in. She hasn't time to daydream about the privileges and luxuries she's left behind. She isn't just putting in hours of "doing good" so that she can go back to the party with the proper righteousness. It's not just that she no longer has a hairdresser; she's gone over to the other side.

Some of her former friends accuse her of sleeping around with workingmen in the neighborhood. Others say she's become a fanatic; after all, she looks terrible, and a person has a duty to eat and keep well. They express concern for her future: What will she *do?* What will become of her?

What would make her do it? She doesn't go to church, says she hasn't gone for months, and that it's hopelessly middle class. Is she just getting back at her father? Wouldn't it have been more sensible to have gotten some government job and done something *effective?* What can she hope to change by doing this?

Perhaps there is something romantic or unhealthy in her decision, but over a bowl of soup at the corner lunch counter she seems quite calm. Tired perhaps, could use some make-up, but she doesn't look unwell. And despite the depressing stories she has of the conditions in which people are living all around her, how is it that she conveys such a sense of hope? Is it something she brought to the neighborhood, or something she found here?

26.

Ayn Rand:

Altruism Condemned*

I swear, by my life—and my love of it—that I will
never live for the sake of another man, nor ask
another man to live for mine.

—John Galt in *Atlas Shrugged*

*There are few contemporary novelists more controversial
than Ayn Rand (1905–   ), author of* The Fountainhead
and Atlas Shrugged. *Acclaimed by her admirers as a brilliant, original, systematic thinker, she is violently attacked
by her opponents.*

*Miss Rand's detractors rarely attack her talent as a
writer. Even the most bitter among them usually balk at
denying the compelling narrative power of her novels. What
they object to is not Ayn Rand the writer, but Ayn Rand
the Objectivist, the champion of rational self-interest and
the unqualified enemy of altruism and self-sacrifice.*

*Objectivism, her philosophy, holds that reason is man's
basic means of survival and his only means of acquiring
knowledge. It holds that man must be guided by a rational,
objectively defined code of morality, whose standard is:
man's life—i.e., that which is required by man's nature for
his survival as a rational being. It holds that the only moral
social system is laissez-faire capitalism, which is based on
the recognition of individual rights, and that the only proper function of the government is the protection of these*

*Ayn Rand, *Atlas Shrugged* (New York: Random House, 1957),
pp. 410–15, 476–77, 478, 479–81.

rights, i.e., the protection of the individual from those who initiate the use of physical force.

The selections which follow are from Miss Rand's philosophic novel *Atlas Shrugged*. This flawlessly written work depicts what happens to the world when the men of the mind—the men of creative ability, the thinkers and producers: the industrialists, the inventors, the artists—go on strike against a collectivist-altruist society.

"So you think that money is the root of all evil?" said Francisco d'Anconia. "Have you ever asked what is the root of money? Money is a tool of exchange, which can't exist unless there are goods produced and men able to produce them. Money is the material shape of the principle that men who wish to deal with one another must deal by trade and give value for value. Money is not the tool of the moochers, who claim your product by tears, or of the looters, who take it from you by force. Money is made possible only by the men who produce. Is this what you consider evil?

"When you accept money in payment for your effort, you do so only on the conviction that you will exchange it for the product of the effort of others. It is not the moochers or the looters who give value to money. Not an ocean of tears nor all the guns in the world can transform those pieces of paper in your wallet into the bread you will need to survive tomorrow. Those pieces of paper, which should have been gold, are a token of honor—your claim upon the energy of the men who produce. Your wallet is your statement of hope that somewhere in the world around you there are men who will not default on that moral principle which is the root of money. Is this what you consider evil?

"Have you ever looked for the root of production? Take a look at an electric generator and dare tell yourself that it was created by the muscular effort of unthinking brutes. Try to grow a seed of wheat without the knowledge left to you by men who had to discover it for the first time. Try to obtain your food by means of nothing but physical motions—and you'll learn that man's mind is the root of all the goods produced and of all the wealth that has ever existed on earth.

"But you say that money is made by the strong at the expense of the weak? What strength do you mean? It is not the strength of guns or muscles. Wealth is the product of man's capacity to think. Then is money made by the man who invents a motor at the expense of those who did not invent it? Is money made by the intelligent at the expense of the fools? By the able at the expense of the incompetent? By the ambitious at the expense of the lazy? Money is *made*—before it can be looted or mooched—made by the effort of every honest man, each to the extent of his ability. An honest man is one who knows that he can't consume more than he has produced.

"To trade by means of money is the code of the men of good will. Money rests on the axiom that every man is the owner of his mind and his effort. Money allows no power to prescribe the value of your effort except the voluntary choice of the man who is willing to trade you his effort in return. Money permits you to obtain for your goods and your labor that which they are worth to the men who buy them, but no more. Money permits no deals except those to mutual benefit by the unforced judgment of the traders. Money demands of you the recognition that men must work for their own benefit, not for their own injury, for their gain, not their loss—the recognition that they are not beasts of burden, born to carry the weight of your misery—that you must offer them values, not wounds—that the common bond among men is not the exchange of suffering, but the exchange of *goods*. Money demands that you sell, not your weakness to men's stupidity, but your talent to their reason; it demands that you buy, not the shoddiest they offer, but the best that your money can find. And when men live by trade—with reason, not force, as their final arbiter—it is the best product that wins, the best performance, the man of best judgment and highest ability—and the degree of a man's productiveness is the degree of his reward. This is the code of existence whose tool and symbol is money. Is this what you consider evil?

"But money is only a tool. It will take you wherever you wish, but it will not replace you as the driver. It will give you the means for the satisfaction of your desires, but it will not provide you with desires. Money is the scourge

of the men who attempt to reverse the law of causality—
the men who seek to replace the mind by seizing the
products of the mind.

"Money will not purchase happiness for the man who
has no concept of what he wants: money will not give
him a code of values, if he's evaded the knowledge of what
to value, and it will not provide him with a purpose, if
he's evaded the choice of what to seek. Money will not buy
intelligence for the fool, or admiration for the coward,
or respect for the incompetent. The man who attempts to
purchase the brains of his superiors to serve him, with
his money replacing his judgment, ends up by becoming
the victim of his inferiors. The men of intelligence desert
him, but the cheats and the frauds come flocking to him,
drawn by a law which he has not discovered: that no
man may be smaller than his money. Is this the reason
why you call it evil?

"Only the man who does not need it, is fit to inherit
wealth—the man who would make his own fortune no
matter where he started. If an heir is equal to his money,
it serves him; if not, it destroys him. But you look on and
you cry that money corrupted him. Did it? Or did he
corrupt his money? Do not envy a worthless heir; his
wealth is not yours and you would have done no better with
it. Do not think that it should have been distributed among
you; loading the world with fifty parasites instead of one,
would not bring back the dead virtue which was the
fortune. Money is a living power that dies without its root.
Money will not serve the mind that cannot match it. Is
this the reason why you call it evil?

"Money is your means of survival. The verdict you pronounce upon the source of your livelihood is the verdict
you pronounce upon your life. If the source is corrupt,
you have damned your own existence. Did you get your
money by fraud? By pandering to men's vices or men's
stupidity? By catering to fools, in the hope of getting more
than your ability deserves? By lowering your standards?
By doing work you despise for purchasers you scorn? If so,
then your money will not give you a moment's or a penny's
worth of joy. Then all the things you buy will become,
not a tribute to you, but a reproach; not an achievement,
but a reminder of shame. Then you'll scream that money
is evil. Evil, because it would not pinch-hit for your self-
respect? Evil, because it would not let you enjoy your
depravity? Is this the root of your hatred of money?

"Money will always remain an effect and refuse to replace you as the cause. Money is the product of virtue, but it will not give you virtue and it will not redeem your vices. Money will not give you the unearned, neither in matter nor in spirit. Is this the root of your hatred of money?

"Or did you say it's the *love* of money that's the root of all evil? To love a thing is to know and love its nature. To love money is to know and love the fact that money is the creation of the best power within you, and your pass-key to trade your effort for the effort of the best among men. It's the person who would sell his soul for a nickel, who is loudest in proclaiming his hatred of money—and he has good reason to hate it. The lovers of money are willing to work for it. They know they are able to deserve it.

"Let me give you a tip on a clue to men's characters: the man who damns money has obtained it dishonorably; the man who respects it has earned it.

"Run for your life from any man who tells you that money is evil. That sentence is the leper's bell of an approaching looter. So long as men live together on earth and need means to deal with one another—their only substitute, if they abandon money, is the muzzle of a gun.

"But money demands of you the highest virtues, if you wish to make it or to keep it. Men who have no courage, pride or self-esteem, men who have no moral sense of their right to their money and are not willing to defend it as they defend their life, men who apologize for being rich—will not remain rich for long. They are the natural bait for the swarms of looters that stay under rocks for centuries, but come crawling out at the first smell of a man who begs to be forgiven for the guilt of owning wealth. They will hasten to relieve him of the guilt—and of his life, as he deserves.

"Then you will see the rise of the men of the double standard—the men who live by force, yet count on those who live by trade to create the value of their looted money—the men who are the hitchhikers of virtue. In a moral society, these are the criminals, and the statutes are written to protect you against them. But when a society establishes criminals-by-right and looters-by-law—men who use force to seize the wealth of *disarmed* victims—then money becomes its creators' avenger. Such looters believe it safe to rob defenseless men, once they've passed a law to disarm them. But their loot becomes the magnet for other looters, who get it from them as they got it. Then the race goes, not to the ablest at production, but to those most ruthless at brutality. When force is the standard, the murderer wins over the pickpocket. And then that society vanishes, in a spread of ruins and slaughter.

"Do you wish to know whether that day is coming? Watch money. Money is the barometer of a society's virtue. When you see that trading is done, not by consent, but by compulsion—when you see that in order to produce, you need to obtain permission from men who produce nothing —when you see that money is flowing to those who deal, not in goods, but in favors—when you see that men get richer by graft and by pull than by work, and your laws don't protect you against them, but protect them against you—when you see corruption being rewarded and honesty becoming a self-sacrifice—you may know that your society is doomed. Money is so noble a medium that it does not compete with guns and it does not make terms with brutality. It will not permit a country to survive as half-property, half-loot.

"Whenever destroyers appear among men, they start by destroying money, for money is men's protection and the base of a moral existence. Destroyers seize gold and leave to its owners a counterfeit pile of paper. This kills all objective standards and delivers men into the arbitrary power of an arbitrary setter of values. Gold was an objective value, an equivalent of wealth produced. Paper is a mortgage on wealth that does not exist, backed by a gun aimed at those who are expected to produce it. Paper is a check drawn by legal looters upon an account which is not theirs: upon the virtue of the victims. Watch for the day when it bounces, marked: 'Account overdrawn.'

"When you have made evil the means of survival, do not expect men to remain good. Do not expect them to stay moral and lose their lives for the purpose of becoming the fodder of the immoral. Do not expect them to produce, when production is punished and looting rewarded. Do not ask, 'Who is destroying the world?' You are.

"You stand in the midst of the greatest achievements of the greatest productive civilization and you wonder why it's crumbling around you, while you're damning its life-blood—money. You look upon money as the savages did before you, and you wonder why the jungle is creeping back to the edge of your cities. Throughout men's history, money was always seized by looters of one brand or another, whose names changed, but whose method remained the same: to seize wealth by force and to keep the producers bound, demeaned, defamed, deprived of honor. That phrase about the evil of money, which you mouth with such righteous recklessness, comes from a time when wealth was produced by the labor of slaves—slaves who repeated the motions once discovered by somebody's mind and left unimproved for centuries. So long as production was ruled by force, and wealth was obtained by conquest, there was little to conquer. Yet through all the centuries of stagnation and starvation, men exalted the looters, as aristocrats of the sword, as aristocrats of birth, as aristocrats of the bureau, and despised the producers, as slaves, as traders, as shopkeepers—as industrialists.

"To the glory of mankind, there was, for the first and only time in history, a *country of money*—and I have no higher, more reverent tribute to pay to America, for this means: a country of reason, justice, freedom, production, achievement. For the first time, man's mind and money were set free, and there were no fortunes-by-conquest, but only fortunes-by-work, and instead of swordsmen and slaves, there appeared the real maker of wealth, the greatest worker, the highest type of human being—the self-made man—the American industrialist.

"If you ask me to name the proudest distinction of Americans, I would choose—because it contains all the others—the fact that they were the people who created the phrase 'to make money.' No other language or nation had ever used these words before; men had always thought of wealth as a static quantity—to be seized, begged, inherited, shared, looted or obtained as a favor. Americans were the first to understand that wealth has to be created. The words 'to make money' hold the essence of human morality.

"Yet these were the words for which Americans were denounced by the rotted cultures of the looters' continents. Now the looters' credo has brought you to regard your proudest achievements as a hallmark of shame, your prosperity as guilt, your greatest men, the industrialists, as blackguards, and your magnificent factories as the product and property of muscular labor, the labor of whip-driven slaves, like the pyramids of Egypt. The rotter who simpers that he sees no difference between the power of the dollar and the power of the whip, ought to learn the difference on his own hide—as, I think, he will.

"Until and unless you discover that money is the root of all good, you ask for your own destruction. When money ceases to be the tool by which men deal with one another, then men become the tools of men. Blood, whips and guns—or dollars. Take your choice—there is no other—and your time is running out." . . .

. . . The newspapers had snarled that the cause of the country's troubles, as this case demonstrated, was the selfish greed of rich industrialists; that it was men like Hank Rearden who were to blame for the shrinking diet, the falling temperature and the cracking roofs in the homes of the nation; that if it had not been for men who broke regulations and hampered the government's plans, prosperity would have been achieved long ago; and that a man like Hank Rearden was prompted by nothing but the profit motive. This last was stated without explanation or elaboration, as if the words "profit motive" were the self-evident brand of ultimate evil.

The crowd remembered that these same newspapers, less than two years ago, had screamed that the production of Rearden Metal should be forbidden, because its producer was endangering people's lives for the sake of his greed; they remembered that the man in gray had ridden in the cab of the first engine to run over a track of his own Metal; and that he was now on trial for the greedy crime of withholding from the public a load of the Metal which it had been his greedy crime to offer in the public market.

According to the procedure established by directives, cases of this kind were not tried by a jury, but by a panel of three judges appointed by the Bureau of Economic Planning and National Resources; the procedure, the directives had stated, was to be informal and democratic. The judge's bench had been removed from the old Philadelphia courtroom for this occasion, and replaced by a table on a wooden platform; it gave the room an atmosphere suggesting the kind of meeting where a presiding body puts something over on a mentally retarded membership.

One of the judges, acting as prosecutor, had read the charges. "You may now offer whatever plea you wish to make in your own defense," he announced.

Facing the platform, his voice inflectionless and peculiarly clear, Hank Rearden answered:

"I have no defense."

"Do you—" The judge stumbled; he had not expected it to be that easy. "Do you throw yourself upon the mercy of this court?"

"I do not recognize this court's right to try me."

"What?"

"I do not recognize this court's right to try me."

"But, Mr. Rearden, this is the legally appointed court to try this particular category of crime."

"I do not recognize my action as a crime."

"But you have admitted that you have broken our regulations controlling the sale of your Metal."

"I do not recognize your right to control the sale of my Metal."

"Is it necessary for me to point out that your recognition was not required?"

"No. I am fully aware of it and I am acting accordingly."

He noted the stillness of the room. By the rules of the complicated pretense which all those people played for one another's benefit, they should have considered his stand as incomprehensible folly; there should have been rustles of astonishment and derision; there were none; they sat still; they understood.

"Do you mean that you are refusing to obey the law?" asked the judge.

"No. I am complying with the law—to the letter. Your law holds that my life, my work and my property may be disposed of without my consent. Very well, you may now dispose of me without my participation in the matter. I will not play the part of defending myself, where no defense is possible, and I will not simulate the illusion of dealing with a tribunal of justice."

"But, Mr. Rearden, the law provides specifically that you are to be given an opportunity to present your side of the case and to defend yourself."

"A prisoner brought to trial can defend himself only if there is an objective principle of justice recognized by his judges, a principle upholding his rights, which they may not violate and which he can invoke. The law, by which you are trying me, holds that there are no principles, that I have no rights and that you may do with me whatever you please. Very well. Do it."

"Mr. Rearden, the law which you are denouncing is based on the highest principle—the principle of the public good."

"Who is the public? What does it hold as its good? There was a time when men believed that 'the good' was a concept to be defined by a code of moral values and that no man had the right to seek his good through the violation of the rights of another. If it is now believed that my fellow men may sacrifice me in any manner they please for the sake of whatever they deem to be their own good, if they believe that they may seize my property simply because they need it—well, so does any burglar. There is only this difference: the burglar does not ask me to sanction his act." . . .

. . . "Are we to understand," asked the judge, "that you hold your own interests above the interests of the public?"

"I hold that such a question can never arise except in a society of cannibals."

"What . . . what do you mean?"

"I hold that there is no clash of interests among men who do not demand the unearned and do not practice human sacrifices."

"Are we to understand that if the public deems it necessary to curtail your profits, you do not recognize its right to do so?"

"Why, yes, I do. The public may curtail my profits any time it wishes—by refusing to buy my product." . . .

. . . The eldest judge leaned forward across the table and his voice became suavely derisive: "You speak as if you were fighting for some sort of principle, Mr. Rearden, but what you're actually fighting for is only your property, isn't it?"

"Yes, of course. I am fighting for my property. Do you know the kind of principle *that* represents?"

"You pose as a champion of freedom, but it's only the freedom to make money that you're after."

"Yes, of course. All I want is the freedom to make money. Do you know what that freedom implies?"

"Surely, Mr. Rearden, you wouldn't want your attitude to be misunderstood. You wouldn't want to give support to the widespread impression that you are a man devoid of social conscience, who feels no concern for the welfare of his fellows and works for nothing but his own profit."

"I work for nothing but my own profit. I earn it."

There was a gasp, not of indignation, but of astonishment, in the crowd behind him and silence from the judges he faced. He went on calmly:

"No, I do not want my attitude to be misunderstood. I shall be glad to state it for the record. I am in full agreement with the facts of everything said about me in the newspapers—with the facts, but not with the evaluation. I work for nothing but my own profit—which I make by selling a product they need to men who are willing and able to buy it. I do not produce it for their benefit at the expense of mine, and they do not buy it for my benefit at the expense of theirs; I do not sacrifice my interests to them nor do they sacrifice theirs to me; we deal as equals by mutual consent to mutual advantage—and I am proud of every penny that I have earned in this manner. I am rich and I am proud of every penny I own. I have made my money by my own effort, in free exchange and through the voluntary consent of every man I dealt with—the voluntary consent of those who employed me when I started, the voluntary consent of those who work for me now, the voluntary consent of those who buy my product. I shall answer all the questions you are afraid to ask me openly. Do I wish to pay my workers more than their services are worth to me? I do not. Do I wish to sell my product for less than my customers are willing to pay me? I do not. Do I wish to sell it at a loss or give it away? I do not. If this is evil, do whatever you please about me, according to whatever standards you hold. These are mine. I am earning my own living, as every honest man must. I refuse to accept as guilt the fact of my own existence and the fact that I must work in order to support it. I refuse to accept as guilt the fact that I am able to do it and to do it well. I refuse to accept as guilt the fact that I am able to do it better than most people—the fact that my work is of greater value than the work of my neighbors and that more men are willing to pay me. I refuse to apologize for my ability—I refuse to apologize for my success—I refuse to apologize for my money. If this is evil, make the most of it. If this is what the public finds harmful to its interests, let the public destroy me. This is my code—and I will accept no other. I could say to you that I have done more good for my fellow men than you can ever hope to accomplish—but I will not say it, because I do not seek the good of others as a sanction for my right to exist, nor do I recognize the good of others as a justification for their seizure of my property or their destruction of my life. I will not say that the good of others was the purpose of my work—my own good was my purpose, and I despise the man who surrenders his. I could say to you that you do not serve the public good—that nobody's good can be achieved at the price of human sacrifices—that when you violate the rights of one man, you have violated the rights of all, and a public of rightless creatures is doomed to destruction. I could say to you that you will and can achieve nothing but universal devastation—as any looter must, when he runs out of victims. I could say it, but I won't. It is not your particular policy that I challenge, but your moral premise. If it were true that men could achieve their good by means of turning some men into sacrificial animals, and I were asked to immolate myself for the sake of creatures who wanted to survive at the price of my blood, if I were asked to serve the interests of society apart from, above and against my own—I would refuse, I would reject it as the most contemptible evil, I would fight it with every power I possess, I would fight the whole of mankind, if one minute were all I could last before I were murdered, I would fight in the full confidence of the justice of my battle and of a living being's right to exist. Let there be no misunderstanding about me. If it is now the belief of my fellow men, who call themselves the public, that their good requires victims, then I say: The public good be damned, I will have no part of it!"

27.

Milton Friedman:
Dissent in a Mixed Economy*

The greatest challenge to the theory and practice of Keynesian economics has come from the "Chicago School," a group of economists who declaim the views of Milton Friedman (1912–   ), a professor of economics at the University of Chicago. Most economists still follow the teachings of Britain's late John Maynard Keynes, who stressed how changes in taxation and government spending can stabilize business cycles and claimed that it was his intention to preserve capitalism by regulating it. Friedman's maverick role has been one of attacking Keynesianism on two fronts: It has not produced the desired results in either stability for the economy or healthy economic growth, and it has diminished essential individual liberty which a free capitalist society alone can offer.

For the past four decades Friedman has had a distinguished career in teaching, research, and writing (fourteen books) in both mathematics and economics. Though he possesses a special talent for abstract and analytical thought, his basic philosophy is simple and unoriginal: personal freedom is the supreme good—in economic, political, and social relations—and most forms of governmental activity infringe on that freedom. Friedman's consistency in applying this formula to all problems renders him a dissenter whose views, depending on the issue, alternately delight and infuriate conservatives, New Left radicals, and groups holding a middle ground. He attacks such things as the regulation of television, the New York Stock Exchange, the

*Milton Friedman, *Capitalism and Freedom* (Chicago: University of Chicago Press, 1962), pp. 7–21. Copyright 1962 by The University of Chicago. Reprinted by permission.

public school system, and the Selective Service System with equal vigor. All repress individual freedom while benefiting the vested interests of unproductive bureaucracy.

In the selection which follows Friedman draws upon historical lessons and makes judgments about capitalism and freedom in an attempt to demonstrate that, like socialism and fascism, a mixed economy, even in a democratic society, is dangerous to human freedom. The reader is encouraged to compare Friedman's views with those advanced by Ayn Rand in the previous selection.

It is widely believed that politics and economics are separate and largely unconnected; that individual freedom is a political problem and material welfare an economic problem; and that any kind of political arrangements can be combined with any kind of economic arrangements. The chief contemporary manifestation of this idea is the advocacy of "democratic socialism" by many who condemn out of hand the restrictions on individual freedom imposed by "totalitarian socialism" in Russia, and who are persuaded that it is possible for a country to adopt the essential features of Russian economic arrangements and yet to ensure individual freedom through political arrangements. The thesis of this chapter is that such a view is a delusion, that there is an intimate connection between economics and politics, that only certain combinations of political and economic arrangements are possible, and that in particular, a society which is socialist cannot also be democratic, in the sense of guaranteeing individual freedom.

Economic arrangements play a dual role in the promotion of a free society. On the one hand, freedom in economic arrangements is itself a component of freedom broadly understood, so economic freedom is an end in itself. In the second place, economic freedom is also an indispensable means toward the achievement of political freedom.

The first of these roles of economic freedom needs special

emphasis because intellectuals in particular have a strong bias against regarding this aspect of freedom as important. They tend to express contempt for what they regard as material aspects of life, and to regard their own pursuit of allegedly higher values as on a different plane of significance and as deserving of special attention. For most citizens of the country, however, if not for the intellectual, the direct importance of economic freedom is at least comparable in significance to the indirect importance of economic freedom as a means to political freedom.

The citizen of Great Britain, who after World War II was not permitted to spend his vacation in the United States because of exchange control, was being deprived of an essential freedom no less than the citizen of the United States, who was denied the opportunity to spend his vacation in Russia because of his political views. The one was ostensibly an economic limitation on freedom and the other a political limitation, yet there is no essential difference between the two.

The citizen of the United States who is compelled by law to devote something like 10 per cent of his income to the purchase of a particular kind of retirement contract, administered by the government, is being deprived of a corresponding part of his personal freedom. How strongly this deprivation may be felt and its closeness to the deprivation of religious freedom, which all would regard as "civil" or "political" rather than "economic," were dramatized by an episode involving a group of farmers of the Amish sect. On grounds of principle, this group regarded compulsory federal old age programs as an infringement of their personal individual freedom and refused to pay taxes or accept benefits. As a result, some of their livestock were sold by auction in order to satisfy claims for social security levies. True, the number of citizens who regard compulsory old age insurance as a deprivation of freedom may be few, but the believer in freedom has never counted noses.

A citizen of the United States who under the laws of various states is not free to follow the occupation of his own choosing unless he can get a license for it, is likewise being deprived of an essential part of his freedom. So is the man who would like to exchange some of his goods with, say, a Swiss for a watch but is prevented from doing so by a quota. So also is the Californian who was thrown into jail for selling Alka Seltzer at a price below that set by the manufacturer under so-called "fair trade" laws. So also is the farmer who cannot grow the amount of wheat he wants. And so on. Clearly, economic freedom, in and of itself, is an extremely important part of total freedom.

Viewed as a means to the end of political freedom, economic arrangements are important because of their effect on the concentration or dispersion of power. The kind of economic organization that provides economic freedom directly, namely, competitive capitalism, also promotes political freedom because it separates economic power from political power and in this way enables the one to offset the other.

Historical evidence speaks with a single voice on the relation between political freedom and a free market. I know of no example in time or place of a society that has been marked by a large measure of political freedom, and that has not also used something comparable to a free market to organize the bulk of economic activity.

Because we live in a largely free society, we tend to forget how limited is the span of time and the part of the globe for which there has ever been anything like political freedom: the typical state of mankind is tyranny, servitude, and misery. The nineteenth century and early twentieth century in the Western world stand out as striking exceptions to the general trend of historical development. Political freedom in this instance clearly came along with the free market and the development of capitalist institutions. So also did political freedom in the golden age of Greece and in the early days of the Roman era. . . .

. . . The triumph of Benthamite liberalism in nineteenth-century England was followed by a reaction toward increasing intervention by government in economic affairs. This tendency to collectivism was greatly accelerated, both in England and elsewhere, by the two World Wars. Welfare rather than freedom became the dominant note in democratic countries. Recognizing the implicit threat to individualism, the intellectual descendants of the Philosophical Radicals—Dicey, Mises, Hayek, and Simons, to mention only a few—feared that a continued movement toward centralized control of economic activity would prove *The Road to Serfdom,* as Hayek entitled his penetrating analysis of the process. Their emphasis was on economic freedom as a means toward political freedom.

Events since the end of World War II display still a different relation between economic and political freedom. Collectivist economic planning has indeed interfered with individual freedom. At least in some countries, however, the result has not been the suppression of freedom, but the reversal of economic policy. England again provides the most striking example. The turning point was perhaps the "control of engagements" order which, despite great misgivings, the Labour party found it necessary to impose in order to carry out its economic policy. Fully enforced and carried through, the law would have involved centralized allocation of individuals to occupations. This conflicted so sharply with personal liberty that it was enforced in a negligible number of cases, and then repealed after the law had been in effect for only a short period. Its repeal ushered in a decided shift in economic policy, marked by reduced reliance on centralized "plans" and "programs," by the dismantling of many controls, and by increased emphasis on the private market. A similar shift in policy occurred in most other democratic countries.

The proximate explanation of these shifts in policy is the limited success of central planning or its outright failure to achieve stated objectives. However, this failure is itself to be attributed, at least in some measure, to the political implications of central planning and to an unwillingness to follow out its logic when doing so requires trampling rough-shod on treasured private rights. It may well be that the shift is only a temporary interruption in the collectivist trend of this century. Even so, it illustrates the close relation between political freedom and economic arrangements.

Historical evidence by itself can never be convincing. Perhaps it was sheer coincidence that the expansion of freedom occurred at the same time as the development of capitalist and market institutions. Why should there be a connection? What are the logical links between economic and political freedom? In discussing these questions we shall consider first the market as a direct component of freedom, and then the indirect relation between market arrangements and political freedom. A by-product will be an outline of the ideal economic arrangements for a free society.

As liberals, we take freedom of the individual, or perhaps the family, as our ultimate goal in judging social arrangements. Freedom as a value in this sense has to do with the interrelations among people; it has no meaning whatsoever to a Robinson Crusoe on an isolated island (without his Man Friday). Robinson Crusoe on his island is subject to "constraint," he has limited "power," and he has only a limited number of alternatives, but there is no problem of freedom in the sense that is relevant to our discussion. Similarly, in a society freedom has nothing to say about what an individual does with his freedom; it is not an all-embracing ethic. Indeed, a major aim of the liberal is to leave the ethical problem for the individual to wrestle with. The "really" important ethical problems are those that face an individual in a free society—what he should do with his freedom. There are thus two sets of values that a liberal will emphasize—the values that are relevant to relations among people, which is the context in which he assigns first priority to freedom; and the values that are relevant to the individual in the exercise of his freedom, which is the realm of individual ethics and philosophy.

The liberal conceives of men as imperfect beings. He regards the problem of social organization to be as much a negative problem of preventing "bad" people from doing harm as of enabling "good" people to do good; and, of course, "bad" and "good" people may be the same people, depending on who is judging them. . . .

. . . Fundamentally, there are only two ways of co-ordinating the economic activities of millions. One is central direction involving the use of coercion—the technique of the army and of the modern totalitarian state. The other is voluntary co-operation of individuals—the technique of the market place.

The possibility of co-ordination through voluntary co-operation rests on the elementary—yet frequently denied— proposition that both parties to an economic transaction benefit from it, *provided the transaction is bi-laterally voluntary and informed.*

Exchange can therefore bring about co-ordination without coercion. A working model of a society organized through voluntary exchange is a *free private enterprise exchange economy*—what we have been calling competitive capitalism.

In its simplest form, such a society consists of a number of independent households—a collection of Robinson Crusoes, as it were. Each household uses the resources it controls to produce goods and services that it exchanges for goods and services produced by other households, on terms mutually acceptable to the two parties to the bargain. It is thereby enabled to satisfy its wants indirectly by producing goods and services for others, rather than directly by producing goods for its own immediate use. The incentive for adopting this indirect route is, of course, the increased product made possible by division of labor and specialization of function. Since the household always has the alternative of producing directly for itself, it need not enter into any exchange unless it benefits from it. Hence, no exchange will take place unless both parties do benefit from it. Co-operation is thereby achieved without coercion.

Specialization of function and division of labor would not go far if the ultimate productive unit were the household. In a modern society, we have gone much farther. We have introduced enterprises which are intermediaries between individuals in their capacities as suppliers of service and as purchasers of goods. And similarly, specialization of function and division of labor could not go very far if we had to continue to rely on the barter of product for product. In consequence, money has been introduced as a means of facilitating exchange, and of enabling the acts of purchase and of sale to be separated into two parts.

Despite the important role of enterprises and of money in our actual economy, and despite the numerous and complex problems they raise, the central characteristic of the market technique of achieving co-ordination is fully displayed in the simple exchange economy that contains neither enterprises nor money. As in that simple model, so in the complex enterprise and money-exchange economy, co-operation is strictly individual and voluntary *provided*: (*a*) that enterprises are private, so that the ultimate contracting parties are individuals and (*b*) that individuals are effectively free to enter or not to enter into any particular exchange, so that every transaction is strictly voluntary. . . .

. . . So long as effective freedom of exchange is maintained, the central feature of the market organization of economic activity is that it prevents one person from interfering with another in respect of most of his activities. The consumer is protected from coercion by the seller because of the presence of other sellers with whom he can deal. The seller is protected from coercion by the consumer because of other consumers to whom he can sell. The employee is protected from coercion by the employer because of other employers for whom he can work, and so on. And the market does this impersonally and without centralized authority.

Indeed, a major source of objection to a free economy is precisely that it does this task so well. It gives people what they want instead of what a particular group thinks they ought to want. Underlying most arguments against the free market is a lack of belief in freedom itself.

The existence of a free market does not of course eliminate the need for government. On the contrary, government is essential both as a forum for determining the "rules of the game" and as an umpire to interpret and enforce the rules decided on. What the market does is to reduce greatly the range of issues that must be decided through political means, and thereby to minimize the extent to which government need participate directly in the game. The characteristic feature of action through political channels is that it tends to require or enforce substantial conformity. The great advantage of the market, on the other hand, is that it permits wide diversity. It is, in political terms, a system of proportional representation. Each man can vote, as it were, for the color of tie he wants and get it; he does not have to see what color the majority wants and then, if he is in the minority, submit.

It is this feature of the market that we refer to when we say that the market provides economic freedom. But this characteristic also has implications that go far beyond the narrowly economic. Political freedom means the absence of coercion of a man by his fellow men. The fundamental threat to freedom is power to coerce, be it in the hands of a monarch, a dictator, an oligarchy, or a momentary majority. The preservation of freedom requires the elimination of such concentration of power to the fullest possible extent and the dispersal and distribution of whatever power cannot be eliminated—a system of checks and balances. By removing the organization of economic activity from the control of political authority, the market eliminates this source of coercive power. It enables economic strength to be a check to political power rather than a reinforcement.

Economic power can be widely dispersed. There is no law of conservation which forces the growth of new centers of economic strength to be at the expense of existing centers. Political power, on the other hand, is more difficult to decentralize. There can be numerous small independent governments. But it is far more difficult to maintain numerous equipotent small centers of political power in a single large government than it is to have numerous centers of economic strength in a single large economy. There can be many millionaires in one large economy. But can there be more than one really outstanding leader, one person on whom the energies and enthusiasms of his countrymen are centered? If the central government gains power, it is likely to be at the expense of local governments. There seems to be something like a fixed total of political power to be distributed. Consequently, if enonomic power is joined to political power, concentration seems almost inevitable. On the other hand, if economic power is kept in separate hands from political power, it can serve as a check and a counter to political power.

The force of this abstract argument can perhaps best be demonstrated by example. Let us consider first, a hypothetical example that may help to bring out the principles involved, and then some actual examples from recent experience that illustrate the way in which the market works to preserve political freedom.

One feature of a free society is surely the freedom of individuals to advocate and propagandize openly for a radical change in the structure of the society—so long as the advocacy is restricted to persuasion and does not include force or other forms of coercion. It is a mark of the political freedom of a capitalist society that men can openly advocate and work for socialism. Equally, political freedom in a socialist society would require that men be free to advocate the introduction of capitalism. How could the freedom to advocate capitalism be preserved and protected in a socialist society?

In order for men to advocate anything, they must in the first place be able to earn a living. This already raises a problem in a socialist society, since all jobs are under the direct control of political authorities. It would take an act of self-denial whose difficulty is underlined by experience in the United States after World War II with the problem of "security" among Federal employees, for a socialist government to permit its employees to advocate policies directly contrary to official doctrine.

But let us suppose this act of self-denial to be achieved. For advocacy of capitalism to mean anything, the proponents must be able to finance their cause—to hold public meetings, publish pamphlets, buy radio time, issue newspapers and magazines, and so on. How could they raise the funds? There might and probably would be men in the socialist society with large incomes, perhaps even large capital sums in the form of government bonds and the like, but these would of necessity be high public officials. It is possible to conceive of a minor socialist official retaining his job although openly advocating capitalism. It strains credulity to imagine the socialist top brass financing such "subversive" activities.

The only recourse for funds would be to raise small amounts from a large number of minor officials. But this

is no real answer. To tap these sources, many people would
already have to be persuaded, and our whole problem is
how to initiate and finance a campaign to do so. Radical
movements in capitalist societies have never been financed
this way. They have typically been supported by a few
wealthy individuals who have become persuaded—by a
Frederick Vanderbilt Field, or an Anita McCormick
Blaine, or a Corliss Lamont, to mention a few names
recently prominent, or by a Friedrich Engels, to go farther
back. This is a role of inequality of wealth in preserving
political freedom that is seldom noted—the role of the
patron.

In a capitalist society, it is only necessary to convince a
few wealthy people to get funds to launch any idea, however strange, and there are many such persons, many
independent foci of support. And, indeed, it is not even
necessary to persuade people or financial institutions with
available funds of the soundness of the ideas to be propa-
gated. It is only necessary to persuade them that the
propagation can be financially successful; that the newspaper or magazine or book or other venture will be profitable. The competitive publisher, for example, cannot afford
to publish only writing with which he personally agrees;
his touchstone must be the likelihood that the market will
be large enough to yield a satisfactory return on his
investment.

In this way, the market breaks the vicious circle and
makes it possible ultimately to finance such ventures by
small amounts from many people without first persuading
them. There are no such possibilities in the socialist society;
there is only the all-powerful state.

Let us stretch our imagination and suppose that a
socialist government is aware of this problem and is composed of people anxious to preserve freedom. Could it
provide the funds? Perhaps, but it is difficult to see how.
It could establish a bureau for subsidizing subversive propaganda. But how could it choose whom to support? If it
gave to all who asked, it would shortly find itself out of
funds, for socialism cannot repeal the elementary economic
law that a sufficiently high price will call forth a large
supply. Make the advocacy of radical causes sufficiently
remunerative, and the supply of advocates will be unlimited.

Moreover, freedom to advocate unpopular causes does
not require that such advocacy be without cost. On the
contrary, no society could be stable if advocacy of radical

change were costless, much less subsidized. It is entirely appropriate that men make sacrifices to advocate causes in which they deeply believe. Indeed, it is important to preserve freedom only for people who are willing to practice self-denial, for otherwise freedom degenerates into license and irresponsibility. What is essential is that the cost of advocating unpopular causes be tolerable and not prohibitive.

But we are not yet through. In a free market society, it is enough to have the funds. The suppliers of paper are as willing to sell it to the *Daily Worker* as to the *Wall Street Journal*. In a socialist society, it would not be enough to have the funds. The hypothetical supporter of capitalism would have to persuade a government factory making paper to sell to him, the government printing press to print his pamphlets, a government post office to distribute them among the people, a government agency to rent him a hall in which to talk, and so on.

Perhaps there is some way in which one could overcome these difficulties and preserve freedom in a socialist society. One cannot say it is utterly impossible. What is clear, however, is that there are very real difficulties in establishing institutions that will effectively preserve the possibility of dissent. So far as I know, none of the people who have been in favor of socialism and also in favor of freedom have really faced up to this issue, or made even a respectable start at developing the institutional arrangements that would permit freedom under socialism. By contrast, it is clear how a free market capitalist society fosters freedom.

A striking practical example of these abstract principles is the experience of Winston Churchill. From 1933 to the outbreak of World War II, Churchill was not permitted to talk over the British radio, which was, of course, a government monopoly administered by the British Broadcasting Corporation. Here was a leading citizen of his country, a Member of Parliament, a former cabinet minister, a man who was desperately trying by every device possible to persuade his countrymen to take steps to ward off the menace of Hitler's Germany. He was not permitted to talk over the radio to the British people because the BBC was a government monopoly and his position was too "controversial." . . .

. . . Another example of the role of the market in preserving political freedom, was revealed in our experience with McCarthyism. Entirely aside from the substantive issues involved, and the merits of the charges made, what protection did individuals, and in particular government employees, have against irresponsible accusations and probings into matters that it went against their conscience to reveal? Their appeal to the Fifth Amendment would have been a hollow mockery without an alternative to government employment.

Their fundamental protection was the existence of a private-market economy in which they could earn a living. Here again, the protection was not absolute. Many potential private employers were, rightly or wrongly, averse to hiring those pilloried. It may well be that there was far less justification for the costs imposed on many of the people involved than for the costs generally imposed on people who advocate unpopular causes. But the important point is that the costs were limited and not prohibitive, as they would have been if government employment had been the only possibility.

It is of interest to note that a disproportionately large fraction of the people involved apparently went into the most competitive sectors of the economy—small business, trade, farming—where the market approaches most closely the ideal free market. No one who buys bread knows whether the wheat from which it is made was grown by a Communist or a Republican, by a constitutionalist or a Fascist, or, for that matter, by a Negro or a white. This illustrates how an impersonal market separates economic activities from political views and protects men from being discriminated against in their economic activities for reasons that are irrelevant to their productivity—whether these reasons are associated with their views or their color.

As this example suggests, the groups in our society that have the most at stake in the preservation and strengthening of competitive capitalism are those minority groups which can most easily become the object of the distrust and enmity of the majority—the Negroes, the Jews, the foreign-born, to mention only the most obvious. Yet, paradoxically enough, the enemies of the free market—the Socialists and Communists—have been recruited in disproportionate measure from these groups. Instead of recognizing that the existence of the market has protected them from the attitudes of their fellow countrymen, they mistakenly attribute the residual discrimination to the market.

28.

James Baldwin:
Opting Out
of Western
Civilization*

*James Baldwin (1924–   ) has established a reputation
on two continents as one of America's most articulate
modern authors. He has written four novels and several
collections of essays, has won numerous fellowships and
distinctions for literary merit, and has taken an important
role in civil rights activities (including membership on the
national advisory board of the Congress of Racial Equality).
Even among fellow writers and scholars who disagree with
much of what he has said, there is a consensus that his is
a voice that well deserves to be heard.*

*Baldwin was born, raised, and spiritually bruised in
Harlem. Nearly all of his written work, sometimes cold,
analytical, often impassioned, reveals the emotional scars
of a tortured soul. He not only claims to know from experience the adversity of the black man's tribulations, but as
well the nature of the white man's own self-deceit. The
stark and brutal impressions of life in Harlem, an evan-
gelical and short-lived calling to the Christian ministry,
careful scrutiny of America's Muslim exhortations, and
literary prominence in the white man's world have all come
to influence Baldwin's attitudes and thoughts on contemporary society. In* The Fire Next Time *(1963), selections
from which appear below, he presents a skillful indictment
of the entire fabric of what we call Western civilization. It*

*Copyright © 1963, 1962 by James Baldwin. Reprinted from
The Fire Next Time by James Baldwin by permission of the
publisher, The Dial Press. Acknowledgment is also made to
Michael Joseph, Ltd.

is a society founded on values and beliefs which are either erroneous or wholly false. For Western civilization is essentially Christian civilization and, despite what the New Testament holds, history has proved Christians incapable of and unwilling to fulfill Christ's teachings. Not only has Western man never treated his fellowman as a brother, he has never seriously considered the inclusion of the black man in that brotherhood. The white man's entire heritage has worked as a complex of values which has left him impotent before the task of reassessing the black man's role. Without any use of dialectical vehicles Baldwin has come to the belief that the general system under which Western man has lived is inevitably doomed because it is distinguished by a rationale originally founded upon an untruth, subsequently perverted by hypocrisy.

The reader must ask himself whether Baldwin is wholly or partially cynical about the future of human relationships for Western man. Does he indeed mean to say that Western civilization is a burning ship from which he wishes to exit before it collapses upon its devoted passengers? If Baldwin's assessment of human inability to live according to New Testament teachings is incorrect, then what alternatives are offered by civil rights leaders in the mold of Martin Luther King?

It is certainly sad that the awakening of one's senses should lead to such a merciless judgment of oneself—to say nothing of the time and anguish one spends in the effort to arrive at any other—but it is also inevitable that a literal attempt to mortify the flesh should be made among black people like those with whom I grew up. Negroes in this country—and Negroes do not, strictly or legally speaking, exist in any other—are taught really to despise themselves from the moment their eyes open on the world. This world is white and they are black. White people hold the power, which means that they are superior to blacks (intrinsically, that is: God decreed it so), and the world has innumerable ways of making this difference known and felt and feared. Long before the Negro child perceives this difference, and even longer before he understands it, he has begun to react to it, he has begun to be controlled by it. Every effort made by the child's elders to prepare him for a fate from which they cannot protect him causes him secretly, in terror, to begin to await, without knowing that he is doing so, his mysterious and inexorable punishment. He must be "good" not only in order to please his parents and not only to avoid being punished by them; behind their authority stands another, nameless and impersonal, infinitely harder to please, and bottomlessly cruel. And this filters into the child's consciousness through his parents' tone of voice as he is being exhorted, punished, or loved; in the sudden, uncontrollable note of fear heard in his mother's or his father's voice when he has strayed beyond some particular boundary. He does not know what the boundary is, and he can get no explanation of it, which is frightening enough, but the fear he hears in the voices of his elders is more frightening still. The fear that I heard in my father's voice, for example, when he realized that I really *believed* I could do anything a white boy could do, and had every intention of proving it, was not at all like the fear I heard when one of us was ill or had fallen down the stairs or strayed too far from the house. It was another fear, a fear that the child, in challenging the white world's assumptions, was putting himself in the path of destruction. A child cannot, thank Heaven, know how vast and how merciless is the nature of power, with what unbelievable cruelty people treat each other. He reacts to the fear in his parents' voices because his parents hold up the world for him and he has no protection without them. I defended myself, as I imagined, against the fear my father made me feel by remembering that he was very old-fashioned. Also, I prided myself on the fact that I already knew how to outwit him. To defend oneself against a fear is simply to insure that one will, one day, be conquered by it; fears must be faced. As for one's wits, it is just not true that one can live by them—not, that is, if one wishes really to live. That summer, in any case, all the fears with which I had grown up, and which were now a part of me and controlled my vision of the world, rose up like a wall between the world and me, and drove me into the church.

. . . All I really remember is the pain, the unspeakable pain; it was as though I were yelling up to Heaven and

Heaven would not hear me. And if Heaven would not hear me, if love could not descend from Heaven—to wash me, to make me clean—then utter disaster was my portion. Yes, it does indeed mean something—something unspeakable—to be born, in a white country, an Anglo-Teutonic, antisexual country, black. You very soon, without knowing it, give up all hope of communion. Black people, mainly, look down or look up but do not look at each other, not at you, and white people, mainly, look away. And the universe is simply a sounding drum; there is no way, no way whatever, so it seemed then and has sometimes seemed since, to get through a life, to love your wife and children, or your friends, or your mother and father, or to be loved. The universe, which is not merely the stars and the moon and the planets, flowers, grass, and trees, but *other people*, has evolved no terms for your existence, has made no room for you, and if love will not swing wide the gates, no other power will or can. And if one despairs—as who has not? —of human love, God's love alone is left. But God—and I felt this even then, so long ago, on that tremendous floor, unwillingly—is white. And if His love was so great, and if He loved all His children, why were we, the blacks, cast down so far? Why? In spite of all I said thereafter, I found no answer on the floor—not *that* answer, anyway— and I was on the floor all night. Over me, to bring me "through," the saints sang and rejoiced and prayed. And in the morning, when they raised me, they told me that I was "saved."

Well, indeed I was, in a way, for I was utterly drained and exhausted, and released, for the first time, from all my guilty torment. I was aware then only of my relief. For many years, I could not ask myself why human relief had to be achieved in a fashion at once so pagan and so desperate—in a fashion at once so unspeakably old and so unutterably new. And by the time I was able to ask myself this question, I was also able to see that the principles governing the rites and customs of the churches in which I grew up did not differ from the principles governing the rites and customs of other churches, white. The principles were Blindness, Loneliness, and Terror, the first principle necessarily and actively cultivated in order to deny the two others. I would love to believe that the principles were Faith, Hope, and Charity, but this is clearly not so for most Christians, or for what we call the Christian world.

. . . And I don't mean to suggest by this the "Elmer

Gantry" sort of hypocrisy concerning sensuality; it was a deeper, deadlier, and more subtle hypocrisy than that, and a little honest sensuality, or a lot, would have been like water in an extremely bitter desert. I knew how to work on a congregation until the last dime was surrendered —it was not very hard to do—and I knew where the money for "the Lord's work" went. I knew, though I did not wish to know it, that I had no respect for the people with whom I worked. I could not have said it then, but I also knew that if I continued I would soon have no respect for myself. And the fact that I was "the young Brother Baldwin" increased my value with those same pimps and racketeers who had helped to stampede me into the church in the first place. They still saw the little boy they intended to take over. They were waiting for me to come to my senses and realize that I was in a very lucrative business. They knew that I did not yet realize this, and also that I had not yet begun to suspect where my own needs, *coming up* (they were very patient), could drive me. They themselves did know the score, and they knew that the odds were in their favor. And, really, I knew it, too. I was even lonelier and more vulnerable than I had been before. And the blood of the Lamb had not cleansed me in any way whatever. I was just as black as I had been the day that I was born. Therefore, when I faced a congregation, it began to take all the strength I had not to stammer, not to curse, not to tell them to throw away their Bibles and get off their knees and go home and organize, for example, a rent strike. When I watched all the children, their copper, brown, and beige faces staring up at me as I taught Sunday school, I felt that I was committing a crime in talking about the gentle Jesus, in telling them to reconcile themselves to their misery on earth in order to gain the crown of eternal life. Were only Negroes to gain this crown? Was Heaven, then, to be merely another ghetto? Perhaps I might have been able to reconcile myself even to this if I had been able to believe that there was any lovingkindness to be found in the haven I represented. But I had been in the pulpit too long and I had seen too many monstrous things. I don't refer merely to the glaring fact that the minister eventually acquires houses and Cadillacs while the faithful continue to scrub floors and drop their dimes and quarters and dollars into the plate. I really mean that there was no love in the church. It was a mask for hatred and self-hatred and despair. The transfiguring power of the Holy Ghost ended when the service ended, and salvation stopped at the church door. When we were told to love everybody, I had thought that meant *everybody*. But no. It applied only to those who believed as we did, and it did not apply to white people at all. I was told by a minister, for example, that I should never, on any public conveyance, under any circumstances, rise and give my seat to a white woman. White men never rose for Negro women. Well that was true enough, in the main—I saw his point. But what was the point, the purpose, of *my* salvation if it did not permit me to behave with love toward others, no matter how they behaved toward me? What others did was their responsibility, for which they would answer when the judgment trumpet sounded. But what *I* did was *my* responsibility, and I would have to answer, too—unless, of course, there was also in Heaven a special dispensation for the benighted black, who was not to be judged in the same way as other human beings, or angels. It probably occurred to me around this time that the vision people hold of the world to come is but a reflection, with predictable wishful distortions, of the world in which they live. And this did not apply only to Negroes, who were no more "simple" or "spontaneous" or "Christian" than anybody else—who were merely more oppressed. In the same way that we, for white people, were the descendants of Ham, and were cursed forever, white people were, for us, the descendants of Cain. And the passion with which we loved the Lord was a measure of how deeply we feared and distrusted and, in the end, hated almost all strangers, always, and avoided and despised ourselves.

But I cannot leave it at that; there is more to it than that. In spite of everything, there was in the life I fled a zest and a joy and a capacity for facing and surviving disaster that are very moving and very rare. Perhaps we were, all of us—pimps, whores, racketeers, church members, and children—bound together by the nature of our oppression, the specific and peculiar complex of risks we had to run; if so, within these limits we sometimes achieved with each other a freedom that was close to love. I remember, anyway, church suppers and outings, and, later, after I left the church, rent and waistline parties where rage and sorrow sat in the darkness and did not stir, and we ate and drank and talked and laughed and danced and forgot all about "the man." We had the liquor, the chicken, the music, and each other, and had no need to pretend to be what we were not. This is the freedom that one hears in some gospel songs, for example, and in jazz. In all jazz, and especially in the blues, there is something tart and ironic, authoritative and double-edged. White Americans seem to feel that happy songs are *happy* and sad songs are *sad,* and that, God help us, is exactly the way most white Americans sing them—sounding, in both cases, so helplessly, defenselessly fatuous that one dare not speculate on the temperature of the deep freeze from which issue their brave and sexless little voices. . . .

White Christians have also forgotten several elementary historical details. They have forgotten that the religion that is now identified with their virtue and their power —"God is on our side," says Dr. Verwoerd—came out of a rocky piece of ground in what is now known as the Middle East before color was invented, and that in order for the Christian church to be established, Christ had to be put to death, by Rome, and that the real architect of the Christian church was not the disreputable, sun-baked Hebrew who gave it his name but the mercilessly fanatical and self-righteous St. Paul. The energy that was buried with the rise of the Christian nations must come back into the world; nothing can prevent it. Many of us, I think, both long to see this happen and are terrified of it, for though this transformation contains the hope of liberation, it also imposes a necessity for great change. But in order to deal with the untapped and dormant force of the previously subjugated, in order to survive as a human, moving, moral weight in the world, America and all the Western nations will be forced to reëxamine themselves and release themselves from many things that are now taken to be sacred, and to discard nearly all the assumptions that have been used to justify their lives and their anguish and their crimes so long.

. . . The struggle, therefore, that now begins in the world is extremely complex, involving the historical role of Christianity in the realm of power—that is, politics—and in the realm of morals. In the realm of power, Christianity has operated with an unmitigated arrogance and cruelty— necessarily, since a religion ordinarily imposes on those who have discovered the true faith the spiritual duty of liberating the infidels. This particular true faith, moreover, is more deeply concerned about the soul than it is about the body, to which fact the flesh (and the corpses) of countless infidels bears witness. It goes without saying, then, that whoever questions the authority of the true faith also contests the right of the nations that hold this

faith to rule over him—contests, in short, their title to his
land. The spreading of the Gospel, regardless of the motives
or the integrity or the heroism of some of the missionaries,
was an absolutely indispensable justification for the plant-
ing of the flag. Priests and nuns and school-teachers helped
to protect and sanctify the power that was so ruthlessly
being used by people who were indeed seeking a city, but
not one in the heavens, and one to be made, very definitely,
by captive hands. The Christian church itself—again, as
distinguished from some of its ministers—sanctified and
rejoiced in the conquests of the flag, and encouraged, if it
did not formulate, the belief that conquest, with the resulting relative well-being of the Western populations, was
proof of the favor of God. God had come a long way
from the desert—but then so had Allah, though in a very
different direction. God, going north, and rising on the
wings of power, had become white, and Allah, out of
power, and on the dark side of Heaven, had become—
for all practical purposes, anyway—black. Thus, in the
realm of morals the role of Christianity has been, at best,
ambivalent. Even leaving out of account the remarkable
arrogance that assumed that the ways and morals of others
were inferior to those of Christians, and that they therefore
had every right, and could use any means, to change them,
the collision between cultures—and the schizophrenia in
the mind of Christendom—had rendered the domain of
morals as chartless as the sea once was, and as treacher-
ous as the sea still is. It is not too much to say that whoever wishes to become a truly moral human being (and let
us not ask whether or not this is possible; I think we must
believe that it is possible) must first divorce himself from
all the prohibitions, crimes, and hypocrisies of the Christian church. If the concept of God has any validity or
any use, it can only be to make us larger, freer, and more
loving. If God cannot do this, then it is time we got rid
of Him.

. . . Again, the terms "civilized" and "Christian" begin
to have a very strange ring, particularly in the ears of
those who have been judged to be neither civilized nor
Christian, when a Christian nation surrenders to a foul and
violent orgy, as Germany did during the Third Reich.
For the crime of their ancestry, millions of people in the
middle of the twentieth century, and in the heart of
Europe—God's citadel—were sent to a death so calculated,
so hideous, and so prolonged that no age before this enlightened one had been able to imagine it, much less

achieve and record it. Furthermore, those beneath the Western heel, unlike those within the West, are aware that Germany's current role in Europe is to act as a bulwark against the "uncivilized" hordes, and since power is what the powerless want, they understand very well what we of the West want to keep, and are not deluded by our talk of a freedom that we have never been willing to share with them. From my own point of view, the fact of the Third Reich alone makes obsolete forever any question of Christian superiority, except in technological terms. White people were, and are, astounded by the holocaust in Germany. They did not know that they could act that way. But I very much doubt whether black people were astounded—at least, in the same way. . . .

. . . "Return to your true religion," Elijah has written. "Throw off the chains of the slavemaster, the devil, and return to the fold. Stop drinking his alcohol, using his dope—protect your women—and forsake the filthy swine." I remembered my buddies of years ago, in the hallways, with their wine and their whiskey and their tears; in hallways still, frozen on the needle; and my brother saying to me once, "If Harlem didn't have so many churches and junkies, there'd be blood flowing in the streets." *Protect your women:* a difficult thing to do in a civilization sexually so pathetic that the white man's masculinity depends on a denial of the masculinity of the blacks. *Protect your women:* in a civilization that emasculates the male and abuses the female, and in which, moreover, the male is forced to depend on the female's bread-winning power. *Protect your women:* in the teeth of the white man's boast "We figure we're doing you folks a favor by pumping some white blood into your kids," and while facing the Southern shotgun and the Northern billy. Years ago, we used to say, *"Yes,* I'm black, goddammit, and I'm beautiful"—in defiance, into the void. But now—now—African kings and heroes have come into the world, out of the past, the past that can now be put to the uses of power. And black has *become* a beautiful color—not because it is loved but because it is feared. And this urgency on the part of American Negroes is *not to be forgotten!* As they watch black men elsewhere rise, the promise held out, at last, that they may walk the earth with the authority with which white men walk, protected by the power that white men shall have no longer, is enough, and more than enough, to empty prisons and pull God down from Heaven. It has happened before, many times, before color was invented, and the hope of Heaven has always been a metaphor for the achievement of this particular state of grace. . . .

. . . One clings then to chimeras, by which one can only be betrayed, and the entire hope—the entire possibility—of freedom disappears. And by destruction I mean precisely the abdication by Americans of any effort really to be free. The Negro can precipitate this abdication because white Americans have never, in all their long history, been able to look on him as a man like themselves. This point need not be labored; it is proved over and over again by the Negro's continuing position here, and his indescribable struggle to defeat the stratagems that white Americans have used, and use, to deny him his humanity. America could have used in other ways the energy that both groups have expended in this conflict. America, of all the Western nations, has been best placed to prove the uselessness and the obsolescence of the concept of color. But it has not dared to accept this opportunity, or even to conceive of it as an opportunity. White Americans have thought of it as their shame, and have envied those more civilized and elegant European nations that were untroubled by the presence of black men on their shores. This is because white Americans have supposed "Europe" and "civilization" to be synonyms—which they are not—and have been distrustful of other standards and other sources of vitality, especially those produced in America itself, and have attempted to behave in all matters as though what was east for Europe was also east for them. What it comes to is that if we, who can scarcely be considered a white nation, persist in thinking of ourselves as one, we condemn ourselves, with the truly white nations, to sterility and decay. . . .

29.

Cohn-Bendit:
Hammering the Establishment*

*"A spectre is haunting Europe—the spectre of student
revolt. All the powers of Old Europe have entered into a
holy alliance to exorcise this spectre: Pope and Central
Committee, Kiesinger [German Chancellor] and de Gaulle,
French Communists and German police-spies." These are
the lines with which Daniel Cohn-Bendit (1946–   ), a
self-styled anarchist popularly known as "Danny the Red,"
opens his book* Obsolete Communism, *selections from
which appear below.*

*Cohn-Bendit, the stateless son of a German-Jewish
couple who took refuge in France during World War II,
attracted international attention in May, 1968, when he
led student rioters at Nanterre and later at the Sorbonne
in violent demonstrations which eventually attracted the
support of the French labor force and grew into a mass
movement of civil and economic disobedience supported
by some ten million Frenchmen. Although no lives were
lost, over a thousand combatants were injured and there
was considerable property damage. The violence abated
only after the Gaullist government conceded that reform
of the university system was "indispensable" and promised
to deal lightly with the affair's leaders.*

*That France's system of higher education has some
monumental problems is undeniable. In comparison to the
United States, relatively few young people gain entrance*

*Daniel and Gabriel Cohn-Bendit, *Obsolete Communism: The
Left-Wing Alternative.* Translated by Arnold Pomerans (London:
André Deutsch Limited, 1968), pp. 41–48, 49–51, 90. Reprinted
by permission of André Deutsch Limited and McGraw Hill Book
Company, publisher of the American edition.

to the universities at all, and nearly 70 percent of those who do either flunk out or give up and quit. The universities are overcrowded (the Sorbonne library has only 4,000 seats for 40,000 students), suffer from an acute shortage of professors, and are administered by an unwieldy bureaucracy that resists change. Yet such problems only assured that the explosion, when it came, would be on a large scale. They are not the issues which prompted Cohn-Bendit and his fellow militants to launch the disturbances of May, 1968. The crucial issue for the radicals was the university curriculum. They wanted a role in determining class content. Hence, shortly before the outbreak of the demonstrations, when a professor offering a course on French society refused to honor a request that he show a film on the strike at the Rhodiceta factory, the radicals threatened to shut down his course.

Cohn-Bendit and his supporters make it clear that their aim is to politicize the university and use it as a hammer against the foundations of what they term the "capitalist-bureaucratic state" as well as against the stodgy apparatus of the parliamentary left (that is, the French Communists). In essence, they seek a vibrant form of student syndicalism reminiscent of Georges Sorel's prescription for French workers over a half-century earlier. And indeed their thrust has enlisted all shades of student activists—including self-proclaimed Maoists, Castroites, and Marxists —under an anti-establishment banner which flaunts such slogans as "Humanity will not be happy until the last capitalist is hanged with the entrails of the last bureaucrat," and "Don't look back now, God, but the world is collapsing behind you! The more I make revolution the more I want to make love!"

In the material which follows, Cohn-Bendit concentrates his rhetoric on the educational structure of the "capitalist-bureaucratic state."

Students and Society

There are 600,000 of us; sometimes treated as mere children, sometimes as adults. We work, but produce nothing. Often we have no money, but few of us are really poor. Although most of us come from the bourgeoisie, we do not always behave like them. The girls among us look like boys but are not sure whether they really want to be boys. We look upon our professors as part father, part boss and part teacher, and can't quite make up our minds about them. Some of us are destined to control the nation, others will become poorly paid intellectual hacks—but every one of us is privileged for all that. . . .

A modern university has two contradictory roles. To begin with, a university must churn out the trained personnel that is so essential for bureaucratic capitalism. The system needs an ever increasing number of engineers, technicians, scientists, teachers, administrators and sociologists to organize production, to "rationalize" industrial methods, to run the gigantic state machine, to "adjust the psychology of individuals and groups" and to preserve their sanity, even to "organize" leisure activities. Now, since the bourgeoisie itself cannot provide enough student material from among its own ranks, increasing numbers of bright lads are recruited from the lower middle classes and even the proletariat and the peasantry. The "right-thinking" Left concentrates its fire on the class structure of French higher education, but stressing that only 6 per cent of the students are the sons of workers, when, in fact, they should be attacking the social function of the university: the production of a managerial élite. If some self-destructive fit should seize the bourgeoisie overnight and persuade it to recruit students exclusively from among the sons of manual workers, the university would become more democratic only in its composition. To the extent that the development of new manufacturing techniques is increasingly eliminating the need for unskilled labour, it is inevitable that pseudo-democratization by the recruitment of working class children to the universities will increase. In the past, the economic depression of the working and lower middle classes meant that sending one child, let alone several children, to the university, imposed an intolerable financial burden on the family, but higher wages and government grants now make it more and more possible. And what all the reformists—be they Communists, Social Democrats or left-wing Gaullists—really mean when they cry for the "democratization" of the universities, is that this process be speeded up.

But in any case it is obvious that, as capitalism increases its demands for graduates, not only the prize pigs, but more and more horses, sheep, even chickens, will all be pressed into the sausage machine. Now this is precisely where the contradiction in the system lies. The production of the maximum number of graduate workers in the minimum time calls for increasingly closer contacts between the universities and industry, for the ever greater adaptation of education to specific industrial needs. But at the same time, the university is supposed to be the supreme guardian of "culture," human reason and disinterested research, of unalloyed truth and objectivity. In brief, the university is supposed to be the temple and eternal repository of the spiritual values of society. Now if, for "spiritual values" we read the "ideology and values of the ruling class," we are left with the role the university has played from the Middle Ages down to the First World War. We might say that during this period the "social" and "cultural" role of the universities more or less overlapped. Society needed a relatively small number of lawyers, doctors, philosophers and professors, and chose them almost exclusively from among the sons of the ruling class. These enjoyed a humanistic and liberal education and were prepared to condone the most glaring social contradictions, while comforting themselves with the thought that the bourgeoisie was a champion of liberalization, democracy, universal education, etcetera. Later, a measure of petty bourgeois radicalism began to filter into the university, but was contained at a purely theoretical level: the crisis of society had not yet really occupied the academies.

Today, it is the economic rather than the theoretical role of the university which is predominant. This explains why the universities have been split up into a set of technical high schools, so many appendages to the major industries. But the system is internally inconsistent—it can only function by trying to suppress its own logic. The "cultural" function of the university is constantly assailed and has constantly to be re-affirmed. After all, even an alienated society cannot allow itself to become alienated to the point of psychosis. Even a totalitarian society, with its determination to subjugate every part of life to the will of the ruling class, group or party, cannot in the long run afford to suppress scientific *objectivity,* and without it, would quickly perish. For the strictest utilitarian reasons, modern societies need fundamental and "disinterested" research—because advances in applied technology depend on them. This the American bourgeoisie has come to realize more and more clearly. . . .

. . . We have seen that the students are a socially heterogeneous group. They are also a transitory one, and their variety of social expectations increases their heterogeneity. Depending on his subject and the importance of his family connexions, a student may end up with a job worth 30,000 francs a month, and quite a few students want nothing better than that.

Their studies take from three to seven years. Hence while the younger students are still irresponsible adolescents, their older colleagues are men with a profession. Nor do these extremes always understand one another.

And yet it was these very students, the most heterogeneous of all social groups, who succeeded in banding together for collective political action, as witness their resistance to war in Algeria and the events of May 1968. The student movement was, in fact, the only "hard" reaction against the war in Algeria, what with violent demonstrations, and constant propaganda campaigns during the later years. It was always given out that "only a minority" participated in these student protests, but this minority represented at least 25 per cent of the French student population. As for the rest of the country, their protests remained largely verbal. The absence of organized protest outside of the universities can be laid squarely at the door of the Communist Party—it was both unwilling and unable to organize effective opposition to the war and support for the Algerian revolutionaries. . . .

The remarkable phenomenon of student opposition was due to several factors, chief among them what so many people call sneeringly "the revolt of modern youth." Now this revolt, which involves ever larger numbers of young people throughout the world, must not be confused with the old "conflict between the generations." The latter, as we know it, particularly in earlier forms of bourgeois society, reflected the impatience of the young to step into the shoes of the old. This impatience often took the form of an attack on the fossilized thinking of the older generation and sometimes crystallized into a liberal, radical or a reformist attitude. In the current revolt of youth, however, very much more is being questioned—the distaste is for the system itself. Modern youth is not so much envious of, as disgusted with, the dead, empty lives of their parents. This feeling began among bourgeois children but has now spread through all levels of society. Daniel Mothé (*Socialisme ou Barbarie* No. 33) has shown clearly how opposed young workers are to both the "values" that capitalist society has to offer them and also to working class values and traditional forms of organization (political parties and trade unions). Factory work, trade union "militancy," verbose party programmes, and the sad, colourless life of their elders are subjects only for their sarcasm and contempt.

The same sort of disdain is the reason why so many students have taken a radical stand, and have made common cause with young workers in the struggle against a repressive society.

Another factor in the student revolt was their own position in the system and the special problems it brings to light.

A minority of students accept the culture which is being dispensed to them, and the knowledge which is being ladled out, with the trust of small children. . . . Another fraction can see through the system, but keep their eyes firmly on the main chance: they are the opportunists, only concerned with their professional future. . . .

. . . But for a third and constantly growing group, university life itself raises a series of fundamental questions. And once they start to analyse their own problems, the logic of their conclusions drives them on ultimately to reject the whole of contemporary society. This is because, as an essential part of the social system, the university necessarily contains all the contradictions, conflicts and paradoxes that characterize society itself.

We have said a university is supposed to be a seat of learning and rational inquiry. Now what young economist, for instance, can seriously believe in the rational character of the contemporary economic scene, whether planned or not? And only a few diehards among their teachers still pretend that the system is even capable of rationalization. How can an economist talk seriously about the rational distribution of goods in view of the glaring contradiction between the affluence of the highly industrialized countries and the misery of the Third World? How can a young industrial psychologist help being led to self-questioning when he sees that the object of his discipline is to "fit the man to the job" and that the job itself is deadly and quite futile? How can a young physicist ignore the theoretical crisis that is shaking the very foundations of contemporary physics and with it all its claims to be an exact science; how can he tell himself that his research is of benefit to humanity, in an age which has produced the H-bomb? Can he really avoid wondering about his personal responsibility when the greatest atomic scientists themselves are beginning to question the function of science and its role in society?

And how can students of social psychology possibly shut their eyes to their professional role: to help in the sacred interest of profit, to break in more workers to the conveyor belt, or to launch yet another useless product on the market?

If these doubts about the value of one's studies are examined, inevitably the system which organizes it is brought into question as well. Subjects for courses are picked out of the hat; there is no logic in the curriculum, other than keeping research subservient to the demands of industry or, perhaps, the professor's next book.

These lectures reduce the student to the role of a listener; he is there to record, to remember, to reproduce in his exam the lecturer's threadbare arguments, opinions and style. The more opportunist a student is, the more he will try to ape his teacher's every word, in the certain knowledge that his final marks will be high. However, many students are becoming increasingly disgusted and sickened not only by this system but by the very culture that produces and fosters it.

There is one last element which should be mentioned in the students' situation: it is the explanation both of the relative ease with which they become involved in political activity and of the often superficial nature of this involvement.

The student, at least, in the modern system of higher education, still preserves a considerable degree of personal freedom, if he chooses to exercise it. He does not have to earn his own living, his studies do not occupy all his time and he has no foreman on his back. He rarely has a wife and children to feed. He can, if he so chooses, take extreme political positions without any personal danger; in general, he is not subjected to formal sanctions or even reprimands. Now, these very factors have an inbuilt inhibiting mechanism: they far too often cause his engagement to lack consistency and force.

However, when a minority of students takes conscious advantage of their freedom to attack the established order, they can become a catalyst activating a larger section of the student population. It is at this stage, and only at this stage, that the struggle becomes transformed qualitatively, and the university authorities feel compelled to call in the police.

The ensuing struggle is especially threatening to the authorities as the student population keeps going up by leaps and bounds. It constantly exceeds the official estimates (the Fourth Plan foresaw 500,000 students for 1971; there were already more than 600,000 by 1968). Pressure is continually increasing: the time-and-motion study boys have already got out their stop watches to calculate how long it takes to teach the Theory of Relativity. Most students will end up as managers and administrators, toiling away amid millions of other workers at their narrow little tasks, without any chance of deciding their place in society, their work, in short, the pattern of their lives. The so-called "liberal" professions will become less and less liberal as the values on which they are ostensibly based are increasingly perverted by the State.

For all that, we are not so much protesting that our education is out of touch with the needs of the future, nor complaining about the shortage of jobs—we totally reject the entire system. Our protest only turns into violent action because the structure of society cannot be smashed by talk or ballot papers. To dream of turning the university into an "island unto itself," where every man will be able to work in independence and peace, is in any case an empty dream because the future "intellectual worker" will not be able to accept the fragmented and alienated life which this dream entails.

As a result, the student movement has become revolutionary and not simply a university protest. It does not rule out reforms (its actions, in fact, provoke them) but it tries beyond its immediate aims to elaborate a strategy that will radically change the whole of society. This strategy will carry the student movement through success and failure, through periods of open conflict and apparent inaction, but as every year passes, and the educational system shows ever more clearly its ideological loyalties and its repressive nature, the student will find himself as alienated from the society in which he lives as the lowest wage earner.

The 22 March Movement

CAPITALISM CAN NO LONGER CONCEAL ITS HAND[1]

"*We must* stop challenging capitalism by means of *outdated* techniques.

"The Socialist Wilson has clamped down on England and now de Gaulle is clamping down on us. It is too late for the kind of peaceful procession organized by the SNESUP (University Teachers' Union) for next Thursday.

"We have to thrash out the problems inside the university and act right where we work.

"We call on you to transform the 29th into a vast debate on

—*Capitalism in 1968 and the workers' struggles*
—*University and Anti-University*
—*The Anti-Imperialist Struggle*
—*The Workers' and Students' Struggle in the East and the West.*

"We shall accordingly occupy Block C and divide for discussions in the various lecture halls.

"As the authorities are becoming more and more brazenly brutal we are forced to become increasingly militant ourselves. We shall demonstrate our determination not to be cowed by holding a demonstration outside the Prefecture of *Hauts-de-Seine.*

"Resolution passed by 142 students, occupying the Administrative Block of Nanterre with 2 against and 3 abstentions."

On reading this proclamation, the university authorities took fright and their fright turned into panic when, by way of preparing for the 29th, we plastered the walls with tracts, placards and slogans, some of which caused a real sensation.

"Professors, you are past it and so is your culture!"

"When examined, answer with questions!"

"Please leave the Communist Party as clean on leaving as you would like to find it on entering."

The challenge of these slogans was one which forced people to take a stand. The authorities, no less than the Stalinists, were furious and tried to incite the staff of the faculty against the "terrorist minority." The library was

[1] The quoted material which follows is from a statement drafted on March 22, 1968, by a group of student protesters at Nanterre. The students had assembled to protest the arrest of six militants of the National Vietnam Committee.

closed in order to stop alleged thefts; there was a stay-in strike by the maintenance staff.

Under pressure from above, from neo-Fascist groups who had sworn to exterminate the revolutionary "rabble," and from reactionary lectures, the Dean, on Thursday, 28 March, one week after the closure of the University of Warsaw, ordered the suspension of lectures and of laboratory work until the following Monday. Three hundred students assembled immediately after this announcement and decided not to leave but to spend the next day drafting a political manifesto to be published on 2 April. Having made up our minds to introduce politics into the campus, we were not going to retreat like a flock of frightened sheep at a bark from the sheepdog.

The weather helped us—the 29 March was a glorious and sunny day. A large police guard ringed the campus, while five hundred students divided into discussion groups on the lawn in front of the closed faculty doors. The gentlemen of the press were completely at a loss to understand what was going on; they had been led to expect a small band of anarchist bomb-throwers with long hair, and what they found instead was more than five hundred students seriously discussing the fundamental problems of our age.

On Monday, 1 April, second year sociology students decided, after a vote, to boycott their current examinations. Then they passed a resolution condemning sociology as a capitalist fraud. Meanwhile the professors themselves were at loggerheads, for while some (particularly in the Faculty of Letters and Social Science) were in favour of opening one of the lecture halls for political discussions, others (Faculty of History) wanted the 'ringleaders' arrested.

Tuesday, 2 April, was a great day for the students. We turned down the small room put at our disposal by the Dean and faced the administration with a *fait accompli*: we took over the large lecture theatre for our inaugural meeting, which was attended by more than 1,200 students including Karl-Dietrich Wolff representing the German SDS. . . .

. . . Students must not fear to make themselves heard and instead of searching for leaders where none can be found, boldly proclaim their principles—principles that are valid for all industrial societies, and for all the oppressed of our time.

These principles are:

To take collective responsibility for one's own affairs, that is, self-government;

To destroy all hierarchies which merely serve to paralyse the initiative of groups and individuals;

To make all those in whom any authority is vested, permanently responsible to the people;

To spread information and ideas throughout the movement;

To put an end to the division of labour and of knowledge, which only serves to isolate people one from the others;

To open the university to all who are at present excluded;

To defend maximum political and intellectual freedom as a basic democratic right.

30.

Perpetual Revolution:
A Guerrilla War Against
the Establishment*

Philosopher and essayist Herbert Marcuse (1898–   ), one of the most controversial figures on the American academic scene, has become in the eyes of much of the public an elderly "pied piper" for student revolutionaries. Born and raised in Germany, he has established a reputation as an effective teacher and productive scholar, has lectured at Columbia, Harvard, and Brandeis Universities, and is the author of several provocative works highly critical of contemporary American society. His best-known works include One-Dimensional Man, Eros and Civilization, Reason and Revolution, *and* Negations.

Marcuse is quick to affirm his ideological outlook as decidedly Marxist, but he has many reservations—given the complex character of modern capitalism—regarding the usefulness of the working class as the pliable vehicle of revolution. Because the "proletariat" has become corrupted (enriched) by capitalism, the chief shock troops of revolution must be the disillusioned, affluent intelligentsia-youth who share Marcuse's revulsion at the exploitative and oppressive qualities of society. Though he does not shrink in principle from sanguinary revolution, he recognizes that such a "solution" is fraught with difficulties, especially in the United States. Instead, he advocates a form of constant guerrilla warfare against every pillar of the "Establishment's" foundation until the entire edifice collapses. Such harsh medicine is justified, nihilistic

*Herbert Marcuse, *An Essay on Liberation* (Boston: Beacon Press, 1969), Chapter 4: "Solidarity," pp. 79–91. Reprinted by permission of the Beacon Press and Penguin Books Ltd., copyright © 1969 by Herbert Marcuse.

as the prescription might be, because all of the descriptives which are used to portray modern American life are no less than hypocritical shams. For Marcuse, terms like "freedom," "democracy," "law and order", and "decency" have become "dirty" words. And all that they stand for in America must be removed by means violent and non-violent alike. He recommends "counterviolence" and "direct action," and proposes that the widespread use of obscenities by youthful radicals be the tool for subverting "the linguistic universe of the Establishment."

In the form and fabric of his rationale for dissent, Marcuse reveals the intellectual influence of several earlier thinkers who declaimed vehemently the need to sweep away existing society in its entirety. He employs Nietzsche's unique phrase in demanding a radical "transvaluation of values," Georges Sorel's exhortation of "direct action," philosophical seasoning from Immanuel Kant, and mixes it all with the abrasive jargon of New Leftists. And in the final analysis he wages unlimited war on what some of the greatest thinkers of the past two centuries would call "civilized" society.

Reprinted below is the concluding chapter of Marcuse's recent book An Essay on Liberation.

The preceding attempt to analyze the present opposition to the society organized by corporate capitalism was focused on the striking contrast between the radical and total character of the rebellion on the one hand, and the absence of a class basis for this radicalism on the other. This situation gives all efforts to evaluate and even discuss the prospects for radical change in the domain of corporate capitalism their abstract, academic, unreal character. The search for specific historical agents of revolutionary change in the advanced capitalist countries is indeed meaningless. Revolutionary forces emerge in the process of change itself; the translation of the potential into the actual is the work of political practice. And just

as little as critical theory can political practice orient itself on a concept of revolution which belongs to the
nineteenth and early twentieth century, and which is
still valid in large areas of the Third World. This concept
envisages the "seizure of power" in the course of a mass
upheaval, led by a revolutionary party acting as the
avant-garde of a revolutionary class and setting up a new
central power which would initiate the basic social
changes. Even in industrial countries where a strong
Marxist party has organized the exploited masses, strategy
is no longer guided by this notion—witness the long-
range Communist policy of "popular fronts." And the concept is altogether inapplicable to those countries in which
the integration of the working class is the result of structural economic-political processes (sustained high productivity; large markets; neo-colonialism; administered
democracy) and where the masses themselves are forces
of conservatism and stabilization. It is the very power
of this society which contains new modes and dimensions
of radical change.

The dynamic of this society has long since passed the
stage where it could grow on its own resources, its own
market, and on normal trade with other areas. It has grown
into an imperialist power which, through economic and
technical penetration and outright military intervention, has
transformed large parts of the Third World into depen-
dencies. Its policy is distinguished from classical imperialism
of the preceding period by effective use of economic and
technical conquests on the one hand, and by the political-
strategic character of intervention on the other: the requirements of the global fight against communism super-
sede those of profitable investments. In any case, by
virtue of the evolution of imperialism, the developments
in the Third World pertain to the dynamic of the First
World, and the forces of change in the former are not
extraneous to the latter; the "external proletariat" is a
basic factor of potential change within the dominion of
corporate capitalism. Here is the coincidence of the historical factors of revolution: this predominantly agrarian
proletariat endures the dual oppression exercised by the
indigenous ruling classes and those of the foreign metropoles. A liberal bourgeoisie which would ally itself with
the poor and lead their struggle does not exist. Kept in
abject material and mental privation, they depend on a
militant leadership. Since the vast majority outside the cities
is unable to mount any concerted economic and political

action which would threaten the existing society, the struggle for liberation will be a predominantly military one, carried out with the support of the local population, and exploiting the advantages of a terrain which impedes traditional methods of suppression. These circumstances, of necessity, make for guerrilla warfare. It is the great chance, and at the same time the terrible danger, for the forces of liberation. The powers that be will not tolerate a repetition of the Cuban example; they will employ ever more effective means and weapons of suppression, and the indigenous dictatorships will be strengthened with the ever more active aid from the imperialist metropoles. It would be romanticism to underrate the strength of this deadly alliance and its resolution to contain subversion. It seems that not the features of the terrain, nor the unimaginable resistance of the men and women of Vietnam, nor considerations of "world opinion," but fear of the other nuclear powers has so far prevented the use of nuclear or seminuclear weapons against a whole people and a whole country.

Under these circumstances, the preconditions for the liberation and development of the Third World must emerge in the advanced capitalist countries. Only the internal weakening of the superpower can finally stop the financing and equipping of suppression in the backward countries. The National Liberation Fronts threaten the life line of imperialism; they are not only a material but also an ideological catalyst of change. The Cuban revolution and the Viet Cong have demonstrated: it can be done; there is a morality, a humanity, a will, and a faith which can resist and deter the gigantic technical and economic force of capitalist expansion. More than the "socialist humanism" of the early Marx, this violent solidarity in defense, this elemental socialism in action, has given form and substance to the radicalism of the New Left; in this ideological respect too, the external revolution has become an essential part of the opposition within the capitalist metropoles. However, the exemplary force, the ideological power of the external revolution, can come to fruition only if the internal structure and cohesion of the capitalist system begin to disintegrate. The chain of exploitation must break at its strongest link.

Corporate capitalism is not immune against economic crisis. The huge "defense" sector of the economy not only places an increasingly heavy burden on the taxpayer, it also is largely responsible for the narrowing margin of profit. The growing opposition against the war in Vietnam points up the necessity of a thorough conversion of the economy, risking the danger of rising unemployment, which is a by-product of technical progress in automation. The "peaceful" creation of additional outlets for the productivity of the metropoles would meet with the intensified resistance in the Third World, and with the contesting and competitive strength of the Soviet orbit. The absorption of unemployment and the maintenance of an adequate rate of profit would thus require the stimulation of demand on an ever larger scale, thereby stimulating the rat race of the competitive struggle for existence through the multiplication of waste, planned obsolescence, parasitic and stupid jobs and services. The higher standard of living, propelled by the growing parasitic sector of the economy, would drive wage demands toward capital's point of no return. But the structural tendencies which determine the development of corporate capitalism do not justify the assumption that aggravated class struggles would terminate in a socialist revolution through organized political action. To be sure, even the most advanced capitalist welfare state remains a class society and therefore a state of conflicting class interests. However, prior to the disintegration of the state power, the apparatus and the suppressive force of the system would keep the class struggle within the capitalist framework. The translation of the economic into the radical political struggle would be the consequence rather than the cause of change. The change itself could then occur in a general, unstructured, unorganized, and diffused process of disintegration. This process may be sparked by a crisis of the system which would activate the resistance not only against the political but also against the mental repression imposed by the society. Its insane features, expression of the ever more blatant contradiction between the available resources for liberation and their use for the perpetuation of servitude, would undermine the daily routine, the repressive conformity, and rationality required for the continued functioning of the society.

The dissolution of social morality may manifest itself in a collapse of work discipline, slowdown, spread of disobedience to rules and regulations, wildcat strikes, boycotts, sabotage, gratuitous acts of noncompliance. The violence built into the system of repression may get out of control, or necessitate ever more totalitarian controls.

Even the most totalitarian technocratic-political administration depends, for its functioning, on what is usually called the "moral fiber": a (relatively) "positive" attitude among the underlying population toward the usefulness of their work and toward the necessity of the repressions exacted by the social organization of work. A society depends on the relatively stable and calculable sanity of the people, sanity defined as the regular, socially coordinated functioning of mind and body—especially at work, in the shops and offices, but also at leisure and fun. Moreover, a society also demands to a considerable extent, belief in one's beliefs (which is part of the required sanity); belief in the operative value of society's values. Operationalism is indeed an indispensable supplement to want and fear as forces of cohesion.

Now it is the strength of this moral fiber, of the operational values (quite apart from their ideational validity), which is likely to wear off under the impact of the growing contradictions within the society. The result would be a spread, not only of discontent and mental sickness, but also of inefficiency, resistance to work, refusal to perform, negligence, indifference—factors of dysfunction which would hit a highly centralized and coordinated apparatus, where breakdown at one point may easily affect large sections of the whole. To be sure, these are subjective factors, but they may assume material force in conjunction with the objective economic and political strains to which the system will be exposed on a global scale. Then, and only then, that political climate would prevail which could provide a mass basis for the new forms of organization required for directing the struggle.

We have indicated the tendencies which threaten the stability of the imperialist society and emphasized the extent to which the liberation movements in the Third World affect the prospective development of this society. It is to an even greater extent affected by the dynamic of "peaceful coexistence" with the old socialist societies, the Soviet orbit. In important aspects, this coexistence has contributed to the stabilization of capitalism: "world communism" has been the Enemy who would have to be invented if he did not exist—the Enemy whose strength justified the "defense economy" and the mobilization of the people in the national interest. Moreover, as the common Enemy of *all* capitalism, communism promoted the organization of a common interest superseding the intercapitalist differences and conflicts. Last but not least, the opposition within the advanced capitalist countries has been seriously weakened by the repressive Stalinist development of socialism, which made socialism not exactly an attractive alternative to capitalism.

More recently, the break in the unity of the communist orbit, the triumph of the Cuban revolution, Vietnam, and the "cultural revolution" in China have changed this picture. The possibility of constructing socialism on a truly popular base, without the Stalinist bureaucratization and the danger of a nuclear war as the imperialist answer to the emergence of this kind of socialist power, has led to some sort of common interest between the Soviet Union on the one side and the United States on the other.

In a sense, this is indeed the community of interests of the "haves" against the "have nots," of the Old against the New. The "collaborationist" policy of the Soviet Union necessitates the pursuance of power politics which increasingly reduces the prospect that Soviet society, by virtue of its basic institutions alone (abolition of private ownership and control of the means of production: planned economy) is still capable of making the transition to a free society. And yet, the very dynamic of imperialist expansion places the Soviet Union in the other camp: would the effective resistance in Vietnam, and the protection of Cuba be possible without Soviet aid?

However, while we reject the unqualified convergence thesis, according to which—at least at present—the assimilation of interests prevails upon the conflict between capitalism and Soviet socialism, we cannot minimize the essential difference between the latter and the new historical efforts to construct socialism by developing and creating a genuine solidarity between the leadership and the liberated victims of exploitation. The actual may considerably deviate from the ideal, the fact remains that, for a whole generation, "freedom," "socialism," and "liberation" are inseparable from Fidel and Ché and the guerrillas—not because their revolutionary struggle could furnish the model for the struggle in the metropoles, but because they have recaptured the truth of these ideas, in the day-to-day fight of men and women for a life as human beings: for a new life.

What kind of life? We are still confronted with the demand to state the "concrete alternative." The demand is meaningless if it asks for a blueprint of the specific institutions and relationships which would be those of the new society: they cannot be determined a priori; they will develop, in trial and error, as the new society develops. If we could form a concrete concept of the alternative today, it would not be that of an alternative; the possibilities of the new society are sufficiently "abstract," i.e., removed from and incongruous with the established universe to defy any attempt to identify them in terms of this universe. However, the question cannot be brushed aside by saying that what matters today is the destruction of the old, of the powers that be, making way for the emergence of the new. Such an answer neglects the essential fact that the old is not simply bad, that it delivers the goods, and that people have a real stake in it. There can be societies which are much worse—there are such societies today. The system of corporate capitalism has the right to insist that those who work for its replacement justify their action.

But the demand to state the concrete alternatives is justified for yet another reason. Negative thinking draws whatever force it may have from its empirical basis: the actual human condition in the given society, and the "given" possibilities to transcend this condition, to enlarge the realm of freedom. In this sense, negative thinking is by virtue of its own internal concepts "positive": oriented toward, and comprehending a future which is "contained" in the present. And in this containment (which is an important aspect of the general containment policy pursued by the established societies), the future appears as possible liberation. It is not the only alternative: the advent of a long period of "civilized" barbarism, with or without the nuclear destruction, is equally contained in the present. Negative thinking, and the praxis guided by it, is the positive and positing effort to prevent this utter negativity.

The concept of the primary, initial institutions of liberation is familiar enough and concrete enough: collective ownership, collective control and planning of the means of production and distribution. This is the foundation, a necessary but not sufficient condition for the alternative: it would make possible the usage of all available resources for the abolition of poverty, which is the prerequisite for the turn from quantity into quality: the creation of a reality in accordance with the new sensitivity and the new consciousness. This goal implies rejection of those policies of reconstruction, no matter how revolutionary, which are bound to perpetuate (or to introduce) the pattern of the unfree societies and their needs. Such false policy is perhaps best summed up in the formula "to catch up with, and to overtake the productivity level of the advanced capitalist countries." What is wrong with this formula is not the emphasis on the rapid improvement of the material conditions but on the model guiding their improvement. The model denies the alternative, the qualitative difference. The latter is not, and cannot be, the result of the fastest possible attainment of capitalist productivity, but rather the development of new modes and ends of production—"new" not only (and perhaps not at all) with respect to technical innovations and production relations, but with respect to the different human needs and the different human relationships in working for the satisfaction of these needs. These new relationships would be the result of a "biological" *solidarity* in work and purpose, expressive of a true harmony between social and individual needs and goals, between recognized necessity and free development—the exact opposite of the administered and enforced harmony organized in the advanced capitalist (and socialist?) countries. It is the image of this solidarity as elemental, instinctual, creative force which the young radicals see in Cuba, in the guerrillas, in the Chinese cultural revolution.

Solidarity and cooperation: not all their forms are liberating. Fascism and militarism have developed a deadly efficient solidarity. Socialist solidarity is autonomy: self-determination begins at home—and that is with every I, and the We whom the I chooses. And this end must indeed appear in the means to attain it, that is to say, in the strategy of those who, within the existing society, work for the new one. If the socialist relationships of production are to be a new way of life, a new Form of life, then their existential quality must show forth, anticipated and demonstrated, in the fight for their realization. Exploitation in all its forms must have disappeared from this fight: from the work relationships among the fighters as well as from their individual relationships. Understanding, tenderness toward each other, the instinctual consciousness of that which is evil, false, the heritage of oppression, would then testify to the authenticity of the rebellion. In short, the economic, political, and cultural features of a classless society must have become the basic needs of those who fight for it. This ingression of the future into the present, this depth dimension of the rebellion accounts, in the last analysis, for the incompatibility with the traditional forms of the political struggle. The new radicalism militates against the centralized bureaucratic communist as well as against the semi-democratic liberal organization. There is a strong element of spontaneity, even anarchism, in this rebellion, expression of the new sensibility, sensitivity against domination: the feeling, the awareness, that the joy of freedom and the need to be free must precede liberation. Therefore the aversion against preestablished Leaders, apparatchiks of all sorts, politicians no matter how leftist. The initiative shifts to small groups, widely diffused, with a high degree of autonomy, mobility, flexibility.

To be sure, within the repressive society, and against its ubiquitous apparatus, spontaneity by itself cannot possibly be a radical and revolutionary force. It can become such a force only as the result of enlightenment, education, political practice—in this sense indeed, as a result of organization. The anarchic element is an essential factor in the struggle against domination: preserved but disciplined in the preparatory political action, it will be freed and *aufgehoben* in the goals of the struggle. Released for the construction of the initial revolutionary institutions, the anti-repressive sensibility, allergic to domination, would militate against the prolongation of the "First Phase," that is, the authoritarian bureaucratic development of the productive forces. The new society could then reach relatively fast the level at which poverty could be abolished (this level could be considerably lower than that of advanced capitalist productivity, which is geared to obscene affluence and waste). Then the development could tend toward a sensuous culture, tangibly contrasting with the gray-on-gray culture of the socialist societies of Eastern Europe. Production would be redirected in defiance of all the rationality of the Performance Principle; socially necessary labor would be diverted to the construction of an aesthetic rather than repressive environment, to parks and gardens rather than highways and parking lots, to the creation of areas of withdrawal rather than massive fun and relaxation. Such redistribution of socially necessary labor (time), incompatible with any society governed by the Profit and Performance Principle, would gradually alter society in all its dimensions—it would mean the ascent of the Aesthetic Principle as Form of the Reality Principle: a culture of receptivity based on the achievements of industrial civilization and initiating the end of its self-propelling productivity.

Not regression to a previous stage of civilization, but return to an imaginary *temps perdu* in the real life of mankind: progress to a stage of civilization where man has learned to ask for the sake of whom or of what he organizes his society; the stage where he checks and perhaps even halts his incessant struggle for existence on an enlarged scale, surveys what has been achieved through centuries of misery and hecatombs of victims, and decides that it is enough, and that it is time to enjoy what he has and what can be reproduced and refined with a minimum of alienated labor: not the arrest or reduction of technical progress, but the elimination of those of its features which perpetuate man's subjection to the apparatus and the intensification of the struggle for existence—to work harder in order to get more of the merchandise that has to be sold. In other words, electrification indeed, and all technical devices which alleviate and protect life, all the mechanization which frees human energy and time, all the standardization which does away with spurious and parasitarian "personalized" services rather than multiplying them and the gadgets and tokens of exploitative affluence. In terms of the latter (and only in terms of the latter), this would certainly be a regression—but freedom from the rule of merchandise over man is a precondition of freedom.

The construction of a free society would create new incentives for work. In the exploitative societies, the so-called work instinct is mainly the (more or less effectively) introjected necessity to perform productively in order to earn a living. But the life instincts themselves strive for the unification and enhancement of life; in nonrepressive sublimation they would provide the libidinal energy for work on the development of a reality which no longer demands the exploitative repression of the Pleasure Principle. The "incentives" would then be built into the instinctual structure of men. Their sensibility would register, as biological reactions, the difference between the ugly and the beautiful, between calm and noise, tenderness and brutality, intelligence and stupidity, joy and fun, and it would correlate this distinction with that between freedom and servitude. Freud's last theoretical conception recognizes the erotic instincts as work instincts—work for the creation of a sensuous environment. The social expression of the liberated work instinct is *cooperation,* which, grounded in solidarity, directs the organization of the realm of necessity and the development of the realm of freedom. And there is an answer to the question which troubles the minds of so many men of good will: what are the people in a free society going to do? The answer which, I believe, strikes at the heart of the matter was given by a young black girl. She said: for the first time in our life, we shall be free to think about what we are going to do.

31.

McGovern:
Resisting "a Cruel,
Self-Defeating War"

Dissent against the war in Vietnam became a persistent theme in the United States during the latter 1960's. In the two selections which follow, United States Senator George S. McGovern of South Dakota expresses his opposition to the conflict. McGovern, who holds a Ph.D. in history and government from Northwestern University, gained national attention with his eleventh-hour antiwar stand at the 1968 National Democratic Convention. A former pilot in the United States Army Air Force, he flew thirty-five combat missions during World War II and was dec-orated with the Distinguished Flying Cross. He is the author of several books, including War Against Want *and* A Time of War/A Time of Peace.

I

*The Lessons of Vietnam**

The responsibility for our present predicament in South-east Asia cannot be placed on any one man or on any single Administration or agency of government. Its roots go back

*George S. McGovern, "The Lessons of Vietnam," *The Progressive,* Vol. 31 (May, 1967), pp. 12–13. Reprinted by permission.

more than twenty years to embrace four Administrations as well as the Congress and the American public.

Senators must bear a portion of the blame for the drift of our policy in Vietnam—for we have been slow to speak clearly or even to ask hard questions about obvious contradictions, poor intelligence, and false prophecies involving the highest officials of our government. Dissent in the Congress and the nation has been sharp and frequent in the last two or three years, but it has come late in the day.

Many of the Senate's most influential members, including the chairmen of powerful committees, have believed for years that the United States made a serious mistake in intervening in Vietnam—first by trying to defeat the Vietnamese independence struggle led by Ho Chi Minh against imperial France, and second, by fostering a divided Vietnam leading to civil conflict after the expulsion of the French. Yet, upon this privately-admitted error a strange syllogism has been constructed:

(1) The United States erred in entering and enlarging the Vietnamese struggle.

(2) We are nevertheless now deeply involved in that struggle.

(3) Therefore, we have no recourse except to see it through at any cost, or force the other side to negotiate on our terms.

It is a strange piece of logic, indeed, which holds that, once committed to error, we must compound the error to salvage the original mistake. It would seem more reasonable, having accepted the premise of error in our involvement, to avoid further widening of the war while devoting our most imaginative efforts to finding a way to end the killing.

Before we take any further steps toward a larger war, or undertake any new ventures of this kind elsewhere in Asia, I would hope that we will reexamine the assumptions that have involved us in what I believe to be a painfully mistaken course. Perhaps the only positive benefit that may come from an otherwise melancholy venture is for us to see the errors of this one clearly enough to avoid being drawn into another one. To assist in stimulating such a reexamination I make the following indictments of our Vietnam policy:

(1) Our Vietnam policy makers have distorted history to justify our intervention in a civil conflict supposedly to defend a free nation against external aggression; actually,

we are backing a dictatorial group in Saigon against a competing group backed by a dictatorial regime in the North.

(2) Our Vietnam policy makers are unwittingly advancing the cause of Communism while seeking to contain it.

(3) While orally calling for negotiations, we are practicing military escalation and diplomatic rigidity in such a fashion as to foreclose negotiations.

(4) Our policy makers have frequently misled the American public; the result has been a serious loss of credibility for the U.S. Government.

(5) We are wasting human and material resources needed for the revitalization of our society.

(6) We are jeopardizing essential U.S. foreign policy interests, including a promising improvement in East-West relations.

(7) We bypassed the United Nations until the eleventh hour and have disregarded the opinion and the sensibilities of the international community.

(8) We are weakening America's moral position and beclouding American idealism.

(9) We are creating at home a climate of intimidation designed to silence dissent and meaningful discussion of policy.

II

End the War Now! *

I cannot accept the diagnosis of some that we are a "sick society"; yet, I cannot find assurance in the state of the union, for our nation is laboring under a double burden—a cruel, self-defeating war abroad and a profoundly troubled domestic society strained by the paradox of affluence and neglect.

It is doubtless simplistic to contend that the malaise of today stems from only one cause—war, racism, technological revolution, or the quickening pace of social change.

*George S. McGovern, "Vietnam: The Time is Now," *The Progressive*, Vol. 33 (September, 1969), pp. 13, 15–16. Reprinted by permission.

Yet, I firmly believe that our involvement in the Vietnam war is at the base of the most acute troubles that beset us today.

Former Secretary of Defense Clark Clifford recently said that his growing doubts about our Vietnam policy have taken on the character of an "obsession." It is obvious that our former great ambassador and chief negotiator, Averell Harriman, and his brilliant deputy, Cyrus Vance, as well as such distinguished generals as Gavin and Shoup, share that obsession. I share it, too, and indeed, for me the war in Vietnam has been a nagging obsession for several years. Early in 1967, in the pages of *The Progressive,* I referred to our deepening war in Asia as "a policy of madness"—"the most tragic diplomatic, military, and moral blunder in our national history."

It may seem ill-timed to repeat that verdict today when we are officially seeking a way out of the Vietnamese morass. But I am increasingly obsessed by the continuing folly that each week kills still more American and Vietnamese youth and wounds several thousand others, and is daily devastating Vietnam while poisoning and dividing our own society. . . .

. . . I plead for us to declare our independence of a monstrous folly that is surely weakening our nation at home and abroad. "A decent respect to the opinions of mankind" commands us "to dissolve the political bands" that have bound the Vietnamese albatross to our backs. Having long ago asserted for ourselves the right to "throw off" a government guilty of "a long train of abuses and usurpations," history demands that we not deny to the people of Vietnam the right to resolve their own struggle with the rulers of Saigon. If we truly seek for ourselves and for others "life, liberty, and the pursuit of happiness," let us in the name of God and our own history end now the slaughter and devastation that at once drain the blood of both Vietnam and America. . . .

. . . If we cannot hear the anguished cries of Vietnam, let us at least look to what we are doing to our own beloved land:

¶ 200,000 young Americans killed or wounded.

¶ $100 billion swallowed in a blood-soaked jungle.

¶ Millions of Americans, especially the young, confused, frustrated or alienated from their own government.

¶ Great American cities and universities caught up in turmoil, violence, and neglect.

¶ Costly wartime inflation, high interest rates, rising taxes, and a continued drain on our dollar and gold reserves.

¶ Perhaps, worst of all, a widespread loss of confidence in ourselves and on the part of others around the globe as to our prudence and humanity.

It is painful in our personal lives, in our business ventures, or in our social enterprises to confess error, to declare bankruptcy, or to seek a reordering of life. It is far easier to begin a war than to end it. It is sometimes more tempting to policy makers to save face than to save lives.

Yet, I am convinced that the overwhelming majority of our people, having taken so many risks for war, are now ready to follow leaders who will take some risks for peace. The one vindication that can console us is that our Vietnam involvement, for all its blood and heartache, may yet be redeemed if we learn from that bitter experience not to repeat it elsewhere. Those brave men who have died in Vietnam—American and Vietnamese alike—can teach us by their too great sacrifice that this is not the way for alien peoples to live on this shrinking planet.

The Biblical wisdom still challenges us: "I have set before you life and death, blessing and cursing; therefore choose life, that both thou and thy seed may live."

I would plead again that we throw off the curse of Vietnam, that we turn away from death without further delay, and set our course toward blessing and toward life.

32.

Martin Luther King:
Virtue in Breaking the Law*

> . . . law to be ethically valid must conform with
> the requirements of the system of rights the pur-
> poses of which the state exists to maintain.
> —Harold J. Laski, *The State in Theory and Prac-
> tice*

*At the time of his death by an assassin's bullet in 1968,
thirty-nine-year-old Martin Luther King, Jr., was probably
the American most admired in many other nations. Born in
1929 in a thirteen-room parsonage in Atlanta, Georgia,
by the early 1960's he had become one of the most
articulate and courageous leaders in the battle for integration.*

*As a young man King had doubts that religion was
intellectually respectable and had leaned toward a career
in medicine or law. But he became captivated by Thoreau's
writings on civil disobedience and decided that the ministry was the only place from which to launch social protest. Accordingly, after being awarded his B.A. from
Morehouse College in 1948, he entered Crozer Theological
Seminary, a Baptist institution in Chester, Pennsylvania,
and became that school's first Negro senior-class president
and top student. In 1955 he received a Ph.D. in theology
from Boston University.*

*At the end of 1955, while serving as pastor of the Dexter
Avenue Baptist Church in Montgomery, Alabama, Dr.*

*"Letter from Birmingham Jail"—April 16, 1963—in *Why We
Can't Wait* by Martin Luther King, Jr. Copyright © 1963 by Martin
Luther King, Jr. Reprinted by permission of Harper & Row,
Publishers, Inc., and Joan Daves.

King assumed leadership of a 381-day Negro boycott of segregated city buses. By the time the boycott succeeded, he was the first nationally known Negro activist. In 1957 he organized the Southern Christian Leadership Conference as a base of operations and during the next decade was increasingly active in voter-registration drives and other desegregation efforts. Many are of the opinion that the protest he led in 1963 for integrated public accommodations and employment in Birmingham, Alabama, and his subsequent spearheading of the March on Washington by 200,000 Negroes and whites led to the 1964 Civil Rights Act. In the year that landmark act was passed Dr. King became the youngest person ever to win the Nobel Peace Prize.

King was both a defender of the duty to disobey unjust laws and an advocate of nonviolent resistance to all forms of racial injustice, even at the risk of imprisonment. As one who took Christ's teaching on love literally, he believed that violence as a way of achieving racial justice is both impractical and immoral. It was his conviction that through nonviolent resistance the Negro will succeed in rising to the noble height of opposing the unjust system while loving its perpetrators.

In his April 16, 1963, "Letter from Birmingham Jail," reprinted below, King responded to a statement by eight Alabama religious leaders which said: "When rights are consistently denied, a cause should be pressed in the courts and in negotiations among local leaders, and not in the streets." Maintaining that "one has a moral responsibility to disobey unjust laws," and that "privileged groups seldom give up their privileges voluntarily," King took the position that the demonstrations taking place in Birmingham were the only alternative left the Negro community by the white power structure.

. . . I am in Birmingham because injustice is here. Just as the prophets of the eighth century B.C. left their villages and carried their "thus saith the Lord" far beyond the boundaries of their home towns, and just as the Apostle Paul left his village of Tarsus and carried the gospel of Jesus Christ to the far corners of the Greco-Roman world, so am I compelled to carry the gospel of freedom beyond my own home town. Like Paul, I must constantly respond to the Macedonian call for aid.

Moreover, I am cognizant of the interrelatedness of all communities and states. I cannot sit idly by in Atlanta and not be concerned about what happens in Birmingham. Injustice anywhere is a threat to justice everywhere. We are caught in an inescapable network of mutuality, tied in a single garment of destiny. Whatever affects one directly, affects all indirectly. Never again can we afford to live with the narrow, provincial "outsider agitator" idea. Anyone who lives inside the United States can never be considered an outsider anywhere within its bounds.

You deplore the demonstrations taking place in Birmingham. But your statement, I am sorry to say, fails to express a similar concern for the conditions that brought about the demonstrations. I am sure that none of you would want to rest content with the superficial kind of social analysis that deals merely with effects and does not grapple with underlying causes. It is unfortunate that demonstrations are taking place in Birmingham, but it is even more unfortunate that the city's white power structure left the Negro community with no alternative.

In any nonviolent campaign there are four basic steps: collection of the facts to determine whether injustices exist; negotiation; self-purification; and direct action. We have gone through all these steps in Birmingham. There can be no gainsaying the fact that racial injustice engulfs this community. Birmingham is probably the most thoroughly segregated city in the United States. Its ugly record of brutality is widely known. Negroes have experienced grossly unjust treatment in the courts. There have been more unsolved bombings of Negro homes and churches in Birmingham than in any other city in the nation. These are the hard, brutal facts of the case. On the basis of these conditions, Negro leaders sought to negotiate with the city fathers. But the latter consistently refused to engage in good-faith negotiation.

Then, last September, came the opportunity to talk with leaders of Birmingham's economic community. In the course of the negotiations, certain promises were made by the merchants—for example, to remove the stores' humiliating racial signs. On the basis of these promises, the Reverend Fred Shuttlesworth and the leaders of the Alabama Christian Movement for Human Rights agreed to a moratorium on all demonstrations. As the weeks and months went by, we realized that we were the victims of a broken promise. A few signs, briefly removed, returned, the others remained.

As in so many past experiences, our hopes had been blasted, and the shadow of deep disappointment settled upon us. We had no alternative except to prepare for direct action, whereby we would present our very bodies as a means of laying our case before the conscience of the local and the national community. Mindful of the difficulties involved, we decided to undertake a process of self-purification. We began a series of workshops on nonviolence, and we repeatedly asked ourselves: "Are you able to accept blows without retaliating?" "Are you able to endure the ordeal of jail?" . . .

. . . You may well ask: "Why direct action? Why sit-ins, marches and so forth? Isn't negotiation a better path?" You are quite right in calling for negotiation. Indeed, this is the very purpose of direct action. Nonviolent direct action seeks to create such a crisis and foster such a tension that a community which has constantly refused to negotiate is forced to confront the issue. It seeks so to dramatize the issue that it can no longer be ignored. My citing the creation of tension as part of the work of the nonviolent-resister may sound rather shocking. But I must confess that I am not afraid of the word "tension." I have earnestly opposed violent tension, but there is a type of constructive, nonviolent tension which is necessary for growth. Just as Socrates felt that it was necessary to create a tension in the mind so that individuals could rise from the bondage of myths and half-truths to the unfettered realm of creative analysis and objective appraisal, so must we see the need for nonviolent gadflies to create the kind of tension in society that will help men rise from the dark depths of prejudice and racism to the majestic heights of understanding and brotherhood.

The purpose of our direct-action program is to create a situation so crisis-packed that it will inevitably open the door to negotiation. I therefore concur with you in your call for negotiation. Too long has our beloved Southland been bogged down in a tragic effort to live in monologue rather than dialogue.

One of the basic points in your statement is that the

action that I and my associates have taken in Birmingham is untimely. Some have asked: "Why didn't you give the new city administration time to act?" The only answer that I can give to this query is that the new Birmingham administration must be prodded about as much as the outgoing one, before it will act. We are sadly mistaken if we feel that the election of Albert Boutwell as mayor will bring the millennium to Birmingham. While Mr. Boutwell is a much more gentle person than Mr. Connor, they are both segregationists, dedicated to maintenance of the status quo. I have hope that Mr. Boutwell will be reasonable enough to see the futility of massive resistance to desegregation. But he will not see this without pressure from devotees of civil rights. My friends, I must say to you that we have not made a single gain in civil rights without determined legal and nonviolent pressure. Lamentably, it is an historical fact that privileged groups seldom give up their privileges voluntarily. Individuals may see the moral light and voluntarily give up their unjust posture; but, as Reinhold Niebuhr has reminded us, groups tend to be more immoral than individuals.

We know through painful experience that freedom is never voluntarily given by the oppressor; it must be demanded by the oppressed. Frankly, I have yet to engage in a direct-action campaign that was "well timed" in the view of those who have not suffered unduly from the disease of segregation. For years now I have heard the word "Wait!" It rings in the ear of every Negro with piercing familiarity. This "Wait" has almost always meant "Never." We must come to see, with one of our distinguished jurists, that "justice too long delayed is justice denied."

We have waited for more than 340 years for our constitutional and God-given rights. The nations of Asia and Africa are moving with jetlike speed toward gaining political independence, but we still creep at horse-and-buggy pace toward gaining a cup of coffee at a lunch counter. Perhaps it is easy for those who have never felt the stinging darts of segregation to say, "Wait." But when you have seen vicious mobs lynch your mothers and fathers at will and drown your sisters and brothers at whim; when you have seen hate-filled policemen curse, kick and even kill your black brothers and sisters; when you see the vast majority of your twenty million Negro brothers smothering in an airtight cage of poverty in the midst of an affluent society; when you suddenly find your tongue twisted and your speech stammering as you seek to explain to your six-year-old daughter why she can't go to the public amusement park that has just been advertised on television, and see tears welling up in her eyes when she is told that Funtown is closed to colored children, and see ominous clouds of inferiority beginning to form in her little mental sky, and see her beginning to distort her personality by developing an unconscious bitterness toward white people; when you have to concoct an answer for a five-year-old son who is asking: "Daddy, why do white people treat colored people so mean?"; when you take a cross-country drive and find it necessary to sleep night after night in the uncomfortable corners of your automobile because no motel will accept you; when you are humiliated day in and day out by nagging signs reading "white" and "colored"; when your first name becomes "nigger," your middle name becomes "boy" (however old you are) and your last name becomes "John," and your wife and mother are never given the respected title "Mrs."; when you are harried by day and haunted by night by the fact that you are a Negro, living constantly at tiptoe stance, never quite knowing what to expect next, and are plagued with inner fears and outer resentments; when you are forever fighting a degenerating sense of "nobodiness"—then you will understand why we find it difficult to wait. There comes a time when the cup of endurance runs over, and men are no longer willing to be plunged into the abyss of despair. I hope, sirs, you can understand our legitimate and unavoidable impatience.

You express a great deal of anxiety over our willingness to break laws. This is certainly a legitimate concern. Since we so diligently urge people to obey the Supreme Court's decision of 1954 outlawing segregation in the public schools, at first glance it may seem rather paradoxical for us consciously to break laws. One may well ask: "How can you advocate breaking some laws and obeying others?" The answer lies in the fact that there are two types of laws: just and unjust. I would be the first to advocate obeying just laws. One has not only a legal but a moral responsibility to obey just laws. Conversely, one has a moral responsibility to disobey unjust laws. I would agree with St. Augustine that "an unjust law is no law at all."

Now, what is the difference between the two? How does one determine whether a law is just or unjust? A just law is a man-made code that squares with the moral law or the law of God. An unjust law is a code that is out of

harmony with the moral law. To put it in the terms of
St. Thomas Aquinas: An unjust law is a human law that
is not rooted in eternal law and natural law. Any law that
uplifts human personality is just. Any law that degrades
human personality is unjust. All segregation statutes are
unjust because segregation distorts the soul and damages
the personality. It gives the segregator a false sense of
superiority and the segregated a false sense of inferiority.
Segregation, to use the terminology of the Jewish philosopher Martin Buber, substitutes an "I-it" relationship
for an "I-thou" relationship and ends up relegating persons to the status of things. Hence segregation is not only
politically, economically and sociologically unsound, it is
morally wrong and sinful. Paul Tillich has said that sin
is separation. Is not segregation an existential expression
of man's tragic separation, his awful estrangement, his
terrible sinfulness? Thus it is that I can urge men to obey
the 1954 decision of the Supreme Court, for it is morally
right; and I can urge them to disobey segregation ordi-
nances, for they are morally wrong.

Let us consider a more concrete example of just and
unjust laws. An unjust law is a code that a numerical
or power majority group compels a minority group to obey
but does not make binding on itself. This is *difference*
made legal. By the same token, a just law is a code that
a majority compels a minority to follow and that it is
willing to follow itself. This is *sameness* made legal.

Let me give another explanation. A law is unjust if it
is inflicted on a minority that, as a result of being denied
the right to vote, had no part in enacting or devising the
law. Who can say that the legislature of Alabama which
set up that state's segregation laws was democratically
elected? Throughout Alabama all sorts of devious methods
are used to prevent Negroes from becoming registered
voters, and there are some counties in which, even though
Negroes constitute a majority of the population, not a
single Negro is registered. Can any law enacted under
such circumstances be considered democratically structured?

Sometimes a law is just on its face and unjust in its
application. For instance, I have been arrested on a
charge of parading without a permit. Now, there is nothing wrong in having an ordinance which requires a permit
for a parade. But such an ordinance becomes unjust when
it is used to maintain segregation and to deny citizens the

First-Amendment privilege of peaceful assembly and protest.

I hope you are able to see the distinction I am trying to point out. In no sense do I advocate evading or defying the law, as would the rabid segregationist. That would lead to anarchy. One who breaks an unjust law must do so openly, lovingly, and with a willingness to accept the penalty. I submit that an individual who breaks a law that conscience tells him is unjust, and who willingly accepts the penalty of imprisonment in order to arouse the conscience of the community over its injustice, is in reality expressing the highest respect for law.

Of course, there is nothing new about this kind of civil disobedience. It was evidenced sublimely in the refusal of Shadrach, Meshach and Abednego to obey the laws of Nebuchadnezzar, on the ground that a higher moral law was at stake. It was practiced superbly by the early Christians, who were willing to face hungry lions and the excruciating pain of chopping blocks rather than submit to certain unjust laws of the Roman Empire. To a degree, academic freedom is a reality today because Socrates practiced civil disobedience. In our own nation, the Boston Tea Party represented a massive act of civil disobedience.

We should never forget that everything Adolf Hitler did in Germany was "legal" and everything the Hungarian freedom fighters did in Hungary was "illegal." It was "illegal" to aid and comfort a Jew in Hitler's Germany. Even so, I am sure that, had I lived in Germany at the time, I would have aided and comforted my Jewish brothers. If today I lived in a communist country where certain principles dear to the Christian faith are suppressed, I would openly advocate disobeying that country's antireligious laws.

I must make two honest confessions to you, my Christian and Jewish brothers. First, I must confess that over the past few years I have been gravely disappointed with the white moderate. I have almost reached the regrettable conclusion that the Negro's great stumbling block in his stride toward freedom is not the White Citizen's Counciler or the Ku Klux Klanner, but the white moderate, who is more devoted to "order" than to justice; who prefers a negative peace which is the absence of tension to a positive peace which is the presence of justice; who constantly says: "I agree with you in the goal you seek, but I cannot agree with your methods of direct action"; who paternalistically believes he can set the timetable for another man's freedom; who lives by a mythical concept of time and who constantly advises the Negro to wait for a "more convenient season." Shallow understanding from people of good will is more frustrating than absolute misunderstanding from people of ill will. Lukewarm acceptance is much more bewildering than outright rejection.

I had hoped that the white moderate would understand that law and order exist for the purpose of establishing justice and that when they fail in this purpose they become the dangerously structured dams that block the flow of social progress. I had hoped that the white moderate would understand that the present tension in the South is a necessary phrase of the transition from an obnoxious negative peace, in which the Negro passively accepted his unjust plight, to a substantive and positive peace, in which all men will respect the dignity and worth of human personality. Actually, we who engage in nonviolent direct action are not the creators of tension. We merely bring to the surface the hidden tension that is already alive. We bring it out in the open, where it can be seen and dealt with. Like a boil that can never be cured so long as it is covered up but must be opened with all its ugliness to the natural medicines of air and light, injustice must be exposed, with all the tension its exposure creates, to the light of human conscience and the air of national opinion before it can be cured.

In your statement you assert that our actions, even though peaceful, must be condemned because they precipitate violence. But is this a logical assertion? Isn't this like condemning a robbed man because his possession of money precipitated the evil act of robbery? Isn't this like condemning Socrates because his unswerving commitment to truth and his philosophical inquiries precipitated the act by the misguided populace in which they made him drink hemlock? Isn't this like condemning Jesus because his unique God-consciousness and never-ceasing devotion to God's will precipitated the evil act of crucifixion? We must come to see that, as the federal courts have consistently affirmed, it is wrong to urge an individual to cease his efforts to gain his basic constitutional rights because the quest may precipitate violence. Society must protect the robbed and punish the robber.

I had also hoped that the white moderate would reject the myth concerning time in relation to the struggle for freedom. I have just received a letter from a white brother in Texas. He writes: "All Christians know that the colored people will receive equal rights eventually, but it is possible that you are in too great a religious hurry. It has taken Christianity almost two thousand years to accomplish what it has. The teachings of Christ take time to come to earth." Such an attitude stems from a tragic misconception of time, from the strangely irrational notion that there is something in the very flow of time that will inevitably cure all ills. Actually, time itself is neutral; it can be used either destructively or constructively. More and more I feel that the people of ill will have used time much more effectively than have the people of good will. We will have to repent in this generation not merely for the hateful words and actions of the bad people but for the appalling silence of the good people. Human progress never rolls in on wheels of inevitability; it comes through the tireless efforts of men willing to be co-workers with God, and without this hard work, time itself becomes an ally of the forces of social stagnation. We must use time creatively, in the knowledge that the time is always ripe to do right. Now is the time to make real the promise of democracy and transform our pending national elegy into a creative psalm of brotherhood. Now is the time to lift our national policy from the quicksand of racial injustice to the solid rock of human dignity.

You speak of our activity in Birmingham as extreme. At first I was rather disappointed that fellow clergymen would see my nonviolent efforts as those of an extremist. I began thinking about the fact that I stand in the middle of two opposing forces in the Negro community. One is a force of complacency, made up in part of Negroes who, as a result of long years of oppression, are so drained of self-respect and a sense of "somebodiness" that they have adjusted to segregation; and in part of a few middle-class Negroes who, because of a degree of academic and economic security and because in some ways they profit by segregation, have become insensitive to the problems of the masses. The other force is one of bitterness and hatred, and it comes perilously close to advocating violence. It is expressed in the various black nationalist groups that are springing up across the nation, the largest and best-known being Elijah Muhammad's Muslim movement. Nourished by the Negro's frustration over the continued existence of racial discrimination, this movement is made up of people who have lost faith in America, who have absolutely repudiated Christianity, and who have concluded that the white man is an incorrigible "devil."

I have tried to stand between these two forces, saying that we need emulate neither the "do-nothingism" of the complacent nor the hatred and despair of the black nationalist. For there is the more excellent way of love and nonviolent protest. I am grateful to God that, through the influence of the Negro church, the way of nonviolence became an integral part of our struggle.

If this philosophy had not emerged, by now many streets of the South would, I am convinced, be flowing with blood. And I am further convinced that if our white brothers dismiss as "rabble-rousers" and "outside agitators" those of us who employ nonviolent direct action, and if they refuse to support our nonviolent efforts, millions of Negroes will, out of frustration and despair, seek solace and security in black-nationalist ideologies—a development that would inevitably lead to a frightening racial nightmare.

Oppressed people cannot remain oppressed forever. The yearning for freedom eventually manifests itself, and that is what has happened to the American Negro. Something within has reminded him of his birthright of freedom, and something without has reminded him that it can be gained. Consciously or unconsciously, he has been caught up by the *Zeitgeist,* and with his black brothers of Africa and his brown and yellow brothers of Asia, South America and the Caribbean, the United States Negro is moving with a sense of great urgency toward the promised land of racial justice. If one recognizes this vital urge that has engulfed the Negro community, one should readily understand why public demonstrations are taking place. The Negro has many pent-up resentments and latent frustrations, and he must release them. So let him march; let him make prayer pilgrimages to the city hall; let him go on freedom rides—and try to understand why he must do so. If his repressed emotions are not released in nonviolent ways, they will seek expression through violence; this is not a threat but a fact of history. So I have not said to my people: "Get rid of your discontent." Rather, I have tried to say that this normal and healthy discontent can be channeled into the creative outlet of nonviolent direct action. And now this approach is being termed extremist.

But though I was initially disappointed at being categorized as an extremist, as I continued to think about the matter I gradually gained a measure of satisfaction from

the label. Was not Jesus an extremist for love: "Love your
enemies, bless them that curse you, do good to them that
hate you, and pray for them which despitefully use you,
and persecute you." Was not Amos an extremist for
justice: "Let justice roll down like waters and righteousness
like an ever-flowing stream." Was not Paul an extremist
for the Christian gospel: "I bear in my body the marks of
the Lord Jesus." Was not Martin Luther an extremist:
"Here I stand; I cannot do otherwise, so help me God."
And John Bunyan: "I will stay in jail to the end of my days
before I make a butchery of my conscience." And Abraham
Lincoln: "This nation cannot survive half slave and half
free." And Thomas Jefferson: "We hold these truths to
be self-evident, that all men are created equal. . . ."
So the question is not whether we will be extremists, but
what kind of extremists we will be. Will we be extremists
for hate or for love? Will we be extremists for the preservation of injustice or for the extension of justice? In that
dramatic scene on Calvary's hill three men were crucified.
We must never forget that all three were crucified for the
same crime—the crime of extremism. Two were extremists
for immorality, and thus fell below their environment.
The other, Jesus Christ, was an extremist for love, truth
and goodness, and thereby rose above his environment.
Perhaps the South, the nation and the world are in dire
need of creative extremists.

I had hoped that the white moderate would see this
need. Perhaps I was too optimistic; perhaps I expected
too much. I suppose I should have realized that few members of the oppressor race can understand the deep groans
and passionate yearnings of the oppressed race, and still
fewer have the vision to see that injustice must be rooted
out by strong, persistent and determined action. I am
thankful, however, that some of our white brothers in the
South have grasped the meaning of this social revolution
and committed themselves to it. They are still all too few in
quantity, but they are big in quality. Some—such as Ralph
McGill, Lillian Smith, Harry Golden, James McBride
Dabbs, Ann Braden and Sarah Patton Boyle—have written
about our struggle in eloquent and prophetic terms. Others
have marched with us down nameless streets of the South.
They have languished in filthy, roach-infested jails, suffering the abuse and brutality of policemen who view
them as "dirty nigger-lovers." Unlike so many of their
moderate brothers and sisters, they have recognized the
urgency of the moment and sensed the need for power-

ful "action" antidotes to combat the disease of segregation.

Let me take note of my other major disappointment. I have been so greatly disappointed with the white church and its leadership. Of course, there are some notable exceptions. I am not unmindful of the fact that each of you has taken some significant stands on this issue. I commend you, Reverend Stallings, for your Christian stand on this past Sunday, in welcoming Negroes to your worship service on a nonsegregated basis. I commend the Catholic leaders of this state for integrating Spring Hill College several years ago.

But despite these notable exceptions, I must honestly reiterate that I have been disappointed with the church. I do not say this as one of those negative critics who can always find something wrong with the church. I say this as a minister of the gospel, who loves the church; who was nurtured in its bosom; who has been sustained by its spiritual blessings and who will remain true to it as long as the cord of life shall lengthen.

When I was suddenly catapulted into the leadership of the bus protest in Montgomery, Alabama, a few years ago, I felt we would be supported by the white church. I felt that the white ministers, priests and rabbis of the South would be among our strongest allies. Instead, some have been outright opponents, refusing to understand the freedom movement and misrepresenting its leaders; all too many others have been more cautious than courageous and have remained silent behind the anesthetizing security of stained-glass windows.

In spite of my shattered dreams, I came to Birmingham with the hope that the white religious leadership of this community would see the justice of our cause and, with deep moral concern, would serve as the channel through which our just grievances could reach the power structure. I had hoped that each of you would understand. But again I have been disappointed.

I have heard numerous southern religious leaders admonish their worshipers to comply with a desegregation decision because it is the law, but I have longed to hear white ministers declare: "Follow this decree because integration is morally right and because the Negro is your brother." In the midst of blatant injustices inflicted upon the Negro, I have watched white churchmen stand on the sideline and mouth pious irrelevancies and sanctimonious trivialities. In the midst of a mighty struggle to rid our nation of racial and economic injustice, I have heard many ministers say: "Those are social issues, with which the gospel has no real concern." And I have watched many churches commit themselves to a completely otherworldly religion which makes a strange, un-Biblical distinction between body and soul, between the sacred and the secular.

I have traveled the length and breadth of Alabama, Mississippi and all the other southern states. On sweltering summer days and crisp autumn mornings I have looked at the South's beautiful churches with their lofty spires pointing heavenward. I have beheld the impressive outlines of her massive religious-education buildings. Over and over I have found myself asking: "What kind of people worship here? Who is their God? Where were their voices when the lips of Governor Barnett dripped with words of interposition and nullification? Where were they when Governor Wallace gave a clarion call for defiance and hatred? Where were their voices of support when bruised and weary Negro men and women decided to rise from the dark dungeons of complacency to the bright hills of creative protest?"

Yes, these questions are still in my mind. In deep disappointment I have wept over the laxity of the church. But be assured that my tears have been tears of love. There can be no deep disappointment where there is not deep love. Yes, I love the church. How could I do otherwise? I am in the rather unique position of being the son, the grandson and the great-grandson of preachers. Yes, I see the church as the body of Christ. But, oh! How we have blemished and scarred that body through social neglect and through fear of being noncomformists.

There was a time when the church was very powerful—in the time when the early Christians rejoiced at being deemed worthy to suffer for what they believed. In those days the church was not merely a thermometer that recorded the ideas and principles of popular opinion; it was a thermostat that transformed the mores of society. Whenever the early Christians entered a town, the people in power became disturbed and immediately sought to convict the Christians for being "disturbers of the peace" and "outside agitators." But the Christians pressed on, in the conviction that they were "a colony of heaven," called to obey God rather than man. Small in number, they were big in commitment. They were too God-intoxicated to be "astronomically intimidated." By their effort and example they brought an end to such ancient evils as infanticide and gladiatorial contests.

Things are different now. So often the contemporary church is a weak, ineffectual voice with an uncertain sound. So often it is an archdefender of the status quo. Far from being disturbed by the presence of the church, the power structure of the average community is consoled by the church's silent—and often even vocal—sanction of things as they are.

But the judgment of God is upon the church as never before. If today's church does not recapture the sacrificial spirit of the early church, it will lose its authenticity, forfeit the loyalty of millions, and be dismissed as an irrelevant social club with no meaning for the twentieth century. Every day I meet young people whose disappointment with the church has turned into outright disgust.

Perhaps I have once again been too optimistic. Is organized religion too inextricably bound to the status quo to save our nation and the world? Perhaps I must turn my faith to the inner spiritual church, the church within the church, as the true *ekklesia* and the hope of the world. But again I am thankful to God that some noble souls from the ranks of organized religion have broken loose from the paralyzing chains of conformity and joined us as active partners in the struggle for freedom. They have left their secure congregations and walked the streets of Albany, Georgia, with us. They have gone down the highways of the South on tortuous rides for freedom. Yes, they have gone to jail with us. Some have been dismissed from their churches, have lost the support of their bishops and fellow ministers. But they have acted in the faith that right defeated is stronger than evil triumphant. Their witness has been the spiritual salt that has preserved the true meaning of the gospel in these troubled times. They have carved a tunnel of hope through the dark mountain of disappointment.

I hope the church as a whole will meet the challenge of this decisive hour. But even if the church does not come to the aid of justice, I have no despair about the future. I have no fear about the outcome of our struggle in Birmingham, even if our motives are at present misunderstood. We will reach the goal of freedom in Birmingham and all over the nation, because the goal of America is freedom. Abused and scorned though we may be, our destiny is tied up with America's destiny. Before the pilgrims landed at Plymouth, we were here. Before the pen of Jefferson etched the majestic words of the Declaration of Independence across the pages of history, we were here.

For more than two centuries our forebears labored in this country without wages; they made cotton king; they built the homes of their masters while suffering gross injustice and shameful humiliation—and yet out of a bottomless vitality they continued to thrive and develop. If the inexpressible cruelties of slavery could not stop us, the opposition we now face will surely fail. We will win our freedom because the sacred heritage of our nation and the eternal will of God are embodied in our echoing demands.

Before closing I feel impelled to mention one other point in your statement that has troubled me profoundly. You warmly commended the Birmingham police for keeping "order" and "preventing violence." I doubt that you would have so warmly commended the police force if you had seen its dogs sinking their teeth into unarmed, nonviolent Negroes. I doubt that you would so quickly commend the policemen if you were to observe their ugly and inhumane treatment of Negroes here in the city jail; if you were to watch them push and curse old Negro women and young Negro girls; if you were to see them slap and kick old Negro men and young boys; if you were to observe them, as they did on two occasions, refuse to give us food because we wanted to sing our grace together. I cannot join you in your praise of the Birmingham police department.

It is true that the police have exercised a degree of discipline in handling the demonstrators. In this sense they have conducted themselves rather "nonviolently" in public. But for what purpose? To preserve the evil system of segregation. Over the past few years I have consistently preached that nonviolence demands that the means we use must be as pure as the ends we seek. I have tried to make clear that it is wrong to use immoral means to attain moral ends. But now I must affirm that it is just as wrong, or perhaps even more so, to use moral means to preserve immoral ends. Perhaps Mr. Connor and his policemen have been rather nonviolent in public, as was Chief Pritchett in Albany, Georgia, but they have used the moral means of nonviolence to maintain the immoral end of racial injustice. As T. S. Eliot has said: "The last temptation is the greatest treason: To do the right deed for the wrong reason."

I wish you had commended the Negro sit-inners and demonstrators of Birmingham for their sublime courage, their willingness to suffer and their amazing discipline in the midst of great provocation. One day the South will recognize its real heroes. They will be the James Merediths, with the noble sense of purpose that enables them to face jeering and hostile mobs, and with the agonizing loneliness that characterizes the life of the pioneer. They will be old, oppressed, battered Negro women, symbolized in a seventy-two-year-old woman in Montgomery, Alabama, who rose up with a sense of dignity and with her people decided not to ride segregated buses, and who responded with ungrammatical profundity to one who inquired about her weariness: "My feets is tired, but my soul is at rest." They will be the young high school and college students, the young ministers of the gospel and a host of their elders, courageously and nonviolently sitting in at lunch counters and willingly going to jail for conscience' sake. One day the South will know that when these disinherited children of God sat down at lunch counters, they were in reality standing up for what is best in the American dream and for the most sacred values in our Judaeo-Christian heritage, thereby bringing our nation back to those great wells of democracy which were dug deep by the founding fathers in their formulation of the Constitution and the Declaration of Independence.

Never before have I written so long a letter. I'm afraid it is much too long to take your precious time. I can assure you that it would have been much shorter if I had been writing from a comfortable desk, but what else can one do when he is alone in a narrow jail cell, other than write long letters, think long thoughts and pray long prayers?

If I have said anything in this letter that overstates the truth and indicates an unreasonable impatience, I beg you to forgive me. If I have said anything that understates the truth and indicates my having a patience that allows me to settle for anything less than brotherhood, I beg God to forgive me.

I hope this letter finds you strong in the faith. I also hope that circumstances will soon make it possible for me to meet each of you, not as an integrationist or a civil-rights leader but as a fellow clergyman and a Christian brother. Let us all hope that the dark clouds of racial prejudice will soon pass away and the deep fog of misunderstanding will be lifted from our fear-drenched communities, and in some not too distant tomorrow the radiant stars of love and brotherhood will shine over our great nation with all their scintillating beauty.

Yours for the cause of Peace and Brotherhood,

33.

Fulbright:
Dissent as a Higher Form
of Patriotism*

In the second quarter of the nineteenth century a Russian aristocrat named Peter Chaadayev was declared insane by order of Czar Nicholas I for publicly describing his country as a backward nation caught up in a narrow and boastful nationalism. Chaadayev subsequently defended his patriotism—and the views which had incurred the Czar's displeasure—in an essay entitled "Apology of a Madman" (1837). "Believe me," he wrote in the concluding paragraph of the essay,

I cherish my country more than any of you. . . . But it is also true that the patriotic feeling which animates me is not exactly the same as the one whose shouts have upset my quiet existence. . . . I have not learned to love my country with my eyes closed, my head bowed, and my mouth shut. I think that one can be useful to one's country only if one sees it clearly; I believe that the age of blind love has passed, and that nowadays one owes one's country the truth. I confess that I do not feel that smug patriotism, that lazy patriotism, which manages to make everything beautiful, which falls asleep on its illusions, and with which unfortunately many of our good souls are afflicted today.

In the selection which follows, United States Senator J. William Fulbright (1905–   ) deplores what he regards as a growing tendency in America to equate expression of dissent with lack of patriotism. Like Chaadayev, he insists

*From J. W. Fulbright, "The Higher Patriotism," *Congressional Record*, CXII, 68 (April 25, 1966).

that to criticize one's country is to do it a service, to per-
form an act of patriotism.

Fulbright is Chairman of the Senate Foreign Relations
Committee. A Rhodes scholar who taught law before as-
suming the presidency of the University of Arkansas at the
age of thirty-four, he has been a Senator since 1945 and
became in 1966 the most outspoken Congressional op-
ponent of the United States involvement in Vietnam.

To criticize one's country is to do it a service and pay
it a compliment. It is a service because it may spur the
country to do better than it is doing; it is a compliment
because it evidences a belief that the country can do
better than it is doing. "This," said Albert Camus in one
of his "Letters to a German Friend," "is what separated
us from you; we made demands. You were satisfied to
serve the power of your nation and we dreamed of giving
ours her truth."

In a democracy dissent is an act of faith. Like medicine,
the test of its value is not its taste but its effects, not how
it makes people feel at the moment, but how it inspires
them to act thereafter. Criticism may embarrass the country's leaders in the short run but strengthen their hand
in the long run; it may destroy a consensus on policy while
expressing a consensus of values. Woodrow Wilson once
said that there was "such a thing as being too proud to
fight;" there is also, or ought to be, such a thing as being
too confident to conform, too strong to be silent in the
face of apparent error. Criticism, in short, is more than
a right; it is an act of patriotism, a higher form of patriotism, I believe, than the familiar rituals of national
adulation.

. . . It is not a pejorative but a tribute to say that America is worthy of criticism. If nonetheless one is charged
with a lack of patriotism, I would reply with Camus, "No,
I didn't love my country, if pointing out what is unjust
in what we love amounts to not loving, if insisting that

what we love should measure up to the finest image we have of her amounts to not loving." . . . .

. . . . The question that I find intriguing . . . is whether a nation so extraordinarily endowed as the United States can overcome that arrogance of power which has afflicted, weakened, and in some cases destroyed great nations in the past.

The causes of the malady are a mystery but its recurrence is one of the uniformities of history; power tends to confuse itself with virtue and a great nation is peculiarly susceptible to the idea that its power is a sign of God's favor, conferring upon it a special responsibility for other nations—to make them richer and happier and wiser, to remake them, that is, in its own shining image. Power confuses itself with virtue and it also tends to take itself for omnipotence. Once imbued with the idea of a mission, a great nation easily assumes that it has the means as well as the duty to do God's work. The Lord, after all, surely would not choose you as His agent and then deny you the sword with which to work His will. German soldiers in the First World War wore belt buckles imprinted with the words: "Gott mit uns." It was approximately under this kind of infatuation—an exaggerated sense of power and an imaginary sense of mission—that the Athenians attacked Syracuse and Napoleon and then Hitler invaded Russia. In plain words, they overextended their commitments and they came to grief.

My question is whether America can overcome the fatal arrogance of power. My hope and my belief are that it can, that it has the human resources to accomplish what few if any great nations have ever accomplished before: to be confident but also tolerant and rich but also generous, to be willing to teach but also willing to learn, to be powerful but also wise. I believe that America is capable of all of these things; I also believe it is falling short of them. Gradually but unmistakably we are succumbing to the arrogance of power. In so doing we are not living up to our capacity and promise; the measure of our falling short is the measure of the patriot's duty of dissent.

The discharge of that most important duty is handicapped in America by an unworthy tendency to fear serious criticism of our Government. In the abstract we celebrate freedom of opinion as a vital part of our patriotic liturgy. It is only when some Americans exercise the right that other Americans are shocked. No one of course ever criticizes the right of dissent; it is always this particular